T0413434

On Exchanges and Mutual Learning among Civilizations

www.royalcollins.com

ON EXCHANGES AND MUTUAL LEARNING
among
CIVILIZATIONS

Teng Wensheng

Books Beyond Boundaries

ROYAL COLLINS

On Exchanges and Mutual Learning among Civilizations

By Teng Wensheng

First published in 2024 by Royal Collins Publishing Group Inc.

Groupe Publication Royal Collins Inc.

550-555 boul. René-Lévesque O Montréal (Québec) H2Z1B1 Canada

10 9 8 7 6 5 4 3 2 1

ISBN: 978-1-4878-1276-8

To find out more about our publications, please visit www.royalcollins.com.

Contents

Preface

This book is a compilation of speeches and presentations I have delivered at various international academic conferences and related events during my tenure at the International Confucian Association (ICA). The manuscripts discussed herein focus on Confucian culture, Chinese historical culture, and Asian civilization, with Confucianism at its core. The central theme revolves around the exchange and mutual learning issues between Confucianism and different cultures worldwide, hence the title *On Exchanges and Mutual Learning among Civilizations*.

The ICA was established in 1994. It was initiated by Confucian cultural organizations from the East Asian Confucian cultural circle, including China, South Korea, Japan, Vietnam, and Singapore, as well as relevant academic and cultural groups from the United States and Germany. It is an international, non-governmental academic and cultural organization that promotes the essence of Confucian culture and the outstanding traditional culture of China, with Confucianism as its core. The association fosters mutual learning and interaction between Confucian culture and Asian civilization and diverse cultures worldwide. Its mission is to contribute to global peace, common development among nations, and the advancement of human civilization.

The ICA has undergone a development journey spanning 25 years since its establishment. Five congresses have been convened in this quarter-century, and the sixth member congress is scheduled for the end of this year. Over the years, the ranks of the ICA have steadily grown, and its work has taken on distinctive features with an increasing impact on the international stage. The membership of the ICA has expanded from the initial 19 organizational members to the current 653 organizational and individual members. These 653 members hail from 80 countries and regions, covering major nations and regions across five continents.

The distinctive features of the ICA's work are primarily manifested in six aspects. Firstly, within the membership, Confucian scholars are combined with scholars from other cultural backgrounds, facilitating comparative research. Secondly, in terms of leadership, the combination of scholarly research and the participation and support of policymakers ensures a mutually reinforcing relationship. Thirdly, in terms of research objectives, integrating academic research and practical application facilitates research for practical use. Fourthly, in terms of research methods, combining individual research and collective discussions encourages collective wisdom. Fifthly, regarding the research timeline, the combination of historical and contemporary studies enables drawing lessons from the past for the present. Lastly, in terms of cultural exchange, integrating research on Confucian culture and the development experiences of Asian civilizations with research on the development experiences of other world cultures allows for mutual complementarity and mutual enlightenment.

In conclusion, through the aforementioned endeavors, the ICA unites scholars of Confucianism and other cultural backgrounds, as well as policymakers from the international community. Together, they are committed to exploring, discovering, assimilating, and drawing inspiration from the strengths, virtues, wisdom, and experiences of Confucian culture, Asian civilizations, and other world cultures. This collective effort aims to facilitate the comprehensive realization and enduring stability of global peace, promote the common development and prosperity of nations, enhance the effective governance of global politics, economy, culture, society, and ecology, advocate for the establishment of a more just and equitable international order, and contribute to the construction of a community with a shared future for mankind. Ultimately, the core mission is to advance human civilization continuously, making the world a better place and wholeheartedly serving this noble cause.

Undoubtedly, this mission is both lofty and honorable. My colleagues at the ICA have the opportunity to dedicate themselves to the common sublime mission of people worldwide and how fortunate and joyful it is! Reflecting on what civilization is, as articulated by the renowned Chinese scholar Kong Yingda (AD 574–648) during the Tang Dynasty, "To govern the heavens and the earth is called civilization; to illuminate and oversee the four directions is called enlightenment." Contributing to the progress of human civilization adds tremendous human value and historical significance. The sense of mission and pride experienced by all those involved in the work of the ICA is undoubtedly profound and uplifting.

In the presence of numerous colleagues, I am merely a "volunteer" and a "novice," learning and working simultaneously. All the manuscripts included in this book are genuinely a "record of a novice," with shortcomings, omissions, and errors undoubtedly present. I sincerely hope that colleagues and readers will not hesitate to offer corrections. I present these manuscripts intending to "offer a humble contribution" and hope to draw forth more valuable insights, like attracting precious jade in the garden of world civilization, making it more vibrant and resplendent. My humble wish is fulfilled if this endeavor can contribute even a little to the enrichment of knowledge.

Author
October 2019

Guiding Principle and Solemn Declaration[*]

Study of President Xi Jinping's Important Speech at the 5th Congress of the ICA

The speech delivered by President Xi Jinping at the 5th Congress of the ICA (hereinafter referred to as the "Speech") is of great importance and far-reaching influence. The Speech has attracted strong responses and favorable comments from home and abroad.

Focusing on the two major issues, which are carrying forward the excellent traditional culture of China and promoting exchanges among civilizations, the Speech made profound elucidation in many aspects. It proposed some far-reaching thoughts and guiding principles.

First, it clarifies that peace and development, remaining the theme of our times, constitute the background and ultimate purpose of inheriting excellent traditional cultures and promoting exchanges among civilizations. The Speech pointed out that since ancient times, the Chinese have been advocates of peaceful ideas, such as "Nations or States coexist in concord," "Loving people and treating neighbors kindly are most valuable to a country," "Within the four seas all men are brothers," "A close neighbor is better than a kinsman afar," "Neighbors wish each other well just as family members do" and "A warlike State, however big it may be, will eventually perish." Peace-loving is embedded in the spiritual world of the Chinese, and today, it is still a cornerstone for China to deal with international

---

[*] Originally published in *Guangming Daily* on September 28, 2015.

relations. The international community must join hands to safeguard world peace and promote common development.

Second, the Chinese traditional culture, including Confucianism, has never ceased to play a vital part for thousands of years in the making and development of Chinese civilization, in making and consolidating the political integration, ethnic unity, and national spirit of China, and in maintaining our national independence and promoting China's social development.

Third, it clarifies the characteristics of Chinese traditional philosophical culture, including Confucianism, such as "harmony without uniformity," "humanistic pragmatism," and "keeping abreast with the times," assuring that the excellent traditional Chinese ideology and culture will not only touch people with culture, but also maintain its enormous vitality.

Fourth, the excellent components of traditional Chinese culture, including Confucianism, proposed profound and valuable philosophies such as "Tao follows spontaneity," "Man is an integral part of nature," "The world for all is the commonwealth of great unity," "Self-discipline and social commitment," "Putting people first and making them live a secured, affluent, and happy life," "One must rule with virtue and moral," "To govern means to rectify," "One should keep improving through reforms and advance with the times," and "One should stay down-to-earth and seek truth from facts." As pointed out in the Speech, these ideologies can inspire people to learn and shape the world, govern and rule their countries, and improve their morality. It also enlightens people to tackle tough issues, such as the continuously widening poverty gap, the insatiable appetite for material extravagance, the vicious inflation of individualism, the diminishing social credibility, the moral bankruptcy, and the worsening relationship between man and nature.

Fifth, how to treat civilizations of different countries and nations and how to treat traditional and modern cultures are essential questions that we must figure out. The Speech also pointed out that we must maintain the diversity of civilization, respect all these civilizations, take an appropriate approach to exchanges and mutual learning, and adopt a scientific attitude toward traditional cultures. By doing this, we will promote exchanges and mutual learning among civilizations, paving the way for a more beautiful world and a better life for people around the world.

Sixth, during their making and development, traditional cultures had to be restrained and influenced by the knowledge level of people, the historical background, and the social system during that period, therefore ending up being outdated or draffy. Therefore, in contrast with copying every traditional culture, we are supposed to get rid of the stale and bring forth freshness when we learn, study, and utilize these traditional cultures.

Seventh, further study of traditional Chinese culture, including Confucianism, becomes a vital path to understanding the national characteristics of the Chinese and the historical origin of their spiritual world. The Speech pointed out that the philosophical culture of China, which has been dominated by Confucianism for a long time, has been marching forward on a track of diversity. These schools of thought embody the view of the world, life, values, and aesthetic standards of the Chinese nation formed and passed down through generations, the kernel of which has become the fundamental cultural DNA of the Chinese nation. It is this DNA that was made when the Chinese people were improving themselves, managing their households, governing their country, staying in the proper position according to the climate, knowing how to apply common sense to different occasions, conforming to the laws of the nature and getting success, and scoring achievements, that distinguishes China from other nations.

Eighth, the Chinese Communists are Marxists who adhere to the scientific theories of Marxism and uphold and promote socialism with Chinese characteristics. The Chinese Communists are neither historical nihilists nor cultural nihilists. We believe that we must adapt the basic tenets of Marxism to China's conditions, take a scientific approach to traditional national cultures and those of other countries, and arm ourselves with all great philosophical cultures created by mankind. The Speech clearly declares that the Communist Party of China (CPC) has always been a loyal follower and advocate of excellent traditional Chinese culture. In a word, only by advancing toward the future with the historical legacy on our shoulders and sustaining the bloodline of our national cultures, can we do our job right today.

President Xi Jinping's speech was concise but comprehensive. It serves as an important principle that guides us to carry forward China's excellent traditional cultures, as well as a solemn declaration that advocates mutual learning among civilizations.

By grasping the spirit of the Speech, we will inherit and carry forward the excellent traditional cultures based on the following historical inspirations.

First, every country and nation serves as a link between past and future, and every modern culture evolves from its traditional forms. We should highly appreciate the contribution of excellent traditional culture in the past. Moreover, we must relate the promotion of excellent traditional cultures to the development of modern ones, so as to make these cultures an integral combination. By doing this, we can shoulder our legacy while propelling progress. We can make our future only when we remember the past. And we shall never plunge into historical nihilism that ruptures history and abandons the dialectics of development.

Second, every traditional ideology inevitably has its historical limitations. We must take their essence and remove the dross from them. What we should uphold is differentiating between good and bad traditional cultures and inheriting their real legacy, so as to draw lessons from the past and contribute to the present.

Third, every traditional ideology and culture was initiated against the specific historical background, social conditions, and historical stage, with its form and content conforming to the historical mission and social needs. The traditional culture, passed down to today, its forms and contents should be coordinated with new historical missions and social needs. We must strive to realize creative transformation and innovative development instead of simply copying every traditional culture.

Fourth, China today is a socialist country founded by the Chinese people under the leadership of the CPC. China aims to build socialism with Chinese characteristics and realize the Chinese dream of national rejuvenation at this stage. We must adhere to the guidance of Marxism as our dominant ideology and mainstream philosophical culture. Marxism epitomizes all the progressive thoughts and cultures of mankind. Featuring "harmony without uniformity," Marxism, along with various excellent traditional cultures and progressive modern thoughts, has formed a unity to serve socialism in today's China. By adhering to the guidance of Marxism, we will not obstruct but facilitate the constructive role of the excellent traditional cultures and progressive modern thoughts in jointly fulfilling the task of our times by touching people with culture. During the feudal society of more than 2,000 years, the predominant ideology of Confucianism did not inhibit other schools of thought from playing their constructive roles. History vividly expounds the dialectical relationship between philosophical cultures, complementing each other and forming a unity with diversity.

By grasping the spirit of this Speech, we should emphasize the following scientific understandings to promote exchanges and mutual learning among civilizations.

First, civilization, especially philosophical culture, is the soul of a country and a nation that should always be cherished. No matter which country or nation it is, it cannot stand tall in the non-appreciation of its philosophical culture and loss of its own soul.

Second, civilizations around the world all have uniqueness and beauty. We must safeguard the civilizational diversity of countries and nations and promote exchanges and mutual learning among civilizations instead of rejecting and displacing each other. Thus, the park of civilization can be lively and covered with colorful blossoms.

Third, the civilization of each country and nation has its own basis during their making and development. They all constitute a part of the modern world community and are supposed to coexist with other civilizations on equal status. The philosophical cultures of different countries and nations have their own features and attributes. None of them can be judged superior to another. We should seek common grounds while setting aside differences and learning from each other, not shutting doors to the outside and exclusively praising ourselves.

Fourth, exchanges and mutual learning among civilizations must be carried out in the context of a country and a nation with the spirit of reciprocal complementing and inclusive absorbing. It does not mean encouraging the picking up of anything without careful selection and screening. On the opposite, we have to reject the dross and internalize the essence.

The ICA will unswervingly take the important thoughts and principles set forth by President Xi Jinping in his speech as a reference. We will strive to carry forward China's excellent traditional culture, including Confucianism, and promote exchanges and dialogues among civilizations around the world. Efforts will be boosted to integrate these works by telling the stories of the inheritance and development of our civilization, as well as the stories of mutual learning among civilizations around the world. By doing this, we will make due contributions to world peace, the common development of all countries, and the construction of a community with a shared future for mankind with win-win cooperation at its core.

Basic Characteristics of Confucianism*

Speech at the International Academic Conference on Confucianism in Seoul

November 25, 2010

The international academic conference on Confucianism held in South Korea this time is a grand event in the international Confucian academic community. Experts and scholars from different countries and regions gathered in Seoul, making it a gathering of eminent individuals. They will engage in discussions and mutual learning on important issues related to Confucianism and contemporary society. Undoubtedly, this will have a positive impact on the development and progress of contemporary society.

A famous historian in China once said, "Confucianism was founded by Confucius and further developed by Mencius, followed by lots of effort by known or unknown scholars to keep it ever-changing and ever-growing." That is a good summary of the creation and development of Confucianism and Confucian culture.

Confucianism, founded by Confucius, is one of the leading schools among the Hundred Schools of Thought during the Spring and Autumn and Warring

---

* This speech was delivered on November 25, 2010, at the International Academic Conference on Confucianism in Seoul, hosted by Sungkyunkwan University and the ICA. The speech focused on Confucianism as an important historical culture with distinctive features such as openness, compatibility, comprehensiveness, and dialectics.

States periods (770–221 BC), both in its influence and number of scholars. Confucianism, along with Taoism, founded by Laozi, Mohism, founded by Mozi, and Legalism, founded by Hanfeizi, competed with, learned from, and influenced each other, making substantial contributions to forming the ideological and cultural environment marked by the "Contention of a Hundred Schools of Thought" during the Spring and Autumn and Warring States periods, and to forming China's multi-ethnic unitary socio-political environment marked by the establishment of the Qin Dynasty (221–207 BC).

Throughout the 2,000-year period from the Qin to the Qing Dynasty (1616–1911), Chinese feudal society witnessed changes of dynasties, Confucianism becoming the guiding philosophy for imperial governance, and Confucian culture becoming the root of Chinese traditional culture. Confucianism and Confucian culture also went through continuous changes and progress during those 2,000 years, including self-renewal, self-rectification, self-enrichment, and self-development. Confucianism experienced two fast developments during the two millennia. The first was during the Han Dynasty (206 BC–AD 220) when there was controversy over Confucian classics in the versions of ancient and modern languages, which ended with Emperor Wu's (156–87 BC) decision to honor Confucianism as the sole governing philosophy, officially making the study of Confucian classics the ruling doctrine at court. That marked a new stage for Confucianism. Another important phase of Confucianism started with the formation and development of Confucian philosophy from the Song and Ming dynasties (AD 960–1644), also known as "Neo-Confucianism of the Song and Ming Dynasties" or the "Song Learning," which included "Chengzhu Philosophy" and "Lu-Wang Theory of Mind." From Confucius and Mencius's teaching to the study of Confucian classics to Neo-Confucianism, Confucianism has gradually developed into a mature ideological system.

It is clear from its development that Confucianism holds an important space in traditional culture with distinctive characteristics, the following ones of which I believe are worth further study.

The first is its openness. Confucius and Mencius were both good at taking the essence of other schools, like Taoism and Mohism, to enrich Confucianism. Confucian scholars after them continued to learn and absorb other teachings, which has made Confucianism and Confucian culture both extensive and profound. For instance, Dong Zhongshu's (179–104 BC) theory of "Harmonious Interaction between Heaven and Man" had some of Gong Yang School's ideas. Another example is Neo-Confucianism, which was developed based on experience learned from other schools like Taoism and the introduction of Buddhism from overseas. In conclusion, one significant feature of Confucianism and Confucian culture is an openness to learning and practice.

The second characteristic is Confucianism's compatibility, its ability to maintain a harmonious relationship with other doctrines despite their differences for their common purpose of good governance. Confucianism was mixed with philosophies such as Legalism, Taoism, and Buddhism for governing the country and society both during the Han Dynasty when it was honored as the sole governing ideology and during the Tang Dynasty when Confucianism, Buddhism, and Taoism were treated equally at the Royal court. Because of this compatibility, Confucianism was regarded as the fundamental governing philosophy for dynasty after dynasty throughout Chinese history.

Another important feature of Confucianism is comprehensiveness. It advocates and adheres to the political view of self-cultivation, family management, regional governance, and peace-keeping of the country. Those four elements are deemed equally important, and each should help improve the others. Confucianism attaches importance to both self-improvement and the governance of the country and society. It's applied both to the ethical ideological study of individuals and social education and to the pursuit of political ideology for governing and politics. Because of this comprehensiveness, Confucianism has maintained its core position in ideology and traditional culture in Chinese history.

Confucianism is also featured by its dialectical nature. Just like other ideologies and cultures, Confucianism and Confucian culture have their defects and flaws despite their strengths and essence. Confucianism requires people to strengthen self-cultivation, overcome their weaknesses, and learn from other people's merits and mistakes. There are quite a few Confucian scholars who are able to critically inherit their own doctrine to different extents, conducting concrete analysis using dialectics to develop the right things and discard the problematic ones. That is not unusual throughout the history of Confucianism.

For example, some Confucian scholars carried out a dialectical analysis on the study of Confucianism classics in both ancient and modern languages and Neo-Confucianism and gave credit to their achievements and also criticized their weaknesses for being either too utilitarian, or too obsessed with details, or too vague. It is because of the dialectical nature that Confucianism and Confucian culture have maintained their vitality and vigor to this day.

Every significant ideology and culture can ensure limitless development and boundless communication as long as they continuously adapt to socio-economic needs and the progress of mankind. Confucianism and Confucian culture have certainly achieved that. Though it originated in China, Confucianism was spread to countries and regions outside of China very early on, first to China's Asian neighbors and then further to countries in Europe, America, and other continents. On the one hand, it integrated with local ideologies and cultures, positively influencing ideological progress and socio-economic development. On the other hand, the ideologies and cultures of other places helped Confucianism grow and mature. Confucianism's diffusion around the world for thousands of years has already become an impressive global cultural phenomenon.

The Republic of Korea, where we are holding this conference, is known for its tradition of etiquette and Confucian culture. Well-known Confucian scholars such as Choe Chiwon, Hyecho, Jeong Mong-ju, Jeong Do-jeon, Ryu Seung-ryong, Lee Toegye, and Lee Er were born on this land. Here, we can also find Andong, the historic city with a rich Confucian tradition, and Sungkyunkwan University, which honors its mission to promote and practice Confucianism. Those are examples of heritage that the Korean people should take pride in and the international Confucian society should praise.

Currently, Confucianism is facing new realities in communication, exchanges, and development, which is no coincidence because of the global status quo, modern society's development, and the problems and challenges ahead. The world is undergoing dramatic changes and rapid development with the deepening of economic globalization and fast scientific progress, bringing challenges along with economic and cultural achievements. If the problems and challenges are not handled properly, the whole world's peace and stability, future economic and social development, and the common cause of mankind will be at risk. When seeking the resolution to problems confronting the international community, more and more visionaries have turned to Confucianism for enlightenment and wisdom. They are truly far-sighted people who can draw on the wisdom of history.

Confucianism and Confucian culture are world cultural heritages with a long history and philosophical achievements that are of great value in solving nations' problems. The two are valuable in the social, economic, and cultural development of today's world and in dealing with relationships between countries, economies, and between humans and nature. Those achievements include righteous thinking that believes in benevolence and justice; people-oriented thinking that regards the general public as the basis of a country with the public's safety secured; governance thinking that values self-cultivation; family management, regional governance and peace-keeping; practical thinking that emphasizes both learning and practice; reform thought that seeks truth and innovation; harmonious thinking that seeks harmony when there are differences; integrity thinking that praises honesty and faithfulness; good-neighborliness thinking that advocates friendly relationships between neighboring countries; and many more. We sincerely hope Confucian scholars of all countries and regions can continue their exploration and interpretation of the Confucian heritage, expressing their own ideas and thinking, generating more results and solutions, and applying the value of Confucianism to practice in contemporary education and economic and social development. Let's make our contribution to maintaining world and regional peace, to the common development of all countries, and to the common cause of humankind.

The Constructive Role of Confucian Culture in Cultivating People and National Governance*

Speech at the Academic Conference on the Development of Confucian Education in the 21st Century

January 11, 2012

At the beginning of 2012, we gathered in Hong Kong and Macao to discuss the development of Confucian education, which is as meaningful as *The Analects of Confucius* said—"to meet our friends on the grounds of culture, and by friendship to help our virtues."

People of every nation and country regard culture as their spiritual home. And Chinese culture is the spiritual home shared by the Chinese nation and all our fellowmen. No matter where we live or at any time in history, we, as part of the Chinese nation, all draw knowledge and ideas from the Chinese culture to cultivate our minds and merits. For thousands of years, Confucian ideas and

---

* In January 2012, the ICA held a symposium themed Development of Confucian Education in the 21st Century in Hong Kong and Macao, which was attended by hundreds of experts and scholars from around China. This speech was delivered at the main hall of the Academic Community Hall of the University of Hong Kong (HKU) on January 11, 2012. It put forward the remarkable strength of Confucianism and Confucian culture, that is, to emphasize both learning and practicing, with the former paving the way for the latter. This called upon scholars to further promote Confucian education, so as to attain greater achievements.

culture, as the backbone of traditional Chinese culture, have been significantly contributing to the development and growth of our nation, as well as the progress and prosperity of China.

In my opinion, one of the remarkable strengths of Confucian philosophy and culture is that they emphasize both learning in school and practicing in society, which are complementary to each other. This is so-called the "integration of learning and practicing" and the "unity of knowing and doing," thus achieving "sageliness within and kingliness without." Since learning paves the way for practical statecraft, Confucian scholars have always attached great importance to education, especially in Confucianism and Sinology, i.e., Chinese learning. Confucius, who initiated Confucianism and passed down his philosophy, spent most of his life in education. Shifting the focus of education from the elite to the common people, he summed up some valuable experiences such as "teaching without discrimination," "teaching students according to their aptitude," and "to teach is to learn." He thus became an outstanding educator in ancient China. Following Confucius, many scholars of fame endeavored in the education of Confucianism and Sinology. They advocated for equal attention to both knowledge accumulation and moral cultivation, which are both indispensable. This is what we know as "excellent in both character and learning" and "equal stress on integrity and ability." Only with such characteristics can people make outstanding contributions to the governance of society and the whole country.

Here, I would like to quote Liang Qichao (1873–1929), a famous modern scholar of Confucianism and Sinology, on education. In his later years, Liang Qichao taught at the Tsinghua Academy of Chinese Learning. Once, he told his students: "Schools today are no more than diploma mills. When they are dying for diplomas and certificates, students show little concern for fortifying their stamina or sharpening independent judgment. This is my biggest concern. I hope that beyond knowledge, moral cultivation should also be your pursuit. As Wang Yangming (a Neo-Confucian philosopher in the Ming Dynasty) proposed, we shall cultivate ourselves through longstanding practice instead of instant success or boasting and bragging. So just march forward, youngsters, to pursue knowledge and cultivate yourselves." Liang Qichao's words implied his concerns and comments on the educational background then, but he still had earnest expectations toward young people. China has so far undergone profound changes over the past 80 years. Yet, the sincere advice from Liang should remain in our minds. His idea of pursuing unity of knowledge and self-cultivation is also the essence of education, which has been verified generation after generation. "What is education? Education is to teach people to keep straight," Liang added. This is an incisive definition. Therefore, whether educating youth or adults, we should always pay equal attention to both the imparting of knowledge and the guidance of morality. History has proved that learning Confucianism and Sinology is indispensable for one's cultivation of thinking and morality.

Hong Kong and Macao have long experiences in practicing Confucian education. And the Chinese mainland has also gained new experience in this regard over the past few years. We can exchange more often to further promote Confucian education across China and utilize Confucian culture to cultivate people and national governance. I also sincerely hope that Confucian scholars from all over China will apply their research to further promote Confucian education.

Since the return of Hong Kong and Macao, we've seen increasing educational and cultural communication between them and the mainland. This academic conference also contributes to such communication. With the support and joint efforts of experts and scholars from the Chinese mainland, Hong Kong, and Macao, we'll enhance educational and cultural communication and cooperation in all forms for further progress and prosperity of Chinese culture.

Explore and Give Play to the Ideological Value of Confucianism[*]

Speech at the Conference on the Foundations of Reason and Morality: A Dialogue between Confucianism and German Philosophy

July 17, 2012

Today, at this conference on "The Foundations of Reason and Morality," we are engaged in a philosophical dialogue between Confucianism and German philosophy. Everyone here today is an accomplished expert in their chosen field of research. We are very fortunate to have so many outstanding people gathered here today.

China and Germany are situated in Asia and Europe, respectively. However, the distance separating them and the differences in their national conditions can-

---

[*] From July 17 to 20, 2012, the ICA, in collaboration with the German Institute for Civic Education, the Department of Philosophy at the University of Cologne, the German International Intercultural Philosophy Association, and the German Confucian Association, jointly organized the "Dialogue between Confucianism and German Philosophy" international academic symposium in Munich. This is an excerpt from the opening speech delivered on July 17, 2012, during the symposium. The speech briefly reviewed the history of intellectual and cultural exchanges between China and Germany, as well as between China and Europe, over the centuries, emphasizing the preciousness of this historical period, which has mutually enriched the development of both sides. The speech proposed that scholars from various countries should collaboratively explore and utilize the philosophical values of Confucianism, seeking wisdom, experience, and historical insights necessary to address the challenges facing the world today.

not impede intellectual and cultural exchanges between China and Germany or between China and other European countries, or keep them from learning from each other. China and Europe have a long history of exchanges and learning from each other. The development of both of them can benefit from the synergetic effect of using the other's strengths to compensate for one's own weaknesses.

Since the late Middle Ages in Europe, Chinese civilization, most prominently exemplified by Confucianism, was brought to Europe by European visitors to China and Chinese visitors to Europe. The Italian Jesuit priest Matteo Ricci was one of the earliest Europeans to introduce Chinese history and culture to Europe. He lived in China for 28 years. In 1594, he disseminated the completed translations of the Four Books (*The Great Learning, The Doctrine of the Mean, The Analects of Confucius,* and *Mencius*) into Latin. In 1626, the French Jesuit priest Nicolas Trigualt translated the Five Classics (*The Book of Songs, The Book of Documents, The Book of Changes, The Book of Rites,* and *The Spring and Autumn Annals*) into Latin. The introduction of the Confucian classics and other historical and cultural classics of China to Europe by Jesuit missionaries who came to China had an enormous effect on intellectual and cultural circles in Europe. For nearly 100 years, from the end of the 17th century until well into the 18th century, the whole of Europe was enveloped in an enthusiasm for Chinese culture. Many famous scholars from Germany, France, England, Italy, Russia, and other European countries were very interested in and constantly studied Chinese philosophy, literature, history, economics, politics, and military affairs. They published many visionary works interpreting and praising Chinese civilization.

French Enlightenment thinkers were the first to study Confucianism and Chinese history and culture and be deeply influenced by it. In order to genuinely understand China, Montesquieu had a long talk with Huang Jialue, a Chinese working in the French Royal Library. Montesquieu's *The Spirit of Laws* and other works were influenced by Confucianism, particularly Neo-Confucianism. Voltaire thought that Confucian philosophy was free of superstition, absurdity, and distortions of nature, so it was the philosophy most suited to human reason. Diderot thought that the fundamental concept of Chinese philosophy was reason and that Confucius advocated ruling the world through morals and reason.

Holbach thought, "China is the only country in the world to integrate politics and ethics." All these thinkers were leading French Encyclopedists. Quesnay, the founder of the French Physiocratic school, also thought that European political and economic thinkers should look to Chinese culture as a model. His Physiocratic theory was influenced by the Confucian thinking of conforming to nature and taking agriculture as the foundation of the state. Turgot, a Physiocrat who served as the French comptroller-general of finance, also suggested that France needed to draw on the experience of Chinese civilization in order to develop.

When Chinese history and culture first entered Germany, German scholars studied it with unprecedented enthusiasm. At that time, many scholars not only read the pre-Qin Confucian classics in Latin translation, but also a German translation of Dong Zhongshu's *Luxuriant Dew of the Spring and Autumn Annals* by Otto Franke. Eminent German intellectuals and philosophers such as Leibniz, Kant, Feuerbach, Goethe, and Schiller studied Chinese history and culture and published many incisive papers. Leibniz was the first great European intellectual to acclaim the usefulness of Chinese civilization for European civilization. Scientific institutes he helped establish in Berlin, Vienna, and St. Petersburg made the investigation of Chinese philosophy and culture a research topic. In a long letter entitled "On Chinese Philosophy," written in 1715, he expressed his admiration for early Chinese philosophers' open-mindedness, independent thinking, speculative acumen, and reliance on reason. He advocated that Europe should study and imbibe China's political and moral culture, and China should study and absorb Europe's theoretical science. Inspired by the Chinese *The Book of Changes*, Leibniz wrote his theory of the binary system, which strengthened the intellectual foundation of dialectics in German philosophy. Inspired by the philosophy of Confucian doctrine, Kant constructed a scientific method for investigating the natural world from a dialectical, connected, and developmental standpoint, and he was a pioneer of classical German philosophy that differed from British empiricism and French rationalism. Feuerbach thought Confucius' dictum, "Do not impose on others what you do not accept for yourself," was a complete, pure, and correct moral system and a kind of noble philosophical ethics. Goethe and Schiller were known as the most dazzling twin stars of German literature; both had a deep interest in Chinese literature, and their writings included Goethe's *Chinese-German Book of Seasons and Hours* and Schiller's *Turandot*.

I don't know whether it's appropriate to say that European intellectuals and political leaders drew upon and used the essence of the philosophy, ethics, and humanistic spirit of the ancient philosophers of the Confucian, Taoist, and other schools and the essence of Chinese material and intangible culture throughout China's long history to smash the theological and political fetters that strangled Europe in the Middle Ages and spur the rise of the European Enlightenment and the development of modern European civilization, or whether this thinking provided intellectual nourishment, political impetus, and material technological conditions represented by the four great inventions that exerted a positive influence on the progress of European civilization. Whenever we think that China might have made such an important contribution to European and world civilization, we feel very honored.

Without a doubt, cultural exchanges, dissemination, and influence are always mutual. China studied and assimilated a great deal of progressive thinking, developmental experience, and advanced technology from Europe in intellectual culture, economics, and science and technology. The essence of European civilization has positively influenced the development of Chinese civilization. We fully realize this.

When Ricci was in China doing his missionary work, many scholars and officials of the Ming Dynasty learned about Europe's intellectual culture and its science and technology. Xu Guangqi (1562–1633) and Li Zhizao (1565–1630) were the most famous scholars. Xu Guangqi was the Minister of Rites in the Ming court and was a prominent agronomist and scientist. He became acquainted with Ricci in 1600 and sought scientific instruction from him with the humble attitude that a Confucian should be ashamed if there is anything he doesn't know. He translated Euclid's *Elements of Geometry* with Ricci and also wrote *Hydrological Methods of the Great West* on the basis of Ricci's lectures, which introduced European hydrology to China. He also compiled the *Calendar Compendium of the Chongzhen Reign* using the latest European astronomical knowledge. He was one of the foremost scholars of the late Ming Dynasty who studied Western science and culture and was a pioneer in Chinese-Western cultural exchanges. Li Zhizao was a foremost astronomer, mathematician, and outstanding late Ming Dynasty scientist. He worked with Ricci in compiling and translating *Illustrated Explanation of the Sphere and the Astrolabe* and *Rules of Arithmetic Common to Cultures* that introduced European astronomy, mathematics, and natural science to China. He also translated Aristotle's *On the Heavens* and *Introduction to Dialectics* together with the Portuguese scholar Francois Furtado. The spread of this cultural and scientific knowledge throughout China made an invaluable contribution to China's social development and progress.

In modern times, various ways of thinking have passed from Europe to China. Many translations of important works from European countries in the humanities and natural sciences, from philosophy, history, literature, and art to economics, politics, law, and science and technology, have been published and distributed in China. These books are vast in number and cover a wide range of fields, almost to the point where we are unable to keep up with them. Works on literature, art, and philosophy by several German masters, in particular, have made a deep impression on the people of China. Goethe's *Faust* and *The Sorrows of Young Werther* and Schiller's *Intrigue and Love* and *Ode to Joy* are popular classics among Chinese cultural circles and people. China's Wang Guowei, Liang Qichao, Lu Xun (1881–1936), and Guo Moruo (1892–1978) have all spoken highly of these works. Immanuel Kant, Ludwig Feuerbach, and Georg Wilhelm Friedrich Hegel are the most frequently studied and most influential German philosophers in China. At the beginning of the 20th century, as the theories of Marx and Engels spread across China, the ideas of Feuerbach and Hegel, whose works were sources of inspiration for Marx and Engels' pioneering thoughts, also became popular in China. In a conversation with the American journalist Edgar Snow on German philosophy, the great leader of China, Mao Zedong, said, "When I was young, I believed in Kant's philosophy and read some of the philosophical works of Feuerbach and Hegel." He commented that Ernst Haeckel's books were "full of rich material" and that he was "actually a materialist." Indeed, Mao Zedong's important philosophical works *On Practice* and *On Contradiction* clearly borrowed the rational core of the philosophies of Feuerbach and Hegel on materialism and dialectical thinking.

Marx and Engels are undoubtedly the Germans who have had the greatest impact on the progress and development of China's modern culture. In the eyes of the Chinese people, they are not only great philosophers, thinkers, and economists, but also great theoreticians who provided a scientific guiding ideology for China's revolution and construction. From February to May 1899, the 121st to 124th issues of *Wanguo Gongbao* (Multinational Communique) serialized a series of articles introducing the main content of the book *Social Evolution* by the British sociologist Benjamin Kidd. These articles were translated by the British missionary Timothy Richard and narrated by the Shanghai native Cai Erkang. In May 1899, these articles were compiled and published as a book titled *Da Tong Xue* (The Great Unity, from which the Chinese people first learned of Marx and Engels and Marxism. Afterward, Li Dazhao (1889–1927), Chen Duxiu (1879–1942), and Li Da (1890–1966), leaders of the CPC during the early period, became the main disseminators of Marxism in China. Once Marxism was integrated with the realities of China, including China's fine traditional culture, it brought earth-shaking historic changes to our country, which had been rendered poor, weak, semi-colonial, and semi-feudal in modern times. The CPC has led the Chinese people, after a long struggle and arduous exploration, to finally succeed in embarking on the broad road of building socialism with Chinese characteristics.

The world has already entered the era of economic globalization, in which new scientific and technological discoveries are made with each passing day, and the world's economies, cultures, and societies are increasingly interdependent. Both materially and spiritually, human civilization has made incredible progress. Nevertheless, economic globalization and the prevalence of neo-liberalism, especially the laissez-faire market economy, give rise to many problems and disadvantages. The unbridled pursuit of profit, endless competition, overuse of resources, high-consumption lifestyles, and unscrupulous financial speculation divorced from the real economy have all resulted in serious resource depletion, environmental pollution, and a variety of conflicts, as well as a greater wealth disparity between nations, regions, and members of societies, greater materialism, moral and spiritual decay, and both economic and social crises. These pressing issues must be settled urgently by the international community. Where do the solutions to these problems lie? Where can we find the necessary historical experience and wisdom to learn from?

Politicians, people of insight, and experts around the world are thinking about and seeking answers to these problems. To find the solutions, every country must strengthen consultations in which the participants are given equal say, and different civilizations must strengthen dialogue and exchanges, so as to assimilate the best aspects each country and each civilization has to offer. Whether it is economic or social development, every country around the world should strive to achieve sustainable development by rationally utilizing resources and protecting the environment. Whether between countries or regions, every country should eliminate military and political conflicts to achieve lasting peace. Whether they are developed or developing countries, every country should seek to create mutual benefits and common prosperity. These are the goals that people around the world wish to achieve.

Confucian culture can play an important role in solving the aforementioned problems. Some people of insight around the world have recognized this point. In 1988, the Nobel laureates held a meeting in Paris with the theme "Facing the 21st Century." During a press conference for the meeting, Sweden's Dr. Hannes Alfven said that if mankind is to survive, it must learn from the wisdom of Confucius. In his book *Megatrends Asia*, the American scholar John Naisbitt also commented that to prevent moral decay, the erosion of professional ethics, hedonistic consumption, individualism, and political fanaticism, there should be a renewed emphasis on Confucian values. Their views have become the consensus among many important political figures, experts, and scholars around the world.

As an ideological and cultural heritage with worldwide influence, Confucianism contains a wealth of ideas. These ideas still have value today, whether it is to help solve problems in national and social governance or economic and cultural development or deal with issues connected to relations between states, economic and social relations, or the relationship between man and nature. For example, Confucianism contains thinking on bringing peace to, enriching and protecting the people and putting them first; thinking on respecting, understanding, and upholding virtue and taking virtue as one's sole source of support; thinking on neutrality, peace, harmony, and on harmony without uniformity; thinking on benevolent love, judging others after oneself, always keeping morality close to one's side, and making all nations live together peacefully; thinking on constantly improving oneself, pursuing great virtue, being frugal in one's comforts for oneself, and the unity of heaven and man; and thinking on not forgetting danger in times of peace, not forgetting chaos in times of order and being prepared for danger in times of safety. From these rich ideas, we can find the wisdom and experience to solve the problems and difficulties presented by economic globalization and neo-liberalism. Our colleagues at the ICA are willing to work with thinkers, politicians, and scholars to this end. This "dialogue between Confucianism and German philosophy" to discuss the "foundations of reason and morality" is also a useful attempt to explore and give play to the ideological value of Confucianism in order to promote world peace and the common development of all countries.

Issues Concerning the Study and Popularization of Confucian Culture[*]

Speech at the Forum for the Chinese Traditional Virtues and the Construction of Socialist Spiritual Civilization & the 5th Popularization Symposium on Confucianism

August 18, 2012

The ICA is an international academic association founded by Confucian research and dissemination groups from nine countries and regions. The aim and task of the ICA are to study, disseminate, popularize, and apply Confucian culture and to facilitate economic and social progress, world peace, and common development of all countries.

ICA President Ye Xuanping has always called on the ICA to adhere to the policy of putting equal emphasis on Confucian research and popularization.

---

[*] From August 18 to 19, 2012, the ICA, the Committee of Culture, History, and Study of the CPPCC National Committee, the CPPCC Shanxi Provincial Committee, the Shanxi Chinese Culture Promotion Society held in Fenyang, Shanxi, the Forum for the Chinese Traditional Virtues and the Construction of Socialist Spiritual Civilization & the 5th Popularization Symposium on Confucianism. This was the invited speech at the opening ceremony on August 18, 2012. It put forward some significant opinions on the study and popularization of Confucian culture in the Chinese mainland, such as "equal importance to both research and popularization," "on upholding Marxism as a guide," "about taking the essence and removing the dross," and "the study and popularization of Confucian culture should be combined with the construction of socialist spiritual civilization."

Domestically, we have paid close attention to both research and popularization for their mutual promotion. Many of our experts and scholars are both researchers and popularizers of Confucian culture. Practice has proved that this policy is correct and has yielded good results.

In the past five years since 2007, the ICA has held a forum on the popularization of Confucianism every year in China, with the aim of exchanging information and achievements in the popularization of Confucianism and summarizing and promoting new successful experiences initiated in different regions. Results tell us that this kind of symposium is very effective. It actually plays a connecting role in the further popularization of Confucian culture.

The progress made in the popularization of Confucian culture in the past five years can be summarized in the following aspects. Firstly, education authorities at all levels have paid more attention to the education of Confucian culture, and Confucian classics are gradually increasing their coverage in the primary and secondary school curriculum, which helps to cultivate the traditional cultural literacy of primary and secondary school students. Secondly, some places were inspired by the form of ancient academies, and new academies were set up by taking into account the conditions today. Results of such exploration show that this new form of academy of classical learning can play a complementary role in the current school education, and it is very useful for students to learn and master the traditional cultural knowledge centered on Confucianism, and to understand and inherit the fine traditions of the Chinese nation. Thirdly, publications about Confucianism culture were released frequently, and Confucianism lectures and forums were held one after another. Fourthly, more Confucian cultural activities were held at the community level, along with increasing volunteers in the dissemination and popularization of Confucian culture. Fifthly, progress has been made in using Confucian culture to educate corporate staff and train entrepreneurs and managers. Sixthly, Confucian culture has been used in the correction of criminals in some places. Seventhly, the popularization of Confucian culture is becoming a part of history education, moral education, and the construction of socialist spiritual civilization in all localities, with importance attached by government leaders at all levels. In a word, there has been a new trend of studying Chinese historical and cultural classics, carrying forward the fine traditions of the Chinese nation and serving the construction of socialism with Chinese characteristics, in which the popularization of Confucian culture plays an important role that should not be underestimated.

Looking back on the research and popularization of Confucian culture over the past few years, I would like to raise the following issues for your discussion. I think that the points below need to be further emphasized and followed.

Firstly, we should attach equal importance to both research and popularization. Any research or study is for application ultimately. Popularizing Confucian culture is also a process of dissemination and application. Through our popularization efforts, we can spread the knowledge of Confucian culture and its essence to the masses and help them know how our ancestors lived and how to govern the family, the society, and the country. This is quite helpful for them to understand the basic principles and experience of their ancestors in doing things and learn how to properly cultivate themselves, manage their own homes, and serve the country in today's socialist society. Confucianism is a kind of historical and cultural heritage. Still, its essence of thought can always play a role in the progress of history, and it will constantly enrich itself with new practices to keep pace with the times. The essence of Confucianism, once grasped and applied in combination with today's social practice, can also become the mental and material power for people to transform the subjective and objective worlds and serve the cause of building socialism. This is what Chairman Mao Zedong called "making the past serve the present." We should attach importance not only to the study of Confucian culture, but also to the popularization of Confucian culture. We should popularize the research results to the masses and enhance the research level through popularization. It is an honor to devote oneself to the study of Confucian culture and its popularization. We hope more and more scholars devote themselves to the popularization effort and make great achievements in both research and popularization. Scholars know best where the essence of Confucianism lies, what is suitable for today's use in Confucianism, and what is lacking in today's masses that can be learned from history and culture. "He who knows the importance of learning is wise, but he who knows people well can be a philosopher." By contributing to popularizing Confucian culture, scholars will see the benefit of "half the work with double results."

Secondly, we should uphold Marxism as a guide. Some people believe that advocating the study of Confucianism and popularizing Confucian culture and education would indicate that Marxism and socialist ideological education have some problems in effectiveness. This is clearly a misunderstanding. We are a socialist country under the leadership and administration of the CPC, and Marxism is our guiding ideology, which occupies a leading position in socialist ideology. This fundamental principle cannot and will not be shaken at any time, and the position of Marxism in China cannot be replaced by other ideologies, so there will be no question of whether Marxism and socialist ideology are still effective. We should not separate the research, dissemination, popularization, and application of Confucian culture from adherence to Marxism's guidance and socialist ideological education, but should make them align with each other. In its long-term struggle, the CPC has always adhered to the combination of the basic principles of Marxism with China's conditions. "China's conditions" include not only the reality but also the historical reality, and naturally also the Chinese historical and cultural reality dominated by Confucianism. The older generation of revolutionaries Mao Zedong, Zhou Enlai, Liu Shaoqi, and Zhu De, among others, have always paid attention to integrating Marxist thought with the actual conditions of Chinese history and culture, and have been using the essence of Chinese history and culture to solve the ideological and cultural development problems in revolution and national building. In the works and speeches by Mao Zedong and other Chinese leaders, there are many quotes from Confucian classics and examples applying the essence of Confucianism. The criticism and denial of Confucius and Confucianism in the "Cultural Revolution" is an abnormality of the special period, which does not represent the overall attitude of the CPC toward Confucianism and other historical cultures. We are now learning from the lesson of the "Cultural Revolution" by advocating the learning, studying, popularizing, and applying of Confucian culture. Strengthening the study and popularization of Confucian culture is an integral part of our socialist cultural work and ideological construction, which, like other cultural work, should be guided by Marxism. Without a doubt, adhering to the guidance of Marxism doesn't mean using Marxism to interfere and label academic and cultural work. Instead, we should apply Marxist viewpoints and methods to analyze problems in the study, dissemination, and application of ideology and culture and give guidance for removing the coarse from the fine, eliminating the false, and preserving the true, so as to make it suitable for socialist modernization. This is very clear.

Thirdly, we should take the essence and remove the dross. "Taking the essence and removing the dross" was put forward by Chairman Mao Zedong and has been advocated ever since, which is a proper policy of the CPC and the country in dealing with history and culture. This policy embodies the scientific attitude of historical materialism. *The Analects of Confucius* says, "There will be good qualities that I can select for imitation and bad ones that will teach me what requires correction in myself," which contains this meaning. During the emergence and development of Confucianism and Confucian culture, we can often see a phenomenon: the works and thoughts of Confucian scholars of the previous generation were not all followed but were scrutinized with critical thinking and enriched by later generations of Confucian scholars. From the Confucius and Mencius thoughts in the pre-Qin period to Confucian classics in the Han Dynasty, to Neo-Confucianism and the Philosophy of the Mind in the Song and Ming dynasties, to Puxue ("unadorned learning") in the Qing Dynasty, we can see a historical context of these changes. Confucian thinking and culture originated in the feudal society of ancient China. As an ideology and culture in the feudal society, it inevitably left an economic, political, and social mark of that era. There must be good thinking in line with the requirements of historical development, social progress, and some backward ideological dross. Therefore, in the study and popularization of Confucian culture, we should adopt a scientific attitude of critical inheritance and continue removing the coarse from the fine and the false from the true. We should not bring it all in without critical analysis. For example, in Confucianism, we should abandon the thoughts involving blind loyalty and filial piety that advocate absolute obedience blindly, the thoughts that oppose social equality and advocate strict hierarchy, the ones that propagate superstition and mysticism, despise manual labor and laborers, discriminate against working women, and hamper the overall development of children. In a word, only by insisting on taking its essence and removing its dross, can the research and popularization of Confucian culture develop soundly and make the past serve the present scientifically.

Fourthly, the study and popularization of Confucian culture should be combined with the construction of a socialist spiritual civilization. This symposium tries to combine the two. The study and popularization of Confucian cultural knowledge and its ideological essence, as part of socialist cultural work, should undoubtedly be combined with the construction of socialist spiritual civilization and included in its developmental planning. In fact, it is encouraging that many places and departments have done or are doing so. An important task of socialist cultural work and the building of socialist spiritual civilization is to strengthen ideological education in patriotism and collectivism among officials and the masses, especially among young people. In Confucian culture, education resources of patriotism and collectivism can be seen a lot. For example, *Zuo Zhuan* said, "Do not forget the country in the face of adversity," "Put the country ahead of oneself," and "As long as it is for the nation, it doesn't matter whether it is life or death." Jia Yi's *New Book* said, "If it's a matter concerning the nation and the public, home and private matters can be put behind." Sima Qian said in *Bao Ren An Shu* (Letter in Response to Ren An), "I'd rather sacrifice myself for the sake of my country" and "go to the public difficult." Cao Zhi's *Miscellaneous Poetry* said, "Leisure is not my ambition; the country is my concern." Cui Hao said in his poems, "It was common to serve the country since the ancient times." Fan Zhongyan's "Yueyanglou Ji" (Note on Yueyang Tower) said, "Be the first to worry about the world's troubles and the last to enjoy its pleasures." Ouyang Xiu's "Pengdang Lun" (Discourse on Factions) said, "When serving the country, we should be concerted with solidarity." Sima Guang's "On Imperial Advisors" said that we should "entirely subordinate our own interests to those of the country." Lu You said in his poems, "A humble position does not mean I will forget my worries about the country." Zhang Juzheng said, "To serve the country with dedication." In Gu Yanwu's *Record of Daily Knowledge*, he said, "The rise and fall of the world is everybody's responsibility." Lin Zexu said in his poems, "I will do whatever it takes to serve my country even at the cost of my own life, regardless of fortune or misfortune to myself," to name just a few. "The world," "country," and "public" mentioned above refer to both the state and the public. In Confucian culture, love of home and motherland and respect for the collective interest are compatible and unified. The patriotic, family-loving, and collective thoughts advocated by the Confucian sages in history should be regarded as the essence of Confucian culture and Chinese history and culture, as well as an invaluable cultural strength. We should creatively apply these ideological resources to the education of patriotism and collectivism among officials, the masses, and young people through the dissemination and popularization of Confucian culture. Our ancestors always spoke of collectivism, esteeming and trusting the wisdom, strength, and function of collectivism. They believed in collective wisdom and solidarity for national success. Today, when building socialism with Chinese characteristics, we should advocate adherence to collectivism among the people. History is created by the people, and socialism is a creative cause of them. This is a basic principle of Marxist historical materialism. Therefore, collectivism must be a core value of socialism. Collectivism and collective strength don't mean that we ignore the important role of individuals. Instead, we are emphasizing that individuals live in a social collective. An individual would accomplish little without the support, wisdom, and strength of the collective, no matter how capable he or she is. We should strengthen the study and popularization of Confucian culture, fully explore and utilize all progressive and valuable ideological resources, and serve our socialist spiritual civilization and socialist modernization.

Dialogue and Mutual Learning between Different Civilizations Is the Path toward Common Progress[*]

Speech at the Dialogue between Confucianism and Russian Civilization International Academic Forum

June 26, 2013

We are gathered here for the "Dialogue between Confucianism and Russian Civilization" International Academic Forum during a bout of pleasant weather in Moscow. Dialogue is a major event in the exchange of the world's cultures and civilizations.

As two great countries with a long history and significant influence on the world, China and Russia are friendly neighbors. The interaction of civilizations between the two countries started long ago, from the ancient Silk Road, across

---

[*] From June 26 to 27, 2013, the ICA, the Far Eastern Research Institute of the Russian Academy of Sciences, and the China Confucius Foundation jointly organized the "Dialogue between Confucianism and Russian Civilization" International Academic Forum in Moscow. Academician Sergey Tikhvinsky, Honorary Chairman of the Russia-China Friendship Association, Academician Mikhail Titarenko, Director of the Far Eastern Research Institute of the Russian Academy of Sciences, and Ambassador Li Hui of China attended the opening ceremony of the forum. This is the keynote speech given on June 26, 2013, during the academic forum. The speech provides a detailed review of the history of cultural and civilizational exchanges between China and Russia since the 17th century, drawing profound historical insights. It expresses the hope to continue exploring all the essence contained in Confucianism, a global cultural treasure, together with Russian scholars, and to creatively apply it.

Central Asia, along the Volga River, and to other significant regions of Russia. The economic ties between China and Russia can be traced back to ancient times, thousands of years ago, when friendships between the two peoples were built.

In the late 16th century, Jesuit missionaries represented by Matteo Ricci preached in China and spread Chinese historical classical works, mainly works of Confucianism, to Europe. At that time, a "Chinese culture fever" set in and lasted for over 100 years, which had a crucial influence on the development of modern civilization in European countries, including Russia. Some scholars stated that the "Chinese culture fever" actually was a "great discovery of culture" after the Age of Discovery. Nolan Pliny Jacobson, Chairman of the Asian Area Studies Program at Winthrop College, once said, "One can hardly imagine a more substantial and many-sided influence than the impact China was having upon 17th and 18th-century Europe."

At that time, a group of well-known European scholars was committed to the research and dissemination of Confucianism and the thinking of a hundred other schools, some of whom were the backbone of the Enlightenment of the 17th and 18th centuries, including Leibniz, Wolff, and Goethe from Germany, Bayle, Voltaire, Quesnay, Diderot, and Baron d'Holbach from France, and Temple from Britain. They praised Chinese historical culture represented by Confucianism, and some even worshiped Confucius and his thinking. Voltaire, for example, hung a portrait of Confucius in his prayer room; Quesnay and Goethe were regarded as the "Confucius of Europe" and "Confucius at Weimar," respectively.

After the 17th century, Russian scholars studying ideology and culture began conducting research on and spreading Confucianism and other bits of Chinese historical culture in their country. These scholars introduced a number of Chinese classical works to Russia. During the regime of Emperor Kangxi (1654–1722) of the Qing Dynasty, some Russian students were sent to China to learn about Chinese culture, including the classics of Confucianism. From 1715 to 1860, 13 groups of Russian missionaries were sent to China to research Chinese historical culture. Among those, some became renowned sinologists and played a significant role in introducing Confucianism to Russia. For example, *The Great Learning*, translated by sinologist Leontyev, was published in 1780; *The Doctrine of the Mean*, translated by Agassenov, was published in 1788; as well as *The Book of Changes*, *The Art of War*, *Collected Better-Known Sayings*, and some other Chinese cultural classics translated by other sinologists. The 18th century witnessed the publishing of over 120 kinds of works related to China by Russia, followed by the 19th century when Russian scholars made great strides in applying Chinese historical culture to the fields of philosophy, religion, history, geography, literature, education, medicine, and architecture; research on Confucianism during this time reached new heights. In this regard, Bichurin and Vasilyev, missionaries of the Eastern Orthodox Church in Beijing, were outstanding representatives of Russian sinologists. Bichurin conducted in-depth research on Chinese philosophy, history, literature, and society in the 14 years he lived in Beijing and translated the Four Books, i.e., *The Great Learning*, *The Doctrine of the Mean*, *The Analects of Confucius*, and *Mencius*, into Russian, which enabled him to be the originator of sinology in Russia. Meanwhile, *Eastern Religions: Confucianism, Buddhism, and Taoism*, and *Outline of the History of Chinese Literature*, written by Vasilyev, also made invaluable contributions to sinology research around the world. At present, we easily remember two great Russian writers, Pushkin and Tolstoy, who are well-known to Chinese people. With great admiration for Chinese historical culture, Pushkin read many classics of Chinese culture in Russian, French, and German, discussed Chinese culture with Bichurin, and promoted the dissemination of the *Three-Character Canon* in Russian. Tolstoy sought wisdom and spiritual strength by reading and studying masterpieces of Confucianism and other Chinese thought. He noted in his diary and a letter to his best friend Chertkov that, regarding Confucianism, "It's hard to believe that these works have reached an extraordinarily spiritual level." He wrote, "I am very much occupied with Chinese wisdom." He called *The Doctrine of the Mean* by Confucius "wonderful." He added that "the *Gospels* will not be complete without the thinking of Confucius and Lao-Tzu." Excellent representatives of Russian civilization like Pushkin and Tolstoy impressed both the Russian and Chinese people with their appreciation and efforts to disseminate Chinese historical culture. In a letter to a Chinese scholar in his late years, Tolstoy also expressed his hope that "in the great transformation of human life, China should play a prominent role in leading oriental nations."

The 17th and 18th centuries witnessed the transformation of Europe from the feudal Middle Ages to a modern capitalist civilization. It was accompanied by the Enlightenment, which advocated morality and ethics, an opposition to brutal government, support for naturalistic reasoning, and fighting theological superstition. At that time, the classics of Confucianism and other Chinese works gained great popularity and became sharp spiritual weapons for Enlightenment thinkers as soon as they were introduced into Europe by Jesuit missionaries; the works exerted profound influences on the modern civilization of Europe in two major aspects.

First, using the morality of Confucianism, Enlightenment thinkers criticized the brutal governing of churches and feudal lords. Tolstoy and Temple thought that the codes of ethics of Confucius and Confucianism guided people to pursue self-cultivation, family harmony, the governing of the country, and peace in the world. Voltaire wrote in *Essaisur les moeurs et l'esprit des nations* that the moral thinking of Confucianism criticized Christian thought, and the monarchs of Europe should imitate the ideas of Confucianism. Baron d'Holbach said that morality is important for the prosperity of a country, and Europe should combine politics and morality, just like China. So, we can find that Confucian morality was an important weapon for European Enlightenment thinkers to object to the autocracy of ideology and politics.

Second, Enlightenment thinkers advocated the rational thinking of Confucianism and opposed church worship of superstition and supernatural powers, thus promoting the development of materialism and atheism in Europe. The pioneer of French Enlightenment, Bayle, thought that the rationalism of Confucianism was opposite to the mysticism of Christianity, and the latter was ridiculous, because atheistic countries were able to create prosperous cultures as well. Diderot, Voltaire, and Quesnay all agreed with Confucius's thinking of valuing and advocating "natural justice and norms" instead of worshiping the wonders of supernatural powers as well as the "odd, puissance, turmoil, and deity." In other words, they thought that natural rules and rationalism provided a wiser foundation for society than the theology of Christianity.

Although some scholars, such as Montesquieu, Rousseau, Kant, and Hegel, disagreed over Confucianism and other facets of Chinese historical culture,

Enlightenment thinkers, represented by the Encyclopedist, idealized Chinese thought and tried to bend it to the reality of the politics and ideology of the time. Because Confucian thought respected rationalism and morality and disapproved of superstition and atrocity, it met the need for a different authority of thinking and culture, which could be used to fight Christian theology and feudal governing. Therefore, from this perspective, the introduction of Confucianism and other aspects of Chinese historical culture played a vital role in Europe's fight against feudalism and desire to escape the spiritual shackles of theology. If the Enlightenment changed the direction of modern European history and facilitated the Industrial Revolution and capitalism, we can say that Confucianism also left a notable impact on the modern civilization of Europe due to its influence on Enlightenment thinkers.

Different cultures and civilizations influence each other in the course of contact, while eliminating difficulties and obstacles, thus giving full play to each other's advantages and realizing common progress by learning from a culture's strong points to offset their own weakness. This is an objective law that cannot be changed by human will, as well as an objective truth repeatedly proven in the development and progress of human civilization.

When Jesuit missionaries such as Matteo Ricci, Johann Adam Schall von Bell, and Ferdinand Verbiest introduced Confucianism and other aspects of Chinese historical culture to Europe, renowned Chinese scholars like Xu Guangqi, Li Zhizao, and Yang Tingjun were absorbing the historical culture and the science and technology of Europe. They translated European works into Chinese for readers back home, with content covering philosophy, calendar science, religion, military affairs, geography, and natural science. It was the first wave of European culture that spread to China, which inspired Chinese scholars to learn, understand, and apply Western culture at home and make a contribution to the birth of capitalism and the economic and social development of China. Interested in Western culture and science and technology, Emperor Kangxi set up the Institute of Mathematics in 1713, where members of the Eight Banners learned about Western culture. The *Siku Quanshu* (Complete Library in Four Branches of Literature) of the Qing Dynasty collected translated versions of masterpieces on Western culture.

Here, I would like to mention the understanding, research, and dissemination of Russian culture in China. When missionaries from the Eastern Orthodox Church in Beijing and Russian students studying in China introduced Chinese culture to Russia, Chinese people also began researching Russian culture. At that time, the government of the Qing Dynasty established the Russian Office in Beijing to help the Eastern Orthodox mission spread the historical culture of Russia, and the Russian School for the government to cultivate research talent on Russian culture. In the 18th century, more and more envoys, scholars, and students were sent to Russia by the Qing government, and many of them wrote books and set up theories about the culture and customs of Russia after returning home, thus becoming important messengers of cultural exchange between China and Russia. *Narrative of the Chinese Embassy to the Khan of the Tourgouth Tartars, in the years 1712, 13, 14, and 15*, written by Tulishen, recorded the culture and customs along the Volga River region during his time in Russia. As the first piece of travel literature on Russia written by a Chinese, this book served as a pioneer for Chinese people to explore and research Russian culture. During some 100 years from the 18th century to the first half of the 19th century, many works about Russian culture written by Chinese scholars were published, such as *Experience in the Western World* written by a man with the alias "Seventy-one," *Haiguo Tuzhi* (Illustrated Treatise on the Maritime Kingdoms) by famous scholar Wei Yuan, *A General View of Russia* by Lin Zexu, and *Shuofang Beicheng*, a book on the relationship between China and Russia by He Qiutao. All these works deepened the Chinese people's understanding of Russian historical culture and its modern development.

In the middle of the 19th century, the First Opium War broke out in 1840 in China. This invasion started when the Western power Britain turned China into a semi-colonial and semi-feudal country from an ancient feudal country. The war was the beginning of China's modern history. At the same time, the European continent had entered into a capitalist industrial civilization after the Bourgeois Revolution. China became the first country to be invaded by Western capitalist countries. Under such circumstances, Confucianism and Chinese historical culture, which once gained great popularity in Europe, were forgotten. However, it was a striking contrast that under the military invasions by Western powers, the Chinese nation started to awaken from hesitation and humiliation. People began to ask how the invasion was possible and how could Western countries be so strong. Some scholars and officials commenced a period of learning from the West. Those in pursuit of progress read books on new modes of Western thought. The number of students sent to Japan and the Occident reached a strikingly high level. The abolition of the thousand-year imperial examination system made it possible for a large number of modern schools to emerge. Many Chinese people were learning from the West for truths, led by Hong Xiuquan, Yan Fu, Wei Yuan, Lin Zexu, Kang Youwei, Liang Qichao, and Sun Yat-sen, among others. Unfortunately, Western learning failed to save the country and make it strong. Although Chinese people learned a lot from Western countries, the application of their knowledge at home often failed, and the invasion of China could not be prevented. Several movements to change the country failed, including the Revolution of 1911, a national movement led by Sun Yat-sen. It was not until the October Revolution in Russia that the Chinese people saw hope.

The October Revolution, led by Lenin, not only fundamentally changed the image of Russia but also opened a new era of human history and civilization. Chairman Mao said that the salvoes of the October Revolution brought us Marxism-Leninism. By then, Chinese people had finally found Marxism and scientific truth from the West. Educated Chinese started to use Marxism as a tool to observe and change China's fate and rethink the problem. A new conclusion about "imitating Russian" was made by the founders and leaders of the CPC early on, by Chen Duxiu and Li Dazhao, and change began in China. Decades later, members of the CPC, represented by Mao Zedong and Deng Xiaoping, led the Chinese people down a revolutionary path and achieved success in a new-democratic revolution. They founded the People's Republic of China, a country where people became their own masters under the guidance of the basic principles of Marxism-Leninism combined with China's circumstances on the ground. After 1949, the Party achieved China's socialist revolution and the construction of Socialism with Chinese characteristics under the guidance of the basic principles of Marxism-Leninism. Those principles were combined with the then-circumstances of the nation and with the experience of the Soviet people responsible for building up their own country. The destiny of the Chinese people and the image of the Chinese nation was forever changed. In brief, after the October Revolution, the Russian people offered substantial support to the Chinese people to realize the independence of the Chinese nation, achieve social liberation, and build a socialist society. Chinese people will never forget the enormous help from the Russian people. It demonstrates how the Chinese people obtained success by learning the truth of the October Revolution and drawing on the experience of building a Soviet Russia.

Over the last 100 years since the early 20th century, the Chinese and Russian people have developed a deep friendship through mutual learning and support, and contact between the two countries has reached an unprecedented level. China has translated a large number of classical works about Russian history, philosophy, politics, and culture. China translated over a thousand pieces of Russian classical works of literature during the half-century before 1949. Famous Chinese writer Lu Xun translated the works of 47 Russian writers in his lifetime. Works of Russian classical and modern writers such as Pushkin, Belinsky, Gogol, Chekhov, Tolstoy, Gorky, Fadeyev, Ostrovsky, and Sholokhov have been widely disseminated in China and had a great influence on the development of Chinese literature and art. Under such an atmosphere, well-known cultural scholars such as Guo Moruo once said that the influence of Russia and its culture was like a rushing river down to China.

During the second half of the 20th century, cultural contact between China and Russia became more active, achieving an unprecedented scale and depth in the history of communication between the two countries. The friendly cooperation between the two countries in the 1950s still remains fresh among the older generation. China has translated and published numerous works of Marxism-Leninism and Russian culture, while Russia has translated and published countless cultural classics on China. Scholars from two countries conducted all-dimensional cultural research in various disciplines, especially in translation and Chinese historical culture; Russian scholars reached new heights in their studies of China. The number of Confucian classics translated by Russia is the largest in the world, and Russia also ranks the top leader in research on Confucianism. We are very glad that the six volumes of the encyclopedia *Spiritual Culture of China*, led by academic Titarenko and compiled by Prof. Lukyanov and other experts and scholars, won the State Prize of the Russian Federation and the State Medal awarded by the President. This great work will be translated into Chinese and published in China by Sichuan University. I would like to take this opportunity to express my sincere gratitude to Titarenko and Prof. Lukyanov! I would also like to pay tribute to all Russian scholars, including Eugene, Federline, Tikhvinski, L. S. Perelomov, Rogachev, and Bronislav, for their outstanding contribution to the introduction, spread, and research of Confucianism and other aspects of Chinese culture and their efforts in promoting cultural exchange and cooperation between China and Russia!

As mentioned above, cultural contact between China and Russia is long-standing and well-established. No other relationship between other countries can compare with the mutual learning between the two peoples of China and Russia. We should cherish and strive to carry forward the sound tradition and valuable experience of our contact and mutual learning.

What are the implications of cultural and civilizational exchanges between China and Russia, as well as the rest of Europe? What profound inspiration can we obtain from these exchanges? I answer these questions below.

First, each culture and civilization is enriched and developed by absorbing all the beneficial and progressive aspects of other cultures and civilizations through exchange and mutual learning. Only through openness can communication be realized; only communication can strengthen the vitality of mutual development. It is unwise for a country to close itself off and reject learning from other cultures and civilizations.

Second, the world is complex, and so is the relationship between nations and countries. The communication between different cultures and civilizations may not always be smooth due to ideological, political, and economic differences. Despite some setbacks, we should never give up the chance for cultural exchange, which can turn instances of negative contact into positive outcomes. This has been demonstrated by the turbulent cultural exchange between China and Russia as well as the rest of Europe.

Third, no culture or civilization is perfect. Each has its own strong points and shortcomings. During cultural communication, we should seek to better understand ourselves and others, enhance advantages while avoiding disadvantages, and absorb the good while discarding the dross. A country will suffer losses if it is blind in communication. This should be avoided in cultural communication. In addition, deeply rooted in its own country, each culture and civilization has unique features and advantages. A country should maintain its own features when it learns from others to strengthen its own advantages; otherwise, it will end up in failure.

Fourth, developing one's own culture and civilization and learning from others are both aimed at pursuing truth and progress for one's own and the good of others. The key to learning from others is applying the good experiences of other countries to the reality of one's own experiences. On the contrary, no matter how effective the experience is, failure to take into account your own circumstances while experiencing positive bouts of contact with other cultures will result in failure. This happened when China drew lessons from the October Revolution and the construction of the Soviet Union.

In this new era of economic globalization, especially with the development of science and technology as well as the Internet, economic, political, cultural, and social relationships are being forged like never before all over the world, which has created favorable conditions for cultural contact. Efforts should be made to facilitate the interaction between cultures and civilizations and enhance the common progress of human civilization. In our global village, however, some believe in a "clash of civilizations" and the "end of history," the meaning of which is abundantly clear. People supporting the "clash of civilizations" theory believe that the coexistence of diversified cultures will surely result in clashes. All cultures except one should give up their existence and integrate with the other; the result will be no clashes in a "civilized world." From the perspective of people believing the theory of the "end of history," the coexistence of various social systems and development models is not good, which will lead to conflict. Therefore, they believe all but one social system and development model should be abandoned. Only one system will be eternal while the others will finally come to an end; there will be no disputes in the world as a result. These two arguments are definitely absurd, and no theoretical foundation or factual basis can be found in the history of human society.

From ancient times, all kinds of cultures and civilizations have disappeared and emerged in the manner of mutual tolerance and mutual promotion. From ancient Egyptian, Mesopotamian, Chinese, Indian, Greco-Roman, and Mayan civilizations to Christian Civilization, Confucianism, Buddhism, Taoism, and Hadarah civilizations, then to modern Western, Oriental, capitalist, socialist, and other civilizations, human society has coexisted in the form of diverse civilizations for a long time. Likewise, there are also periods of coexistence of different social systems during a transition period, from the primitive communal system, slavery system, and feudal system of ancient times to the capitalist system and socialist system of today. Not all systems may be identical; there cannot be a single existence. Just as sunlight has seven colors, human society and the world are composed of an array of dazzling colors as well. President Xi Jinping of China said in his speech on a trip to Mexico that the world is colorful and diversified. Different civilizations and cultures can prosper only if they maintain their own features and also tolerate others. Different cultures should learn from each other through mutual exchange and will thrive and progress when doing so.

The coexistence of different cultures and civilizations we are talking about today is identical to the thinking of "harmony in diversity" by Chinese Confucian thinkers two thousand years ago, which laid the theoretical foundation for today's speech. Confucius said, "Gentlemen seek harmony but not uniformity; mean men seek uniformity but not harmony." Mencius also stated, "Things are born to be different." Such thinking of "harmony in diversity" had been clearly clarified by Shi Bo before Confucius. He thought, "Harmony actually fosters new things, and similarity doesn't sustain." That is to say, all things are comprised of contradictory sides in the unity of opposites. Different sides can transform into one another under certain conditions and create new things. If all sides of a thing are the same with each other, there will be no transformations and new things. In Shi Bo's view, all things conform to the rules of "Harmony actually fosters new things and similarity doesn't sustain," in which harmony is different from similarity. Such thinking is conformed with the philosophical idea of the "unity of opposites," which is the fundamental rule for the development of all things in the universe as well as the dialectics of human civilization and society. We adhere to the coexistence, common development, and prosperity of different civilizations, which completely conforms with dialectic thoughts. President Jiang Zemin expressed this when he visited the United States in 2002, saying that "harmony in diversity" is an important rule for social development, the norm for human behaviors, and the truth for the coordinated development of diversified civilizations.

The extensive and profound ideology of Confucianism has spread to and influenced every corner of the world during the past thousand years and provided considerable momentum for the progress of human civilization. Having origized from China, Confucianism was delivered to countries and regions in East Asia in a very short time. Then, it struck root in those countries, absorbing the essence of local culture while enriching and developing itself. At the same time, an East Asian civilization centered on Confucianism was formed. Afterward, Confucianism was introduced to Europe and other regions of the world. Sinologists and others were inspired by Confucianism and greatly enriched it. We should show our sincere gratitude to the people who made the effort to research, spread, apply, and develop Confucianism.

With the world stepping into a new era of economic globalization, it is no surprise that Confucianism is a focus on the international stage. Government leaders and others hope to find solutions in Confucianism to solve problems and difficulties in politics, economy, culture, society, and environment. There is wisdom to be found in Confucianism to solve a number of global affairs, including the inundation of neoliberalism, terrible economic risks and threats, unprecedented gaps between the rich and the poor, high consumption and extravagance, hegemony, extreme expansion of individualism, a collapse of ethics and morality, and serious degradation of resources and the environment.

The former President of France, Chirac, once said, "This world is still hesitating between stability and disorder." He quoted a famous Confucian saying, "If two people act as one, their strength can break iron," to express his hope that countries should enhance cooperation to reduce global risks. Helmut Schmidt, former Chancellor of West Germany, stated that the economy of Western countries had been developing fast while their morality collapsed. The judicial system of the West should combine with the Confucian tradition of China, so as to form a firm ethical and moral system centered on humans rather than capital. Moreover, the Minister Mentor of Singapore, Lee Kuan Yew, said that the government of Singapore and everyday Singaporeans benefited from the influence of Confucianism, especially when applied to those who put their personal interests before the social interest; Confucianism stood in stark contrast to unbridled individualism. And the Secretary General of the United Nations, Ban Ki-moon, said, "During my lifetime, I have been influenced and taught many of the good teachings of Confucius and Mencius. I am still guided by many of the good teachings of Confucius."

Plenty of experts, scholars, and news media outlets have commented on the positive role Confucianism can play in international affairs to solve problems and difficulties faced by all of humanity. For instance, Prof. Hans Küng of the University of Tübingen said that behind the global economic crisis was the collapse of ethics and morality, which reflected an urgent need for a universal moral and ethical standard. He believed that morality and ethics were more important than economics and politics and that Confucian thought would not only promote the development of China but also help to create international morality. The American sociologist Burger holds the opinion that the modernization of the West is based on individualism, but the experience of the Orient has proven that individualism is not the only means to achieve modernization. Confucianism, which is embedded deep in everyone's heart, has been a great force in the economic development of East Asia. Moreover, the tycoon of Japanese modern industry, Shibusawa Eiichi, wrote a book titled *The Analects of Confucius and the Abacus* in the 1930s, in which he held the opinion that the use of the abacus should be based on *The Analects of Confucius*. He explained that, on the one hand, we could not realize the prosperity of a nation without the expansion of business. On the other hand, national prosperity would not last without virtue and morality. It was urgently necessary that we combine the abacus with *The Analects of Confucius*. The *Washington Post* also commented that although Confucius lived over two thousand years ago, his teachings still provided a source of guidance for many. At the assembly of Nobel Prize winners in 1988 in Paris under the theme "Facing the 21st Century," Hannes Alfvén, a Swedish physicist, said that If mankind was to survive in the 21st century, we must go back to more than 2,500 years ago to draw on the wisdom of Confucius and the teachings of Confucianism.

Government leaders and scholars all over the world encourage giving further play for Confucianism in the contemporary world to solve its many difficulties, which is something worth considering if we care about the future of humanity.

This past March, President Xi Jinping's successful state visit to Russia further consolidated and strengthened China and Russia's comprehensive strategic cooperation and partnership. It placed great emphasis on the importance of the promotion of cultural communication in enhancing friendships between two peoples. We believe that friendly interaction and mutually beneficial cooperation between China and Russia will more broadly develop and exert profound influence on the international community. As mentioned by Russian President Vladimir Putin on the phone with President Xi Jinping on June 15, both the level of mutual trust and the quality of cooperation between Russia and China have reached an unprecedented level, and the development of the Russia-China relationship is of long-standing and strategic importance. My colleagues at the ICA would like to take advantage of the driving force of the China-Russia friendship to continue to explore further the essence of Confucianism, combine it with the realities on the ground in China and Russia as well as the rest of the world, and creatively apply it, so as to make new contributions to the shared prosperity of both countries and the lasting peace and common development of the world.

The Spread and Development of Confucianism in East Asia in History[*]

Speech at "The Spread and Practice of Contemporary Confucian Culture" International Academic Conference and the 7th Promotion Work Conference of the ICA

July 5, 2014

Today, we all gathered together in the well-known city of Kuching in Malaysia to discuss the promotion and practice of Confucian culture, which is a great event for the international Confucianism community. Zeng Zi, a famous ancient Chinese thinker, said, "Friends are made through academic communication; self-improvement is made through making friends." Just like our conference today, we will "Make friends through academic communication," and I hope we all can achieve great "self-improvement" after the conference.

This year marks the 2565th anniversary of the birth of Confucius, the founder of international Confucianism and a great philosopher and educator in China's ancient history. During the Spring and Autumn and Warring States periods in

---

[*] From July 5 to 8, 2014, the ICA, together with the Malaysia Confucian Studies Association and the China Confucius Foundation, jointly organized "The Spread and Practice of Contemporary Confucian Culture" International Academic Seminar and the 7th Promotion Work Conference of the ICA in Kuching, Malaysia. The keynote speech at the opening ceremony on July 5, 2014, reviewed the historical context of the dissemination and development of Confucianism in East Asian countries and regions. It then summarized the historical insights into the transmission and development of Confucian culture.

China more than 2,000 years ago, ancient philosophers like Confucius and Mencius founded Confucianism and later the Confucian school on the basis of previous achievements in philosophy and culture as well as ideas from other schools of that period, paving the road for the development of Confucian culture afterward. Confucianism contains profound philosophic thinking and rich political, economic, cultural, educational, and ethnic thinking. The truthful essence of Confucianism is our absolutely precious spiritual treasure.

As the root of Chinese traditional culture, Confucianism has had a profound influence on cultural development and social progress in China's history. When it was spread to other regions in Asia, Europe, and other continents, it merged with local cultures and became a significant source of world cultures, playing a crucial role in advancing the progress of human civilization. Therefore, although it originated and formed in China, Confucianism has gone beyond China's borders to become an international culture. People in China have made pioneering contributions to Confucianism. But it's undeniable that people from other countries and regions also made their share of contribution to its communication and development.

China is a significant country in the Asia-Pacific region. There have been exchanges in physical and spiritual cultures and mutual influence between China and its Asian neighbors since ancient times. Thus, Confucianism also traveled to the countries of Northeast and Southeast Asia early on and developed into a Confucianism with local characteristics in each country.

I. The Spread and Development of Confucianism in the Korean Peninsula in History

According to the *Dongguk Tonggam*, compiled in Korea in 1485, as early as the 11th century BC, Prince Ji Zi of Shang led "five thousand people to enter Korea" during the Western Zhou Dynasty and China's poetry, books, rites, and music "all followed and spread there." During the unification of the six states by Qin Shi Huang (the first emperor of Qin), people from regions such as Yan, Qi, and Zhao frequently traveled to the Korean Peninsula, bringing China's material culture and Confucian ritual and music culture. By the Western Han period, the Confucian classic *The Analects of Confucius* had been introduced to the Korean Peninsula. From that time onward, for over two thousand years, the cultural exchange between China and the Korean Peninsula in Confucianism has become increasingly widespread and profound.

During the Western Jin Dynasty in China, "Taixue," an education institute, was set up in the Goguryeo Kingdom on the Korean Peninsula in AD 372, teaching mainly Confucian philosophy. During the Sui and Tang dynasties in China, the Korean Peninsula went through a period of transition from the division among the three kingdoms of Goguryeo, Baekje, and Silla to the unification under Silla. In the period before unification, Goguryeo, which existed before the unification, received Chinese classics such as the Five Classics and historical texts like *Records of the Grand Historian, Book of Han, Book of the Later Han,* and *Records of the Three Kingdoms.* At the same time, Baekje also adopted Chinese works such as the *"Five Classics,* classics, and historical records." After the Silla Kingdom unified the Korean Peninsula, Confucian culture continued to spread. In AD 682, another institution, "Guoxue," was established, teaching the Five Classics and *The Analects of Confucius.* Every Silla King went to "Guoxue" to study Confucian classics. Emperor Xuanzong of Tang Dynasty (AD 685–762) called Silla "the Kingdom of Junzi (Man of Virtues)." In the year 737, he dispatched a scholar named Xing Shu to visit Silla, with the primary mission of teaching Confucian classics and introducing the prosperity of Confucianism in China. During the period of Silla's unification, the number of Korean Peninsula students studying in China increased significantly. In the year 837 alone, over 200 students went to the Tang Dynasty, with 58 successfully passing the imperial examinations and becoming officials. Upon their return, these scholars played an active role in promoting the development of Confucianism. One of the most famous among these students was Choe Chiwon, who served in various official positions in the Tang Dynasty and later became a prominent Confucian scholar in the Korean Peninsula after returning home.

During the late Tang Dynasty and the period of the Five Dynasties and Ten Kingdoms in China, the Korean Peninsula underwent a transition from the "Unified Silla Period" to the "Goryeo Unified Period." After Wang Geon, the founder of Goryeo, unified the Korean Peninsula in 936, he emphasized the establishment of schools with a primary focus on teaching Confucian classics. His successor, King Hyejong, advocated Confucian governance, establishing a "National Academy" in the capital and local "Village Schools" and implementing the civil service examination system. King Seongjong sent envoys to study Confucian classics at the National Academy in Northern Song China and, in 992, established the National Academy in Goryeo, later known as Sungkyunkwan, serving as a dedicated institution for Confucian education and research. King Yejong personally presided over lectures at the National Academy, fostering a culture of respecting and studying Confucian classics. Throughout the Goryeo Dynasty, a governing philosophy of "placing the people first" and "governing through virtue" prevailed. Scholars such as An Hyang, Baek Yi-jeong, Yi Je-hyeon, Yi Seok, Jeong Mong-ju, Jeong Do-jeon, and Gwon Geun emerged as prominent Confucian figures during this period. In 1290, An Hyang brought a copy of *The Complete Works of Zhu Xi* from China to Korea, marking the gradual adoption of Neo-Confucianism as the core content of Confucian education, research, and practice on the Korean Peninsula.

In 1392, Lee Seong-gye established the Joseon Dynasty in Korea, implementing Confucian governance as its guiding ideology. Subsequent monarchs of the Joseon Dynasty adhered to this guiding ideology, considering Confucianism, particularly the Cheng-Zhu school of Neo-Confucianism, as the central philosophical framework for statecraft. Over the more than five centuries of the Joseon Dynasty, numerous distinguished Confucian scholars emerged, including figures like Kim Jong-jik, Jeong Yeo-chang, Jo Gwang-jo, Yi Toegye, Gi Gobong, Seong Woogye, and Yi Yulgok.

The commitment to developing Confucian education and research with a distinctive Korean Peninsula flavor, integrating it with indigenous culture, and applying uniquely Korean Confucian thought to governance, societal management, and personal cultivation has become a longstanding tradition on the Korean Peninsula, enduring through the centuries to the present day.

II. The Spread and Development of Confucianism in Japan in History

According to historical records, in the late 3rd century AD, Wani of the Korean Peninsula introduced *The Analects of Confucius* to Japan and assisted in establishing scholars of the Five Classics. At that time, the crown prince of Emperor Ojin in Japan even studied under Wani and "mastered all the classics under Wani, comprehending everything." This marks the recorded beginning of Confucianism being transmitted to Japan. Before the Sui and Tang dynasties, cultural exchanges between China and Japan were mainly facilitated through scholars from the Korean Peninsula, highlighting the peninsula's role as a bridge in cultural interactions between the two countries. Starting from the Sui and Tang dynasties, cultural connections between Japan and China were more directly conducted through mutual visits by individuals.

The end of the Sui Dynasty and the beginning of the Tang Dynasty in China coincided with the reign of Empress Suiko in Japan. During this period, Prince Shōtoku, influenced by Confucian ideas such as "virtue, benevolence, ritual, trust, righteousness, and wisdom," formulated a constitution comprising 17 articles and implemented reforms in Japanese society. Historical records indicate that Japan sent four missions to the Sui Dynasty and over ten missions to the Tang Dynasty, with a large number of students and monks accompanying the envoys. The largest delegation consisted of 651 members, while the smallest had 120 members. During the Sui and Tang dynasties in China, cultural exchanges between China and Japan reached their first peak, leaving behind numerous noteworthy events. For instance, in AD 607, scholars Takamuko no Kuromaro and the monk Min, who accompanied the first Japanese envoy to China, witnessed the decline of the Sui Dynasty and the prosperity of the Tang Dynasty. Upon their return, they both served as advisers to the emperor—Kuni no hakase (National Scholar). In AD 645, Emperor Kotoku, with their assistance, presided over the renowned "Taika Reforms." The Taika Reforms involved adopting the Confucian concept of "great unification" from China and the legal system of the Tang Dynasty, establishing a centralized feudal state in Japan. For example, Kibi no Makibi, who played a significant role in creating Japanese characters by drawing inspiration from the Chinese characters' forms, studied in China for 17 years during the reign of Emperor Xuanzong. He achieved considerable success in studying Chinese Confucian classics, history, law, and other fields. Additionally, various literary works such as poems, lyrics, songs, essays, novels, and artistic expressions like calligraphy, painting, and other skills deeply infused with Confucian ideology from China were transmitted to Japan through Japanese students and scholars who studied in China. This had a profound impact on the development of Japanese literature and culture. An outstanding example is Abe no Nakamaro, also known as Chao Heng, a Japanese student who developed close friendships with major Tang Dynasty poets like Li Bai and Wang Wei, creating a well-known story in the annals of Sino-Japanese cultural exchange.

After the Song Dynasty in China, cultural exchanges between China and Japan continued to progress, especially during China's Ming and Qing periods, which corresponded to Japan's Edo period. During the Edo period, the Tokugawa shogunate was in power. At the establishment of the shogunate, Tokugawa Ieyasu designated Confucianism as Japan's official doctrine. With a strong foundation in Confucianism himself, Ieyasu personally convened scholars to teach Confucianism and Chinese cultural classics. He supervised the publication of works such as *Kongzi Jiayu* (The School Sayings of Confucius), *Qunshu Zhiyao* (The Compilation of Books and Writings on the Important Governing Principles), *Zhenguan Zhengyao* (Essentials about Politics from the Zhenguan Reign), *Liu Tao* (Six Secret Teachings), and *San Lue* (Three Strategies of Huang Shigong), using these as reference materials for educating the people and governing the country. The fifth shogun, Tokugawa Tsunayoshi, established Confucian officials within the shogunate and personally lectured on *The Analects of Confucius*. The eighth shogun, Tokugawa Yoshimune, further promoted "Confucianism in governance." The flourishing of Confucianism in Japan during the Edo period was closely related to the development of maritime trade between China and Japan. Maritime trade facilitated the spread of Chinese historical and cultural elements, including Confucianism, in Japan. From 1693 to 1803, a total of 4,181 different Chinese cultural books were imported to Japan through merchant ships. It can be said that education and academic culture in Japan during the Edo period were predominantly centered around Confucianism, making it a crucial guiding ideology for the social development of that time.

Regarding the dissemination of Chinese historical culture, primarily Confucianism, to Japan and its impact and role in Japan's cultural development and societal progress, numerous renowned Japanese scholars have offered extensive commentary throughout history. They believe that through continuous absorption of the merits of Chinese culture, "after refining, digesting, and assimilating, Japan finally produced a beautiful and elegant culture, particularly after the mid-Heian period," stating that "as China progressed, so did Japan." Modern Japanese sinologist Naito Konan noted that Japanese culture "is a continuation of ancient Chinese culture; to understand the roots of Japanese culture, one must first comprehend Chinese culture." Similarly, contemporary Japanese sinologist Okamura Shigeru pointed out that "Japanese culture is formed on the foundation of Chinese culture" and that "by studying and inheriting classical Chinese culture and philosophy, Japan can maintain its unique cultural identity."

III. The Spread and Development of Confucianism in Vietnam in History

There are two main periods of Vietnam's ancient history: the Bắc thuộc (Belonging to the North) period, according to Vietnamese history books, and the independent period of Vietnam. After the unification of China by Qin Shi Huang, he established administrative regions in the southern areas beyond the Five Ridges, including Guilin, Nanhai, and Xiang commanderies. Among them, Xiang Commandery encompassed Vietnam's present-day northern and central regions. At that time, there was a man called Li Wengzhong who had been to Xianyang to study Confucian classics. During the period of Nanyue Kingdom founded by Zhao Tuo, Confucianism was already spread to and practiced in the middle and northern parts of today's Vietnam. Proof can be found from the words in the history books, "The Xiang Commandery was influenced by culture and education, with Confucian classics cultivating customs and righteousness strengthening solidarity." In 111 BC, Confucianism was further popularized in the area of Vietnam after Emperor Wu of Han Dynasty took over Nanyue and established the three commanderies of Jiaozhi, Jiuzhen, and Rinan in the middle and northern parts of today's Vietnam. In the early years of the Eastern Han Dynasty, the governors of Jiaozhi, Xi Guang, and Jiuzhen, Ren Yan, persisted in conducting Confucian education with the principle of "guiding through rituals" in their respective administered regions. During the Three Kingdoms period, Shi Xie, who served as the governor of Jiaozhi, was well-versed in Confucian classics such as *Zuo Zhuan* and *The Book of Documents*. While governing Jiaozhi, a significant number of literati and Confucian scholars from the Central Plains sought refuge under his administration. Through their efforts in spreading knowledge and promoting Confucian values, there emerged a situation in Jiaozhi where "customs were refined through poetry and books, and people's hearts were cultivated through rituals and music," leading to a period of "forty years of internal peace." Entering the Sui and Tang periods, Confucianism experienced a renewed development in the Lingnan region, including the central and northern parts of present-day Vietnam. In the Vietnamese region, individuals such as Jiang Gongfu (姜公辅), Jiang Gongfu (姜公复), and Liao Youfang all passed the imperial examination, with Jiang Gongfu even serving as a chancellor during the Tang Dynasty, earning the title of "eternal literary sage." Eminent officials and scholars from the Tang Dynasty, including Chu Suiliang, Du Shenyan, Shen Quanqi, Song Zhiwen, and Liu Yuxi, successively sought refuge in the Vietnamese region. Wang Bo's father, Wang Fuzhi, also held the position of Jiaozhi magistrate, contributing to the dissemination and development of Confucianism in the Vietnamese region.

In AD 939, Ngo Quyen established the Ngo Dynasty, declaring independence. By AD 968, Dinh Bo Linh unified the Vietnamese region, founding the Dai Co Viet state and marking the beginning of Vietnam's independent statehood. During the early periods of the Ngo, Dinh, and the Early Le dynasties, there was a "promote Buddhism, suppress Confucianism" policy in place. However, the promotion and practice of Confucianism in Vietnam did not cease. The Ly Dynasty, established in 1009, and the Tran Dynasty, established in 1226, adopted a policy of "respecting Confucianism, Buddhism, and Taoism," elevating the status of Confucianism. The rulers of the Ly and Tran dynasties considered Confucianism the political ideology for governing the country. In 1126, the Ly Dynasty held a grand ceremony to commemorate the "Five Classics." During the Tran Dynasty, Vietnam established national academies, state schools, universities, and academies, implementing the imperial examination system comprehensively. The societal standing of Confucian culture continued to rise. The renowned Confucian scholar Chu Van An from the Tran Dynasty dedicated his life to Confucian education and research, authoring Four Books Annotations and being hailed as a "Confucian sage" of his time. In AD 1400, Ho Quy Ly established the Ho Dynasty, implementing a policy of "limiting Buddhism and honoring Confucianism." Ho Quy Ly personally wrote *The Book of Mingdao*, translated *The Book of Documents*, and compiled *Annotations on the Songs of the States*, promoting the dissemination of Confucian knowledge.

In AD 1428, after Le Loi established the Later Le Dynasty, Vietnam entered a period of "Confucianism supremacy." Le Loi, also known as Le Thai To, stipulated a triennial imperial examination where all examination sites had to include tests on the "Four Books." He also ordered the nationwide engraving of *Complete Works of the Four Books*. Later, Le emperors, particularly Le Thanh Tong, implemented policies centered on Confucianism in politics, legislation, and cultural education across Vietnam. The flourishing of Confucianism drove prosperity in historiography and literature, and the well-known historical book *Complete Annals of Dai Viet*, written by the imperial historian Ngo Si Lien during this period, embodies Confucian thought. The Nguyen Dynasty, established in 1778, continued to uphold Confucianism. The Chong Zheng Academy, headed by the renowned Confucian scholar Nguyen Thiep, was established to translate *Xiao Xue* and the "Four Books" into Vietnamese characters (Nom) and printed the Poetry Classic Phonology for easier dissemination. The Nguyen Dynasty, established by Nguyen Phuc Anh in 1802, was the last feudal dynasty in Vietnamese history. The Nguyen Dynasty persisted in the national policy of "Confucianism supremacy," spreading Confucianism from the north to the Mekong Delta and implementing it throughout Vietnam. Emperors Minh Mang, Thieu Tri, and Tu Duc of the Nguyen Dynasty personally studied Confucianism.

In the early years of the Nguyen Dynasty, Confucian scholars such as Phạm Đăng Hưng wrote *Interpretation of the Great Learning*, and another Confucian scholar, Nhữ Bá Sĩ, wrote *Explanation of the Changes* and *Round Discussions on the Great Learning*. Historical works compiled by the Nguyen Dynasty National Historical Archives, such as *Chronicles of Vietnamese History*, *Imperial Records of Dai Nam*, and *Biographies of Dai Nam*, all carry the central theme of "Confucian spirit" and have become essential reading materials for studying Vietnamese history and culture. During the Nguyen Dynasty era, it can be said that Confucian research, education, dissemination, and application in Vietnam reached their zenith.

Concerning the impact and influence of Confucianism on the development of Vietnamese history after its introduction from China to Vietnam, Vietnamese scholars have expressed insightful perspectives. First, the dissemination and development of Confucianism in Vietnam played a crucial guiding role in the country's independence, state-building, and governance. Prof. Nguyen Ngoc Tho from the Ho Chi Minh National University stated, "Since the introduction of Confucianism, the official social and political ideology in Chinese history, into Vietnam, it has provided crucial cultural elements to supplement Vietnamese indigenous culture." He emphasized its direct influence on the formation of the feudal societal thought system in Vietnam and its involvement in national organization and governance. Secondly, over centuries of education and dissemination in Vietnamese society, Confucianism has permeated and integrated into people's daily lives, influencing their lifestyles and customs. The impact of Confucian thought on people's daily lives can be clearly seen in Vietnamese historical records regarding "family genealogy, village compacts, clan rules, family teachings, family rituals, and family agreements." Thirdly, Confucian culture also serves as a source of thought for modern and contemporary revolutions in Vietnam. Revolutionary leader Ho Chi Minh once remarked, "The merits of Confucianism lie in personal moral cultivation." He incorporated Confucian moral thoughts, innovating and proposing Vietnam's four revolutionary virtues: "diligence, frugality, strictness, and rectitude." He also introduced a new concept of loyalty and filial piety: "Loyalty to the country" and "Filial piety to the people." Vietnamese scholars argue that Confucianism blended with local culture and formed its distinctive characteristics after its introduction to Vietnam. For instance, using Vietnamese-created Nom characters for phonetic annotation, translation, and interpretation of Confucian classics represents a creative aspect of Vietnamese Confucianism. Prof. Nguyen Kim Son from the Hanoi National University stated, "Vietnamese Confucian literature has a long and deep-rooted history," describing it as the result of the localization of Confucianism in Vietnam and an essential component of East Asian Confucianism.

IV. The Spread and Development of Confucianism in Southeast Asia in History

During the Western Han period in China, there was already some level of contact and interaction with regions in Southeast Asia beyond Vietnam. Archaeological findings suggest that in the 1st century BC, people from China had already settled in what is now Sumatra, Indonesia. Ever since the Han Dynasty, with the expansion and upgrading of the Maritime Silk Road and land transportation, connections have grown closer between China and other Southeast Asian countries like Myanmar, Cambodia, Thailand, the Philippines, Malaysia, Singapore, Indonesia, and Brunei, and exchanges are more frequent. There were mainly two channels of communication. One was exchanges between envoys, officials, scholars, and monks, and the other was trade and business communication and people-to-people exchanges.

The **exchanges between envoys and officials.** From the Chinese perspective, during the Three Kingdoms period, envoys Zhu Ying and Kang Tai were sent from the Wu Kingdom. In the Southern Song Dynasty, Zhou Qufei traveled abroad. During the Yuan Dynasty, Zhou Daguan and the navigator Wang Dayuan visited various regions that now belong to Cambodia, Thailand, Malaysia, Indonesia, and other countries. Upon their return, they wrote books such as *Foreign Relations of the Wu Period, Answers beyond the Ridge, Records of the Customs of Zhenla*, and *A Brief Account of the Barbarous Islands*, describing the political, economic, cultural, and local conditions of the regions they visited. From the perspective of Southeast Asia, historical records about their envoys and officials visiting China are relatively abundant. During the Eastern Han Dynasty, the kings of present-day Cambodia, the Shan State in present-day eastern Burma, and the Yehtiao State in present-day

Indonesia all sent envoys to China for political, economic, and cultural exchanges. During the Tang Dynasty, from around AD 620 during the reign of Emperor Gaozu to around AD 870 during the reign of Emperor Yizong, countries such as Pyu in present-day Myanmar, Funan and Zhenla in present-day Cambodia, Panpan in present-day Malaysia, and Srivijaya in present-day Indonesia, sent envoys to the Tang court multiple times. In AD 801, the King of Pyu, Yongqiang, sent his son to visit China with a Pyu musical ensemble of over 30 people. They performed 12 Pyu songs in the Chang'an court for several days, creating a sensation. The poet Bai Juyi wrote a poem titled "New Music Bureau · Pyu Music," "The son of Yongqiang, Shu Nantuo, came to present Southern music to celebrate the New Year." Emperor Dezong even wrote a letter to Yongqiang, expressing a sense of "gentleness from afar." From the Tang to the Ming and Qing dynasties, instances of envoys, officials, and even kings from various Southeast Asian regions visiting China became numerous.

The exchanges between scholars and monks. Taking China as an example, in the late Eastern Jin Dynasty, the eminent monk Faxian traveled to India to obtain Buddhist scriptures. On his return, he stayed in the kingdom of Yavadvipa, present-day Indonesia, for five months, engaging in preaching activities and learning about the local customs and conditions. During the Tang Dynasty, the venerable monk Huining went to places like Java and Srivijaya in present-day Indonesia to study and propagate Buddhism. Another Tang Dynasty monk, Yijing, also visited the Indonesian region and resided in Srivijaya for nearly ten years, accompanied by nearly 20 other monks who arrived in Indonesia around the same time. Chinese scholars visiting or traveling to Southeast Asia have been common for centuries. In the late Qing Dynasty, two renowned scholars, Zuo Binglong and Huang Zunxian, visited the region of Singapore. Zuo Binglong stayed in Singapore for a decade, organizing local scholars to study Confucian classics and playing a role in promoting Confucian studies in the region. Huang Zunxian established the "Tunanshe" in Singapore and served as its superintendent, guiding Chinese students in studying ancient Chinese classics, exploring Confucian thought, and addressing local social issues.

Trade and business communication and people-to-people exchanges. Taking China as an example, from the Han Dynasty to the Ming and Qing dynasties, people from China engaged in business and sought livelihoods in Southeast Asia in a continuous stream. This trend showed a growing momentum, especially reaching its peak from the 15th and 16th centuries to the 18th and 19th centuries. According to historical records, Chinese immigrants who settled in Malaysia through business and employment on Penang Island numbered over 1,400 by the mid-18th century, increasing to 3,000 by the late 18th century and surpassing 7,000 by the early 19th century. In Malacca, the Chinese population had exceeded 3,000 by the end of the 18th century. In the Indonesian region, during the Tang Dynasty, a group of Chinese people migrated overseas to Sumatra to escape conflicts, ultimately settling there. By the Yuan Dynasty, Chinese communities had appeared in villages like Makassar and Belitung in Java. During the Ming Dynasty, Chinese settlers in the Palembang region numbered no less than 10,000. By 1860, the Chinese diaspora in Indonesia had reached 220,000, increasing to 340,000 by 1880 and reaching 530,000 by 1900.

Through over 2,000 years of exchanges, China and other Southeast Asian countries have become good neighbors who learn from each other and grow together. The mutual exchange of people and political and economic interactions between the two regions undoubtedly drive and promote cultural exchanges. China has benefited a lot from Southeast Asian cultures. At the same time, Chinese traditional culture, with Confucianism as its core, has also made contributions to the social development of all countries in this region.

It was in the 18th and 19th centuries when Confucian culture bloomed and flourished in Southeast Asia. After 1840, China, faced with aggression and oppression from Western powers, experienced accumulated poverty and weakness, and its people endured profound suffering. In this situation, an unprecedented number of Chinese were compelled to migrate to Southeast Asia. Many sought livelihoods, some engaged in business, and others participated in academic and cultural activities. Additionally, some individuals sought political and economic support in Southeast Asia for China's salvation. The significant concentration of overseas Chinese in Southeast Asia during this period is evident in the statistics mentioned earlier for Malaysia and Indonesia. As the number of overseas Chinese increased in Southeast Asia, a lot of Chinese schools teaching Confucian classics and Chinese history and culture were set up, along with more academic cultural events by Chinese scholars. In the realm of Confucian education, it was primarily conducted through formal school systems. Taking Malaysia and Singapore as an example, in Chinese communities in the 18th and 19th centuries, traditional Chinese schools were built, including charity schools, private schools, academies, and reading institutes. In 1815, there were already nine Chinese vernacular schools (华文私塾) in the Malacca region with approximately 160 students. Around 1820, there were four Chinese schools in Penang. By 1829, there were three Chinese vernacular schools in Singapore. In 1849 and 1854, overseas Chinese Tan Kim Seng established Chung Wen Pagoda and Chui Eng Free School in Singapore, and in 1889, he founded Nan Hua Yixue in Penang. By the early 20th century, a batch of modern Chinese schools emerged, such as the "Confucian Chinese School," "Lok Yuk," and "Zhongxi" schools. In the traditional schools, the educational focus was steeped in Confucian cultural values. Chung Wen Pagoda, for instance, explicitly aimed at "reading the books of Confucius and exploring the profundities of Luo and Min." In modern schools, the education of Confucian knowledge remained a significant component. Whether traditional or modern, Chinese schools served as fundamental channels for the education and dissemination of Confucian cultural values. They made important contributions to the development of Confucian culture in the Chinese communities of Southeast Asia, including Malaysia and Singapore.

In the field of Confucian studies, we have already mentioned the influential roles played by Chinese scholars Zuo Binglong and Huang Zunxian in the late 19th-century Confucian research in Singapore. Concurrently, in Malaysia and Singapore, several prominent Chinese scholars, including Khoo Seok Wan, Lim Boon Keng, Chong Hak Sin, Lie Kim Hok, Kwee Tek Hoay, and Chan Kim Boon, made unique contributions to the study and dissemination of Confucianism. Khoo Seok Wan, taking it upon himself to promote Confucianism and Chinese culture, consecutively established Lize and Lequn Shushe in 1896 and 1897. Later, together with Lim Boon Keng and others, he advocated for Confucian research by establishing schools, garnering a widespread response and creating a prevailing trend. In 1898, he also founded the *Thien Nan Shin Pao*, publishing numerous articles promoting Confucian ideas. In 1900, the newspaper consecutively published articles by Guangdong scholar Wang Xiaocang and the renowned late Qing poet Qiu Fengjia, causing a "sensation" in the Chinese communities in Southeast Asia. The combination of promoting Confucian research through the establishment of schools and propagating Confucianism through the creation of newspapers to foster the prosperity of Confucian culture was the first characteristic of Confucian development in the Malaysia and Singapore regions at that time. The second characteristic is the integration of Confucian education and research with the translation and interpretation of Confucian classics into local languages and vernacular, as well as the compilation of introductory Confucian knowledge primers. Scholars such as Chong Hak Sin, Lie Kim Hok, and Kwee Tek Hoay made particularly diligent efforts and notable contributions in this regard. Chong Hak Sin believed that the teachings of Confucius, despite being profound, were extensive, and even traditional scholars found it challenging to grasp the essence, not to mention farmers, laborers, and merchants. To make Confucian principles easily understood by literate individuals and facilitate transmission, he authored *Essentials of Confucianism in Vernacular*, the earliest vernacular Confucian primer in Southeast Asia. Lie Kim Hok, known locally as the "Father of Chinese Malay," wrote *The Life of the Sage Confucius*, the first monograph on Confucius written in Malay. Kwee Tek Hoay, proficient in Chinese, Malay, and English, translated *The Great Learning* and *The Doctrine of the Mean* into Malay. The third characteristic involves combining Confucian education and research with the translation of Chinese classical and popular novels infused with Confucian ideological spirit into local languages to increase interest in learning Confucian culture. In this regard, the notable achievement of Chinese scholar Chan Kim Boon, born in Penang, stands out. He spent five years translating and publishing the complete *Romance of the Three Kingdoms* in Malay. Simultaneously, he translated other Chinese classical novels such as *Water Margin*, *The Story of the Western Wing*, and *The Romance of Sui and Tang*. These characteristics reflect the innovative spirit of Chinese scholars in Malaysia and Singapore in promoting Confucian education and research. It also underscores their significant contributions to the dissemination and development of Confucian culture in Southeast Asia, particularly Malaysia and Singapore.

V. A Few Lessons and Insights from History

What lessons can we learn and what insights can we gain from two thousand years of cultural communication between China, and other countries and regions in Northeast Asia and Southeast Asia, and from the history of Confucianism on the Korean Peninsula, and in Japan, Vietnam and other regions in Southeast Asian while enriching itself at the same time? The following are some of my personal views, which are open for discussion and correction.

The historic achievements of East Asian civilization with Confucianism as its major cultural signature deserve full recognition. People often compare and distinguish East Asian civilization from European civilization and Eastern civilization from Western civilization precisely because the cultures of East Asian and Eastern civilizations have Confucianism as a significant component, offering unique characteristics and distinctive advantages that differ from the cultures of European and Western civilizations. East Asian civilization, also known as the "East Asian Confucian Cultural Circle," was created, nurtured, and developed by people in China and all the countries and regions of East Asia. It has been among the world's many civilizations and enjoys worldwide praise for its continuous contribution of wisdom and strength to human civilization overall. People in East Asia should all share in this glory. Kong Yingda, a Chinese scholar during the Tang Dynasty, made the following interpretation of "civilization": "Civilization should be able to guide the development of all and to shed light on the world." That explains the historical meaning of every great civilization. The "light" of East Asian civilization has shone not only on Asian regions, but also everywhere in the world. And its light continues to glow to this day. The historical achievements of East Asian countries related to the economy, culture, and social development are all good examples. Furthermore, more and more visionaries have resorted to Confucian culture and East Asian civilization for enlightenment, wisdom, and solutions to the many problems we face in economic and social development today. That's why we have to treasure, practice, and promote Confucian culture and East Asian civilization so that its philosophies and wisdom can continue to benefit people in East Asia, all of Asia, and the world.

The only way for any culture to have lasting development is through constant communication and mutual learning with other cultures. Any culture, wherever it is from, has its characteristics and advantages, which are all inherited and developed through circulation and openness. Self-confinement drains vitality. It is an objective law for every culture's development that only through constant communication, opening up across time, and absorbing useful ingredients from other cultures can one culture maintain its strength, grow its vitality, and continue to shine. The fact that Confucian culture traveled from China through Northeast Asia to Southeast Asia and finally developed into a unique cultural signature of East Asian civilization serves as proof of this law.

Excellent cultures introduced from overseas must be able to meet local conditions and blend in with local cultures to be a success. The historic process of Confucian culture spreading from China to other countries and regions in East Asia shows that the Korean Peninsula, Japan, Vietnam, and other countries in Southeast Asia are good at learning and practicing Confucianism based on the reality of their own society and cultures, which enabled them to add the characteristics of their country and nationality to Confucianism resulting in changes and innovation, making Confucian culture a crucial part of their own culture. This is also the fundamental reason and essence that allows Confucianism to play a lasting role in the development of various countries and regions in East Asia. In our efforts to promote Confucianism globally in education, research, dissemination, and practice, we should especially apply and utilize this fundamental experience of combining practical learning and the application of Confucianism. This can serve as an indispensable method for the continued development of Confucianism.

It is crucial to closely integrate the dissemination and development of spiritual culture with the exchange and development of material culture, ensuring their mutual support and simultaneous progress. Material culture serves as the foundation and prerequisite for developing spiritual culture. Spiritual culture, in turn, fulfills the mission of meeting people's spiritual needs while serving and supporting the development and prosperity of material culture. The relationship between the two is inseparable and mutually reinforcing. The historical interactions between China and other countries and regions in East Asia, as well as their interactions with each other, illustrate that over the ages, not only the exchanges of envoys, officials, and scholars contributed significantly to the dissemination and development of Confucianism and other cultures, but economic and trade exchanges also played a crucial role. Cultural exchanges between countries and ethnic groups often begin at the level of material culture. The exchange of material culture inevitably drives the dissemination of spiritual culture. Throughout history, China's exquisite silk, porcelain, and tea, as well as technological products like papermaking, printing, gunpowder, and the compass, were transported worldwide through both overland and maritime routes of the Silk Road, spreading China's profound cultural and philosophical ideas to different parts of the world. During the Edo period in Japan, the widespread dissemination and development of Confucian culture were closely linked to the concurrent growth and prosperity of maritime trade between China and Japan. Similarly, in the 18th and 19th centuries in Southeast Asia, including Malaysia and Indonesia, the development of overseas Chinese in economic and trade ventures went hand in hand with the development of Confucian cultural endeavors. Undoubtedly, in today's efforts to promote the dissemination and development of Confucian culture globally, we should fully leverage the crucial role of material culture exchange and development in facilitating the dissemination and development of spiritual culture. In fact, many regions and countries are already doing so, with numerous entrepreneurs joining the ranks of those contributing to the development of Confucian culture, becoming essential driving forces in its dissemination and practice. This is indeed a heartening development.

It has always been the essential requirement of Confucian culture to uphold the principle of the harmonious coexistence between different things and the peaceful coexistence between countries. There's an important philosophy in Confucianism: "Harmony in diversity, and harmony generates vitality." "Harmony in diversity" means harmonious coexistence in one unity of different things. In their coexistence, they create new things and a new unity through integration and transformation, which is explained by the idea that "Harmony generates vitality." We can easily find examples in the "Contention of a Hundred Schools of

Thought" during the pre-Qin period and in the Han Dynasty when Confucianism, Buddhism, and Taoism coexisted in a harmonious cultural environment. Another important political philosophy of Confucianism is that "All nations live in peace and harmony" and "Peace is the best option," advocating building friendly and peaceful relationships with neighboring countries. As it is said in *Zuo Zhuan*, "A harmonious and peaceful relationship with its neighbors is a country's blessing." We should always uphold this precious principle. When we look back at history, there has always been mutual respect, mutual learning, and mutual improvement among East Asian countries. Peaceful coexistence has been the mainstream of our relationships, which has a lot to do with the widespread guidance of Confucian culture. Matteo Ricci, the Italian Jesuit priest who came to China for missionary work at the end of the 16th century, once said about Zheng He's voyages overseas as a cultural ambassador to spread peace and friendship: "It seems surprising that in a kingdom with boundless territory, countless population and amazingly rich resources, the emperor and his people never thought about starting an invasion, despite their fine weapons that could easily conquer any ground or navy forces in its neighboring countries, which is totally different from European countries." The famous "Five Principles of Peaceful Coexistence," which has already been deemed as the only proven principle in handling state-to-state relations, was jointly advocated by China, India, and Myanmar and made known to the world at the Bandung Conference in 1955. It is no coincidence that this famous principle originated in Asia and the East. So, as we can see, the philosophies of "Building peaceful and friendly relations with your neighbors" and "Peaceful coexistence" are major contributions made by Confucian culture and East Asian culture to the peaceful development of humankind. These philosophies should always be treasured in the future to maintain relations between countries in East Asia, Asia, and the world.

Scholars of Confucianism bear the historical responsibility of Confucian education, dissemination, and practice. The renowned Confucian philosopher and synthesizer of Neo-Confucianism, Zhu Xi, once said, "Scholars shall shoulder the responsibility of current affairs." This means that scholars, in addition to academic research, have an "immediate task" to disseminate the essence of the thoughts contained in the classics of Confucianism and other historical cultures, widely spreading them among officials and the public through lectures, discussions, and the creation of popularized textbooks. Zhu Xi advocated for this, and he practiced what he preached. Zhu Xi devoted immense effort to writing *The Collected Annotations on the Four Books*, which became a must-read Confucian primer for officials, scholars, students, and others in various dynasties after the Song Dynasty and in many East Asian countries. He also participated in lectures and academic discussions at prominent academies in contemporary China, imparting knowledge and thoughts on Confucianism and other historical cultures. In his later years, he established the Kaocheng School in the Jianyang region of Fujian Province, China, where he continued teaching and established a new school of thought. Zhu Xi believed that "editing and arranging ritual books" was only "one aspect" for scholars and a "shallow surface" of Confucian classics. He emphasized that the ritual books should be used to govern the state and secure the people, considering them the "source." Consequently, he advocated that officials at the county level should simplify the prevailing "Political Harmony and Five Rites," adapt them to local conditions, and post them in urban and rural areas every January, striving to make them widely known among the common people. Zhu Xi's advocacy of the idea that "scholars shall shoulder the responsibility of current affairs" and his practical efforts became a consensus and a way of practice among Confucian scholars and other scholars in Chinese history. Many scholars served as researchers, educators, disseminators, and practitioners of cultural and ideological studies. This tradition continued in other East Asian countries and regions throughout history. As mentioned earlier, the Chinese scholars in Malaysia and Singapore in the late 19th century, such as Khoo Seok Wan, Lim Boon Keng, Chong Hak Sin, Lie Kim Hok, Kwee Tek Hoay, and Chan Kim Boon, also played multiple roles. They were not only researchers of Confucianism but also educators, disseminators, and practitioners. Many scholars devoted to the cause of Confucian culture in various countries and regions continue to uphold and expand this fine tradition, making significant contributions to the international development of Confucianism. Their wisdom and efforts shine brightly, earning admiration and respect.

There is an old Chinese saying that goes, "If something withstood time, it will last long; if something has achieved a lot, it will achieve more." Confucianism is a glorious cultural achievement that has withstood the change of time over a long history. As one non-withering flower in the garden of the world's cultures, its color and fragrance are bound to last long. All the scholars and workers involved in inheriting the magnificent heritage of Confucian culture and promoting a contemporary Confucianism spirit will see their achievements thrive.

Speech at the 5th Congress and the Board Member Meeting of the ICA*

September 25, 2014

First of all, I would like to express my heartfelt thanks for the support and trust of all the members and councilors who attended the meeting. Thank you for electing me as the 5th chairman of the ICA.

In the past ten years, under the leadership of Chairman Ye Xuanping, ICA and our fellow professionals in Confucianism worked together to effectively push forward the study, spread, and application of Confucianism. We've made impressive and well-recognized achievements. Chairman Ye is open-minded; he has come up with a series of strategic thoughts focusing on future development and built the framework of ICA; he is deliberate and resolute, with some of his decisions playing a vital role in both the work of ICA and the spread of Confucianism; he has a big circle of friends and makes the best use of people's talent, providing a large sum of material and mental wealth to ICA's facility and long-term development. In a word, Chairman Ye is our role model, an erudite man with infinite wisdom, extensive experience, and a graceful demeanor. In the past decade, Mr. Yang Bo successively served as the executive vice-chairman and vice-chairman of ICA. Despite his age, he devoted himself to the running of the

---

* From September 24 to 27, 2014, the ICA held the International Conference in Commemorating the 2565th Anniversary of Confucius's Birth and the 5th Congress of the ICA in Beijing. Chinese President Xi Jinping attended the opening ceremony and delivered an important speech. The conference elected the new leadership members of the ICA. This speech was delivered on September 25, 2014, after being elected president of the ICA.

association. All of us should learn from him, not only because of his achievements but also because of his thoughts and manners. We can see Mr. Yang's wisdom in nearly every part of ICA's work, be it the decision-making and implementation process or the improvement and achievements that have been made. So, on behalf of the new leadership and all the colleagues of ICA and in my own name, I would like to express our gratitude and respect to Chairman Ye Xuanping and Vice-Chairman Yang Bo for their tremendous efforts and contributions to the association.

At the meeting, a number of members and advisors of the 4th ICA Council and Executive Committee retired from their positions. Our thanks and respect also go to them. In the past five years, they have been our colleagues and also our friends. We worked together and made due contribution to the development of ICA. Here, I would like to quote a poem line by Gu Yanwu, a Chinese scholar in the Qing Dynasty, "The dragon god continues to perform its duty of rainfall even when the day is nearly over; an old tree still blooms though spring ends soon." I sincerely hope that all the leaving retirees continue to support the development of ICA. And I wish all of them enjoy the happy years ahead.

I remembered what Fan Zhongyan, a Chinese scholar in the Northern Song Dynasty, said when he complimented a distinguished man in the Eastern Han Dynasty, "Your integrity is like the towering mountains and mighty rivers." I think this classic poem line can be used to honor the founders and pioneers of ICA. Mr. Gu Mu, Mr. Ye Xuanping, Mr. Yang Bo, Mr. Tang Yu, Mr. Xu Zhengdun, and others who used to work at the ICA or are about to leave there. They are a group of talented and distinguished scholars. The achievements they have made, the mental legacy they have left, and the righteousness and nobility they possess will have a profound impact on the development of both ICA and Confucianism, just like the towering mountains and flowing streams I have mentioned. We will carry forward the achievements and legacy they've created. We will also learn from them about how to be a noble person.

Honestly speaking, when I knew that Mr. Ye recommended me as the next chairman, I felt humbled by this position. So, I tried to persuade Chairman Ye to stay in his position for another five years. However, he refused. Although

I have been elected as the new chairman, I know well the significance of my responsibility and the challenge ahead. When I was in college, my major was modern Chinese history. Therefore, I was not quite familiar with ancient Chinese history and needed to put more effort into Confucianism and the hundreds of schools of thought. To some extent, I was an outsider. After starting at ICA, I learned Confucianism from scratch through books, experts, and scholars. After the past few years, I've made some progress but still far from gaining a profound understanding, with the others even out of reach. This is why I said the job is a big challenge for me. It's nothing about modesty. As the chairman of ICA, I will continue working diligently with all the members to promote the development of ICA and meet your expectations. Confucius once said: "To know what you know and what you do not know, that is true knowledge." This is a principle that I will uphold when learning from books, practice, predecessors of ICA, and experts in Confucianism. I will strive to reach an expert level in Confucianism.

The Book of Documents says, "Have forbearance, and your virtue will be great." Yuan Keli, an official in the Ming Dynasty, put it this way: "Modesty brings in virtue, and forbearance is a great virtue." Lin Zexu, a prominent official in the Qing Dynasty, said: "The sea is great because it accepts hundreds of rivers; a man is gracious because he is forbearing." Inclusivity is not only a moral standard of Confucianism but also a principle we should uphold in our work, research, and career, including the development of both the ICA and Confucianism. Only if we adhere to this principle in the process of researching, spreading, popularizing, and applying can we see a dynamic Confucianism circle with harmony in diversity. "Seeking common ground" is conducive to forming consensus; "Reserving differences" is beneficial to promoting transformation and innovation. Only if we uphold the principle of inclusivity can we make our association a place that draws on collective wisdom. I would like to take the lead in treating people's academic views equally and be a good listener to colleagues' advice with an open mind. Chairman Ye mentioned at the opening ceremony that we needed to adopt advice from different people, draw on collective wisdom, and unite the power of the association. So, my dear friends, let us work together to advance the development of ICA to a new stage.

Speech at the Celebration of the 20th Anniversary of the Founding of the ICA[*]

September 25, 2014

Tonight, the banquet hall is filled with distinguished guests and friends. We are here to celebrate the 20th anniversary of the founding of the ICA. On behalf of ICA and in my own name, I would like to extend a warm welcome and heartfelt thanks to all the ICA leaders present here, to representatives of relevant departments of the Chinese government, and to friends and guests who have come all the way here from around the world. Also, I would like to extend warm congratulations to the councilors, members, and fellow professionals of ICA and my sincere greetings to the experts, scholars, and people from all walks of life who contribute to the cause of Confucianism development.

It will be remembered that 30 years ago, on the initiative of Deng Yingchao, chairman of the CPPCC National Committee, the Chinese government approved the establishment of the China Confucius Foundation, the predecessor of the ICA; 20 years ago, advocated and coordinated by Mr. Gu Mu, former vice chairman of the CPPCC National Committee, and promoted by a number of international Confucian societies and scholars, the ICA was successfully registered in China and formally established in Beijing on October 15, 1994. "When drinking water, one must not forget its source." Hereby, we would like to pay tribute to the late

---

[*] During the International Conference in Commemorating the 2565th anniversary of Confucius's Birth and the 5th Congress of the ICA, the newly-elected leaders of ICA hereby held the 20th anniversary since its founding. This speech was delivered at the celebration ceremony on September 25, 2014.

Chairman Deng Yingchao, the first President of ICA Gu Mu, and all the societies, experts, and scholars who have made historic contributions to the founding of the ICA.

For 20 years, under the great leadership and cultivation of Presidents Gu Mu and Ye Xuanping, Board Directors Cui Gende, Tang Yu, and Xu Zhengdun, Vice Chairmans Yang Bo, Gong Dafei, Zhou Nan, and Liu Zhongde, and all the other leaders of ICA, the Association has grown from scratch into an authoritative and international Confucian society recognized by the international community. It is with their pioneering achievements that ICA attains today's success.

Over the past 20 years, the CPC, the Chinese government, and the people have rendered great support and assistance to the ICA. The Party and state leaders visited each congress of ICA, met with the delegates, and addressed their speeches. Yesterday, Xi Jinping, general secretary of the CPC Central Committee, president of the People's Republic of China, and chairman of the Central Military Commission, attended the opening ceremony of the 5th Congress of the ICA and delivered an important speech, which once again demonstrated the great importance the Party, government and people attached to the work of ICA and the international development of Confucianism. The Chinese government disburses funds every year and instructs the Ministry of Culture, the Ministry of Civil Affairs, and other ministries to pay close attention to and support the work of ICA. With the strong support of the Party, the government, and our fellowmen, ICA carries out the international development of Confucianism in such ascendant today.

Over the past 20 years, the councilors, members, researchers, and other staff of ICA have engaged in various academic and promotional activities around the world. According to the current situation and development needs of international politics, economics, culture, education, etc., they carried out Confucian research, education, and publicity, promoting and facilitating the use of Confucianism. They have brought up great achievements. Their works are based on the principles of Confucianism, such as "humanistic pragmatism" and "the unity of knowledge and practice." Besides conducting research, they also endeavor to popularize and apply Confucianism. Cao Pi, emperor of the State of Wei in the Three Kingdoms period, once proposed: "Writing essays remains a great undertaking and an immortal event of the state." Confucian cultural workers, together with those of other cultural areas, have followed this instruction and made glorious deeds. Thanks to their efforts and contributions from home and abroad, ICA has now exerted a profound influence on the international community, and Confucian culture has also spread to all parts of the world.

Twenty years of grope, upstream progress, and hard work constitute a journey marked by both setbacks and glory. Even though our predecessors proposed: "Ask not what you paid, ask what you obtained," our efforts will always pay off. After 20 years, the international development of Confucianism presents us with a prosperous picture—academic research on Confucianism is springing up in China and beyond; Confucian research institutions and publicity organizations are being established; Confucian study, education, and dissemination are gaining popularity. The development of Confucian culture is now beaming with vigor and vitality. This is rather gratifying and encouraging, especially for those who engage in promoting international Confucianism.

Confucian culture was initiated and developed in China, but it had spread to East Asia since early times and formed its cultural circle there. Then, it gradually spread to Europe and other parts of the world, becoming an important source and component of world culture. Therefore, it not only profoundly affected the Chinese civilization, but also greatly contributed to the development of world civilization. It is a treasure house of Chinese and world culture, whose thoughts, values, and functions serve both history and modern times. Through creative transformation and development, Confucianism will serve today's society and write a new chapter for the benefit of mankind. Now, the journey for the international development of Confucian culture has begun. Let us, as well as those who support and devote themselves to the cause of Confucianism, join our efforts to make greater contributions.

Speech at the Closing Ceremony of the International Conference in Commemorating the 2565th Anniversary of Confucius's Birth and the 5th Congress of the ICA*

September 27, 2014

Through the joint efforts of all the members, directors, and representatives, we have completed the agenda of the Beijing session. We will soon go to Qufu, the hometown of Confucius, Shandong Province, to start the next session. Representatives from the seven subgroups summarized their discussions, which concluded this academic conference.

This meeting is a milestone. There is something new at the meeting. Firstly, an unprecedented number of more than 300 experts and scholars are attending the conference, including prominent figures such as former Peruvian President Garcia and Tanzanian President Mkapa. This indicates that some national dignitaries

---

also care about and support Confucian cultural development. They even directly participate in the research, dissemination, and application of Confucian culture. This is an encouraging phenomenon. In particular, Chinese President Xi Jinping's speech at the opening ceremony attracted warm responses that can be seen from media reports and comments in China and around the world. As many experts and scholars said at the seminar, President Xi Jinping's speech pointed out the direction of efforts for the study, education, dissemination, and application of international Confucianism, and its significance and influence will be far-reaching.

The meeting was broadly representative. The number of delegates attending the conference increased from a previous maximum of 20 countries and regions to 50 from five continents. This is the first time nearly 30 countries have joined the meeting, including India, Myanmar, Mongolia, Slovenia, Bahrain, Egypt, South Africa, Italy, Finland, and Argentina. Alongside experts, scholars, and promoters of Confucianism, many historians, philosophers, political scientists, and educationalists also attended the conference. This shows that the ICA is expanding its work area, while attracting more support and participation for the development of international Confucianism. Among the attendees are a number of prestigious experts of the older generation and a few emerging scholars of the younger generation. The older experts represent our longtime strength, while the younger scholars have brought in new vitality. In a word, this conference is a grand gathering of new and old friends to exchange knowledge with each other.

This conference proved to be very inspiring, with a high academic level. The conference received nearly 200 research papers. Focusing on the issue of peace and development, we've discussed the interaction between Confucianism and contemporary economic and social development, contemporary political and international relations, contemporary culture and civilizations, world and regional peace, education, and environmental protection. We also talked about the rule of virtue in Confucianism, the spread of Confucianism around the world, and so on, and gave many valuable academic opinions. Among them are profound philosophical thoughts, insightful viewpoints, new breakthroughs, and thought-provoking explorations. During the discussion, everyone expressed their views and consulted on an equal footing, reflecting the spirit of academic democracy. In particular, the speeches by some well-known international scholars at the conference fully demonstrated their erudite knowledge and academic attainments. They also showed their philosophy of "contributing to society with a global perspective." This is a good idea for all of us to share.

During the Spring and Autumn and Warring States periods in China more than 2,000 years ago, Confucius, Mencius, Xun Zi, and other philosophers of pre-Qin Confucianism summed up the thinking achievements of predecessors and created profound Confucianism in an era of vassal disputes, morality degradation, and social upheaval. This was a theoretical guide for China's unification and economic and cultural development. In the meantime, Confucianism contributed to cultural prosperity featuring "harmony in diversity" and "Hundred Schools of Thought" in mutual learning with other schools of thought. Together, they inherited and developed the ancient Chinese civilization. Today's situation is similar to the Spring and Autumn and Warring States periods in China, which occurred more than 2,000 years ago. The world is changing with rapid development, but countries and regions are also facing many problems and difficulties. Because of this, more and more far-sighted people, including many national dignitaries, turn to Confucian culture, hoping to find inspiration and wisdom to help solve these problems. For example, Dr. Taylor of UNESCO pointed out, "Today's prosperous and successful society is still largely based on many of the values established and articulated by Confucius. These values transcend national boundaries and the times. They belong to both China and the world, both the past, today, and the future." Many scholars at this conference also stressed that the value and wisdom of Confucian culture provide a realistic possibility for solving global problems. As Confucian researchers and professionals, we should be duty-bound to stand in the forefront of the times. We should not only strengthen the study and exploration of the value and wisdom contained in the Confucian culture, but also disseminate and apply them to social development and governance, so as to make greater contributions to solving the common problems and difficulties facing mankind and promoting world peace and common development of all countries.

After this conference, the new leadership of the ICA will begin its work. We should take the 20th anniversary of the founding of the ICA as an opportunity to ride on the momentum built at this conference and seize the favorable opportunity for the development of Confucianism. With concerted efforts, we should seize the opportunity to play a good role in organizing, coordinating, serving, and promoting the development of international Confucianism and culture, strengthen the unity and interconnection with Confucian organizations, Confucian researchers and professionals all over the world, and work tirelessly to jointly open up a new prospect for the research, education, dissemination, and application of international Confucianism.

Communication and Mutual Influence between Asia and Europe and between China and Europe in History and Confucian Characteristics, Values, and Prospects[*]

Presentation for the International Confucianism Forum · Academic Conference in Venice

September 19, 2015

---

[*] From September 19 to 20, 2015, the ICA, in collaboration with Beijing Foreign Studies University, Venice International University, and the University of Venice, jointly organized the International Confucianism Forum · Academic Conference in Venice in Italy. Nearly 30 scholars from countries including China, Italy, Germany, France, Slovenia, New Zealand, the United States, India, and Singapore attended the conference. The theme was "Dialogue between Confucian Culture and European Culture—Decline or Prosperity of Confucianism in an Age of Globalization." This is the keynote speech given at the conference on September 19, 2015. The speech reviewed and analyzed the general historical course of communication between Asian-European and Central-European civilizations, especially the exchange of ideological and cultural ideas over the past two millennia. Based on this, the speech summarized how to correctly understand the historical status, role, and mutual relationships of various civilizations worldwide and advocated principles for promoting exchange and mutual learning among different world civilizations. It also analyzed and expounded on the contemporary value and essential characteristics of Confucianism and subsequently proposed some principles that should be adhered to in the study, research, and application of Confucian culture.

Today, we are gathered in the beautiful water city of Venice, the hometown of Marco Polo, to hold this International Confucianism Forum. It can be said that this is a grand occasion for the exchange of Eastern and Western cultures. In March 1999, I had the honor of visiting Venice with Comrade Jiang Zemin, who was then the President of China. We rode on the unique "gondola," drifting on the azure waters, appreciating the profound historical culture of Venice and the picturesque scenery of sea and sky. The scenes from that time still vividly linger in my memory. Having the opportunity to return to Venice once again is like revisiting an old friend, and it brings me great joy.

This academic conference of the ICA, held in Venice, Italy, is themed "Dialogue between Confucian Culture and European Culture—Decline or Prosperity of Confucianism in an Age of Globalization," which illustrates the humanistic feelings that exist between Chinese and European culture and care for the prospects of Confucianism. This is a very significant theme. I believe this conference will be very beneficial in promoting communication and reference between China and Europe and the East and the West.

Now, I want to take this opportunity to share my views on four areas to serve as an exploratory written speech for seeking advice from all present experts and scholars.

I. Contributions Made by China and Italy Regarding the Formation and Development of Asian and European Civilizations

Confucian culture, born in China, is the main source of Chinese civilization's formation and development. It has spread to East Asia and other regions of Asia, and then to Europe and other regions of the world, and thus is a significant part of world culture. China, as one of the Four Great Ancient Civilizations, has had an uninterrupted civilization for thousands of years, which has made great contributions to both Asian civilization and world civilization. In the 1930s, English scholar Reginald Johnston pointed out that "Confucianism is fully qualified as a 'great tradition' of the Chinese nation" and "Confucianism is the most important factor that makes the Chinese nation breed in an endless succession and makes China one of the countries with the longest history in the world."

As early as 300 or 400 years before and after AD, Confucian culture had spread to the Korean Peninsula, Japan, and the northern regions of Vietnam, where the East Asian cultural circle was gradually formed. As Nishijima Sadao, a scholar of Japan, said in the *Formation of the East Asian World*, "The East Asian World is formed based on the development and formation of Chinese civilization, and as Chinese civilization developed, a self-realized cultural circle was formed with the Chinese civilization as the core." Thousands of years later, Chinese historic civilization dominated by Confucianism has played an indelible role in mutual exchange with Southeast Asia civilization, South Asia civilization, West Asian civilization, and Central Asian civilization, and in the formation and development of Asian and Eastern civilizations overall.

If we say that China is an important source of Asian civilization, which has made a unique contribution to the development of Asian civilization, then we can say that Italy is the birthplace of European civilization, which has made a unique contribution to the formation and development of European civilization. The Roman Empire and the Renaissance are two examples.

The Roman Empire, an ancient empire across Africa and Asia, originated from Italy and gradually expanded. It made two important contributions to European civilization. One is Latin, which later became the mother of European languages. After the collapse of the Roman Empire, European countries developed their national languages on the basis of Latin; another contribution was Roman laws, which served as the guidance and reference for the enactment of laws of later European countries and even the rest of the world. It is on the basis of inheriting Roman law that the Continental Law System, one of the two law systems in the world today, has gradually formed. It is also called the Roman Law System.

The Renaissance was a cultural movement developed in Europe in the 14th century. It promoted the vigorous development of European thought, science, culture, and art. The Renaissance began in Italy and later spread to the rest of Europe, reaching its height in the 16th century. The so-called Renaissance, originally referred to as the "regeneration of Greek and Roman classical culture," was not a simple recovery. It was instead a great movement for ideological and cultural liberation initiated to meet the political and economic demands of the rising bourgeoisie of Europe and their demands against feudal rule in the field of ideology and culture, under the banner and call of inheriting Greek and Roman classical culture. The representative figures of the Renaissance thought that under the rule of medieval theology for a continuous one thousand years, Europe had been in a divided, backward, and chaotic state, and human nature and humanities were destroyed. They required that the restraints of theology on human thinking be broken, along with the despotic rule of religion and feudal hierarchy. They argued the need to fight against "theocracy" with "human rights" and advocated personal liberation, equality, and freedom. They called for the learning and mastering of scientific and technological knowledge. This prepared the way for political and cultural change and the mass conditions needed for a European Bourgeois Revolution and the Industrial Revolution. Therefore, the Renaissance not only became an important symbol that marked the end of the Dark Middle Ages in Europe and the opening of a modern historical prelude for European countries, but also an important symbol that marked a shift in the world from the ancient civilization of feudal societies to the modern civilization of a capitalist society.

This movement for the emancipation of ideology and culture first originated in Florence in northern Italy. Its initial representatives included Dante, Giotto, Petrarch, Boccaccio, Brunelleschi, Ghiberti, and others. Later, in Italy, outstanding celebrities such as Machiavelli, Leonardo da Vinci, Raphael, Michelangelo, and Palestrina sprung up and became another group of pioneering figures that led the Renaissance movement.

As this movement spread to the rest of Europe, great cultural masters such as Thomas Moore, Martin Luther, Rabelais, Lassus, Montaigne, Cervantes, and Shakespeare sprung up in the UK, Germany, France, Spain, and elsewhere. Cultural giants appeared one after another. As Engels pointed out: "This is the greatest and progressive change that humans have ever experienced; the need is a giant one and had a giant—in the ability to think, passion and character, versatility and knowledge in giant times." Among these giants, Dante, Leonardo da Vinci, and Shakespeare were the most outstanding. Because the Renaissance originated in Italy, where the highest number of leading figures in the movement existed, it is often said that Italy is the firstborn of modern Europe.

From the above, we can clearly see the historical position of Italy in the Roman Empire and the Renaissance, which also clearly shows Italy's important contribution to the formation and development of European civilization.

II. General Process of Mutual Exchange and Learning between Asian and European Civilizations and between Chinese and European Civilizations and Their Mutual Influence

During over two thousand years of mutual exchange between Asian and European civilizations, every Asian and European country played a significant role and made their contributions, especially China and Italy. Great exchange and reference occurred between these two great civilizations, in addition to the role played by merchants, religious figures, and scholars. Italy was home to the Roman Curia and thus sent more religious people and scholars to Asia and the East; China, with its developed economy and culture during ancient times, opened up the Silk Road as the main channel for communication between the East and the West, which became an important force in the exchange between Asia and Europe.

Since ancient times, contact between the two great civilizations has occurred in various channels and forms. Exchange first took place in the form of material culture through commercial activities, although historical records in this area are scarce.

By contrast, there are a large number of historical records on the spiritual and cultural exchanges between Asian and European civilizations. According to China's historical chronology and stages, I think that the course of communication between the two civilizations on ideology and culture can be generally divided into two stages. The first stage began in the pre-Qin period and continued through the Yuan Dynasty, during which the Qin, Han, Tang, and Song dynasties existed.

During this period of over one thousand years, mutual direct contact and exchange of ideology and culture between West Asian, Central Asian, and South Asian civilizations and European civilization was underway and had been increasingly frequent. However, such direct contact and exchange were not completely equal and harmonious and sometimes were passive through mutual conflict and war, such as in the Greco-Persian Wars and Alexander's Anabasis.

For over one thousand years, Chinese and East Asian civilizations ideologically and culturally communicated with Italian and European civilizations, mostly through Central Asia, South Asia, and West Asia, although their direct contact and communication were rare.

During the Western Han Dynasty in China from 138 BC to 126 BC and from 119 BC to 115 BC, Emperor Wu had twice sent Zhang Qian to the Western Regions. Zhang only reached as far as today's Central Asia and failed to make direct contact with Greece at that time. During the Eastern Han Dynasty in AD 73 to AD 102, Ban Chao served as an envoy and stayed in the Western Regions for 30 years, but he mainly moved about in today's Xinjiang region of China. Though he sent his assistant superintendent, Gan Ying, to visit Daqin, namely the Roman Empire, in AD 97, Gan Ying was dissuaded by Parthians on the excuse of a strong sea wind when he arrived at the east coast of the Mediterranean. So, he failed to reach European areas on the north coast of the Mediterranean. In AD 166, during the last years of the Eastern Han Dynasty, the King of Daqin sent envoys who arrived in China via Rinan (now central Vietnam). This period was under the rule of the Roman Emperor Marcus Aurelius. This was recorded in the *Book of the Later Han* in China, but there was no record of it in Latin literature. Some scholars thought that perhaps some West Asia merchants pretended to be envoys. In AD 751, the Tang Empire went to war with the Arab Empire in Talas, Central Asia, and the Tang suffered a crushing defeat, with many people captured. Among the captured was a scholar named Du Huan, who followed the Arabs to West Asia, North Africa, and other places and then went back to China in AD 762 by the Maritime Silk Road. He wrote a book called *Record of Travels*, but he also failed to arrive in Spain, Portugal, Italy, and other European countries. In AD 1255, during the Southern Song Dynasty, Zhao Rushi, a scholar who held office in Quanzhou, Fujian Province, wrote a book titled *Records of Foreign Countries* according to the introductions by merchants from Italy and West Asia who came to Quanzhou and other places in China to do business. But he hadn't been to Europe personally. In the book, an island named "Sijia Liye" was described in detail, including its close proximity to the state of "Lumei." "Sijia Liye" island is today's Sicilia, and "Lumei" is Rome. This is an earlier book that records Italy and other European countries among Chinese historical records.

On the whole, over a thousand years before the Yuan Dynasty, China and East Asia hadn't directly communicated with Italy and Europe ideologically or culturally. Although both sides had heard a lot about each other and used goods from each other's civilizations, their understanding and acquaintance were limited to hearing instead of direct contact. Their understanding of each other was still in a hazy and mysterious state. The European region where the Roman Empire was located had long been known as "Daqin," "Liqian," "Lixuan," "Fulin," or "Fulang" in China's historical records. At the same time, China had long been called "Serica," i.e., a country of silk, in Europe. Although both sides wanted to become acquainted with each other, a long period passed, and such a desire failed to come to fruition, and the moment finally arrived in China's Yuan Dynasty. From the Yuan to Ming and Qing dynasties, ideological and cultural communication between Asia and Europe and China and Europe had entered its second stage.

During this stage, the communication between both sides experienced three flowering periods in the late Yuan, late Ming and early Qing, and the late Qing dynasties, respectively. In the nearly seven hundred years from the Yuan Dynasty to the Qing Dynasty, namely, from the middle of the 13th century to the beginning of the 20th century, material communication was in full swing and developed rapidly. Meanwhile, ideological and cultural communication was also direct, frequent, and comprehensive. From ideological and cultural exchanges between China and Europe, we can clearly see the rapid development of contact between Asian civilization and European civilization over seven centuries.

Ideological and cultural communication between China and Europe before the eve and after the founding of the Yuan Dynasty. China's Yuan Dynasty was founded in 1271. Before its establishment, two big events occurred in Asia and Europe at that time: one was the Sixth Crusade launched by the Roman Curia and European kings against the Arab Islamic countries of West Asia; the second was the outward expansion launched by the emerging Mongol Empire in East Asia to Europe. In order to understand the political situation, military power, cultural customs, and intentions of the western expedition of the Mongol Empire and also to coordinate it with the Crusades and further understand the eastward expansion, the Roman Curia, Italy, and other European countries sent over a batch of Franciscan missionaries and some merchants familiar with West Asia and East Asia. The great khans of the Mongol Empire and the kings who established China's Yuan Dynasty personally met these Western missionaries and merchants. Chinese rulers at that time understood the Roman Curia and the situation of the European countries through these people. Meanwhile, they sent these missionaries and merchants back as their own messengers to promote their national prestige and desire to communicate with Europe.

Among the European missionaries to East Asia, Franciscan Jean de Plan Carpin and Rubruck successively went to the Mongol Empire in 1245 and 1253; John of Montecorvino, Odoric of Pordenone, Andre, Delhi, Marignolli, and so on, successively came to China's Yuan Dynasty. Except for Rubruck, who was Flemish, the rest were all Italians. The merchants who visited during the Yuan Dynasty included Andaloda Savignone, Marco Polo and his father and uncle, Pietro Lucalongo, Luchetto Duodo, Giovanni Loredan, Franceschino Loredan and so on, all of whom were Italians. Many of them wrote books on the Mongol Empire and Chinese history, for example, Jean de Plan Carpin's *Mongolian History*, Rubruck's *The Journey of William of Rubruk to the Eastern Parts*, Marco Polo's *Travels of Marco Polo*, Marignolli's *History of Bohemia*, Odoric of Pordenone's *Odoric's Itinerarium*, and so on. When these European missionaries and merchants came to the East, Rabban Bar Sauma, a Chinese religious man who was born in a Uighur family, set out from the Great Capital of the Yuan Dynasty (now Beijing) as an envoy of the Yuan Dynasty in 1278 to Europe via West Asia. He successively met the pope of Rome and the kings of France and Britain and wrote the *Travels* about his time in Europe.

Here, I want to specifically talk about Marco Polo and his *Travels of Marco Polo* with the account of his experiences in China. Marco Polo's father, Niccolò, and his uncle, Maffeo, were merchants of Venice who were engaged in trade between the East and the West. The brothers had been to the Mongolian Empire around 1265 and met Kublai Khan, who later became the first emperor of China's Yuan Dynasty. Kublai Khan sent them to the Roman Curia. In 1271, Marco Polo and his father and uncle accompanied papal envoys to the Far East and arrived in Xanadu in 1275. Later, Marco Polo was appointed by Kublai Khan as an advisor and traveled to many places in China. In 1292, he left China and returned to Italy, writing his well-known *Travels of Marco Polo*. From then on, Europeans clearly understood that the "Serica" they heard about far away in the East was an ancient civilization with a several thousand-year history. Some scholars believe that the historical culture and the economic and social situation of China written in the book opened "a window for Europe and the West to know China" and widened Europeans' horizons, enriched their knowledge of geography, and aroused their great enthusiasm to explore China and the East personally. Since then, a large number of European navigators, travelers, and explorers headed east.

All in all, during the Yuan Dynasty, European missionaries and merchants who came to the East introduced the historic culture of Europe to China. Also, they spread the historic culture of China to Europe, which opened a new stage of direct contact and mutual understanding between the two and formed the first wave of ideological and cultural communication. Italians made a great contribution in this period.

Ideological and cultural communication between China and Europe in the late Ming and early Qing dynasties. The late Ming and early Qing dynasties refer to the period of two hundred years, from the middle of the 16th century to the middle of the 18th century. At this time, Europe had experienced the Renaissance, geographical discovery, and Martin Luther's reformation, all of which marked Europe's entry into the beginnings of capitalism. The emergence and development of European capitalism inevitably required the external expansion of commodity markets and sources of raw materials needed for industry. The opening of the new sea route and the great progress of European science and technology, especially navigation technology, provided the technical conditions for Europe's overseas development and expansion. To this end, the Roman Curia and political rulers of some major countries of Europe first cast their eyes on Asian countries with large populations, abundant resources, and long histories, such as China and India. Such economic and political background contributed to the arrival of the second wave of ideological and cultural exchange between the East and the West, especially between China and Europe.

The main force that assumed the mission of ideological and cultural communication was still religious people, merchants, scholars, some officials, and ambassadors of both sides, especially the European side. But religious people at this time were mainly Jesuit missionaries instead of the past Franciscans, among which, the number of Italian Jesuit missionaries were most, including Michele Ruggieri, Matteo Ricci, Alessandro Valignano, Nicholas Longobardi, Lazzaro Cattaneo, Sabatino de Ursis, Jules Aleni, Giacomo Rho, Frarcuis Brancati, Lodovico Buglio, Martino Martini, Prospero Intorcetta, Domingo Fernández Navarrete, Matteo Ripa, Cunevari Pierre, Jean-François Ronusi de Ferrariis, and so on. They were the first in Europe to systematically learn the Chinese language and culture, and they first built a bridge of ideological, scientific, and cultural exchanges between China and Europe. After the Italians, a group of French Jesuit missionaries came to China. Among them, French King Louis XIV directly sent six persons, i.e., Jean de Fontaney, Joachim Bouvet, Jean-François Gerbillon, Claude de Visdelou, Louis le Comte, and Guy Tachard. French Jesuit missionaries also included Joseph de Premare, Michel Benoist, Nicolas Trigault, Du Halde, Artus de Lionne, Antoine Gaubil, Moyriac de Mailla, Jean Baptiste Regis, Jean Francoise Foucquet, Jean Baborier, Pierre Foureau, and so on. During this period of contact between China and Europe during the late Ming and early Qing dynasties, French Jesuit missionaries also played an important role. In addition to Italy and France, Jesuit missionaries of other European countries also came to China, such as the Germans Johann Adam Schall von Bell, Johann Schreck, Ignatius Koegler, and Bernhard Diestel, the Belgians Ferdinand Verbiest, Philippe Couplet, and Francesco Sambiasi, the British Joseph Edkins, Austrian Jean Grueber, Spanish Diego de Pantoja and Portuguese Gabriel Magaillans, among others. Among them, Matteo Ricci was an important pioneer. He studied the Chinese language, history, and culture and integrated Confucianism and Christian thoughts. The famous Italian sinologist Jake Obetsebi Lamptey once said, "Matteo Ricci can be regarded as the first Chinese scientist among Westerners, and he is the only European person whose biography is worthy of recording on the history of the Ming Dynasty."

These European Jesuit missionaries came to China to spread Christianity with the intention of expanding Europe's presence abroad. We should not have any objection in this regard. To preach in China, however, they should know about

China and make China know about Europe. So, plenty of work was done related to culture and science and technology. Many of the missionaries were astronomers, mathematicians, geographers, philosophers, hydraulicians, artists, and musicians. They mainly conducted the following activities.

Firstly, they established relationships with all levels of feudal society in China, from emperors to officials, scholars, religious believers, and others.

Secondly, they learned the Chinese language and understood China's history, culture, national traditions, folk customs, and social reality.

Thirdly, they introduced and propagated "Western learning" to Chinese people. So-called Western learning refers to learning about European history, ideologies, culture, science and technology, folk customs, national conditions, etc. First of all, with the assistance of Chinese scholars, they translated European historical and cultural classics into Chinese and then published these classics in China, such as Euclid's *Elements* and ancient Greek classics like *Gougu Yi* (Pythagorean Theorem), *Celiang Fayi* (Complete Principle of Measurement), *Tongwen Suanzhi* (Epitome Arithmetical Practice), and *Huanrong Jiaoyi* (Comments on Spheres). Moreover, they wrote academic literature in Chinese on European history, ideologies, culture, and science and technology. For example, in astronomy and calendar, they wrote *Gujin Jiaoshi Kao* (Research on Ancient and Modern Eclipse), *Ce Shi Shuo* (Eclipse Observation Theory), and *Hengxing Chumo* (On Stellar); in military, they wrote *Huo Gong Qie Yao* (Elements of Fire Attack) and *Kunyu Tushuo* (Illustrated Explanation of the World), as well as the *Xifang Yaoji* (Record of Western Countries) for more general knowledge. Giulio Alenio, an Italian Jesuit missionary, wrote 23 books introducing "Western learning." Among these books are *Zhifang Waiji* (Record of Foreign Lands), *Xi Xue Fan* (An Introduction to Western Learning), and *Xi Xue Da Wen* (Questions and Answers to Western Learning). They introduced the philosophy, art, geography, religion, and social systems of Western countries. Furthermore, they taught Western learning to Chinese emperors, officials, scholars, and religious believers. For instance, French Jesuits like Joachim Bouvet and Jean-François Gerbillon lectured to Emperor Kangxi on Western geometry, philosophy, medical science, and pharmacology. Meanwhile, they built a bridge of communication between Emperor Kangxi of China and King Louis XIV of France. Joachim Bouvet once wrote a report with nearly 100,000 words on what he saw and heard in China, and then he presented it to King Louis XIV. In addition, they passed on and applied Europe's latest scientific and technological knowledge and achievements to China. For example, they helped China revise its calendars, make astronomical instruments and maps, make artillery and pass on its usage, etc. The revised calendars include *Chongzhen Calendar* and *Shixian Calendar*, and maps made by them include *Kunyu Wanguo Quantu* (Great Universal Geographic Map), *Zhongguo Xin Ditu Ji* (Atlas of China), *Huangyu Quan Lan Tu* (Map of China in the Kangxi Reign), and *Qianlong Shisanpai Ditu* (Map of China in the Qianlong Reign).

Fourthly, they introduced "Chinese learning" to the Europeans. This included learning about China's history, ideologies, culture, political system, national traditions, and folk customs. When introducing and spreading Chinese learning, they accomplished the following. First of all, they translated Chinese historical and cultural classics into Latin and published them in Europe. For instance, they translated *The Book of Documents*, *The Book of Songs*, *The Book of Changes*, *The Great Learning*, *The Doctrine of Mean*, *The Analects of Confucius*, *Tao Te Ching*, *The Six Books of China*, *Tong Jian Gang Mu*, and Yuanqu (a type of verse popular in the Yuan Dynasty) like *The Orphan of Zhao*, as well as novels like *Biographies of Good Spouses*. Moreover, they wrote and published various books in Latin, introducing Chinese history, culture, and social reality. These books include *The History of Expedition to China*, *The History of Ancient China*, *The Ancient China*, *The History of Tang Dynasty*, *The General History of China*, *Imperial History of China*, *Overview of Imperial China*, *New Survey of China*, *New History of China*, *Interpretation of "The Book of Changes," Confucius Sinarum Philosophus*, *Military Strategy and Tactics of China*, etc. According to incomplete data, during the nearly one hundred years dating from 1687 to 1773, a total of 176 books about China were written in Latin by Jesuits who came to China, including 48 on comprehensive knowledge, 14 on history, 54 on astronomy and geography, 40 on philosophy and religion, and 20 on language. Furthermore, they wrote a lot of reports and other material introducing China and their perceptions of China's history and reality. These reports were presented to the Roman Curia, political leaders, and scholars.

In addition, they recommended or even led some Chinese officials, Christians, scholars, and students to Europe for further investigation and study. Among those were Chen Ande, Christians like Shen Fuzong, Fan Shouyi, Hu Ruowang, Liu Baolu, Lan Fangji, Huang Jialue, and young students like Wu Jun, Yin Ruowang, Huang Batong, Gu Wenrao, Gao Leisi, Yang Wangde, etc. In particular, Huang Jialue followed Artus de Lionne, a French missionary, to Rome in 1702. Afterward, he went to France and became the King's Chinese translator. He was also familiar with Montesquieu, and they often discussed China's history, politics, and law. Undoubtedly, these Chinese people played an important role in introducing China to Europe.

What were the distinguishing features of ideological and cultural exchange between China and the countries of Europe during the late Ming and early Qing dynasties? What about their status and significance in the civilization exchange between Asia and Europe? For these two questions, I would like to make the following comments.

Firstly, before the 16th century, if the direct exchange between Asian and European civilizations in ideology and culture was dominated by the exchange between countries of West Asia and Europe in Islamic civilization and Christian civilization, then, after the middle of the 16th century, it was dominated by the exchange between China in East Asia and Europe in ancient Chinese civilization and modern European civilization.

Secondly, before the middle of the 16th century, if the exchange between Chinese civilization and European civilization was mainly the exchange of material civilization, then, after the middle of the 16th century, it entered into the period when the exchange of material civilization and spiritual civilization developed simultaneously. The proportion of the exchange of spiritual civilization continuously increased.

Thirdly, if the direct exchange between China and Europe during the Yuan Dynasty of China was just beginning and was limited between Chinese emperors and the popes and the kings of some European countries, which was mainly related to religious culture, the breadth and depth of the exchange was greatly expanded. This happened due to the support of the current political rulers of both sides, especially the active participation and promotion of many scholars such as

Xu Guangqi, Li Zhizao, Yang Tingjun, and Wang Zheng from China and Leibniz, Voltaire, Goethe, and Quesnay from Europe. Therefore, the exchange at this time was truly about the "westward transmission of Chinese culture" and "eastward transmission of Western culture," which saw the mutual integration, learning, reference, complementation, and mutual improvement of Chinese culture and Western culture. This signified that the exchange between Chinese civilization and European culture entered into a new period.

Fourthly, the exchange of ideology and culture between China and Europe at this time had a far-reaching impact on both China and Europe. As for Europe, with the westward transmission of Chinese culture, "Chinese culture fever" developed, which lasted for one century from the end of the 17th century to the end of the 18th century. This cultural phenomenon was not only shown in Europeans' admiration and pursuit of Chinese cultural products; it was further shown in the learning and referencing of Chinese ideology and culture. How exactly did this "fever" pan out? Quite well, in fact. For example, Friedrich II, king of Prussia, invited Voltaire to Prussia to help to carry out a Chinese style of politics at court; when inspecting Oxford, James II, King of England, used to ask an orientalist whether there were works of Confucius translated by Jesuits; Louis XIV of France received Shen Fuzong, a Chinese Jesuit to better understand China, which led to the dispatch of French Jesuits to China to investigate Chinese culture to supplement a shortage of European culture; Jesuit Joseph Mastropaolo translated the Yuanqu *The Orphan of Zhao* into English, which was performed all over Europe, and Voltaire also rewrote it into *The Chinese Orphan*, which was performed in Paris.

Here, we should talk about the research, cognition, and evaluation of Chinese ideology and culture by three European Enlightenment thinkers, Leibniz, Voltaire, and Quesnay. After researching Chinese ideology and culture and comparing it with that of Europe, Leibniz thought that "No one of us ever believed that there was any other nation in the world that had better ethics and better ways of conducting themselves, and now China in the East just awakens us." "If we are neck to neck with China in technology and ahead of China in speculative philosophy, I am sure China is beyond us in practical philosophy, moral commandments, and politics applicable to real life. He said, "Chinese people had mastered the compass, gunpowder, and knowledge about many herbal medicines in front of us," and "Undoubtedly, I believe that there are still a lot of things worth learning from them." Voltaire was the European Enlightenment thinker who researched, understood, and talked about China most at that time. He discussed China in nearly 80 works and more than 200 letters. He thought, "China is the only country that combines politics with ethics" and "the Chinese people are the most rational people among all people." He said, "We had no idea about China in the past, and it had been distorted for a long time in our eyes." Furthermore, "The Hindu and the Chinese people had held an important position long before the formation of other nations" and "Why don't we pay attention to understand their spirits? When you try to understand the world as a philosopher, you should first look to the East, which is the cradle of art and gives many things to the West." Voltaire also regarded the aphorisms "Do not do unto others what you would not have done unto yourself" and "Be kind to others before they do to you and be tolerant to others before they do to you" as his mottos. Chief thinker Quesnay of the physiocratic school also paid much attention to the research of Chinese ideology and culture. To collect data for his research, he asked 52 questions to Gao Leisi and Yang Dewang, two young students studying in France. Quesnay believed that "the political system and moral system of the vast empire of China was established on the basis of science and natural law" and "China is not an object of admiration that is visible but unattainable, but it is a model that can be imitated." The physiocratic school also thought that "no other place in the world has more advanced agriculture than China" and "the advanced agriculture of China is owed to the government. The deep and unshakable foundation of the Chinese government is established on the basis of rationality." Voltaire and Quesnay were referred to as the "Confucius of Europe."

In a word, the "Chinese culture fever" in Europe from the end of the 17th century to the end of the 18th century could be summarized by the words of two Western scholars. French scholar Maurice Robain said, "China was everywhere in the West at the Age of Enlightenment." American scholar L. S. Stavrianos said, "In the 17th century and the beginning of the 18th century, China had much greater influence on Europe than Europe had on China. The Western people were totally fascinated after learning about Chinese history, art, philosophy, and politics" and Chinese civilization "began to be regarded as the model civilization." Many

European Enlightenment thinkers, represented by Leibniz, Voltaire, and Quesnay, carefully analyzed information about Chinese ideology and culture provided by Jesuits and compared Chinese culture with European culture and absorbed the beneficial parts, which facilitated the development of European ideology and culture such as philosophy, literature, ethics, and politics. It provided a weapon of thought and wisdom for the rise of the European Enlightenment and the outbreak of the French Revolution. A Western scholar, Jacques Gernet, once pointed out: "The discovery and understanding of China played a decisive role in the development of 18th-century European philosophy, and it was this philosophy that laid the groundwork for the French Revolution."

Although there was no "Europe fever" in China, the eastward transmission of Western culture had a far-reaching influence. The latest science and technology transmitted from Europe played an important role as an accoucheur in the breeding of the sprouts of capitalism in China and the emergence of science and technology and industry in modern China. Meanwhile, modern political thought transmitted from Europe injected new light into the ideology and culture of China, which was governed by feudal autocracy. It provided mental preparation for the rise of Western ideological trends dominated by science and democracy in China afterward.

Fifthly, during the exchange of ideology and culture exchange, though there was "Rites Controversy," the dispute was soon resolved due to the attention, support, and tolerance of the political rulers, thus allowing the exchange to carry on in an atmosphere of mutual respect. This also provided a beneficial historical experience for later generations to engage in dialogue and exchange among different civilizations.

As the second climax of exchange and mutual reference between Chinese and European civilizations, its great significance and far-reaching influence can be clearly seen from the above analysis of basic information, main features, and the historical experience of ideology and cultural exchange between China and Europe during the late Ming and early Qing dynasties. During this time of exchange, the role of the bridge played by European Jesuits can't be ignored.

Information about the ideology and culture exchange between China and Europe during the late Ming and early Qing dynasties. The year 1840 was a historical turning point for ancient and modern China. This year, England launched the First Opium War against China; in 1856, England and France launched the Second Opium War against China. The two wars shocked both China and the whole East. From then on, China entered into a semi-colonial and semi-feudal society jointly governed by Western capitalist imperialism and China's feudalism, and the Chinese people were caught in an unprecedentedly severe national crisis; the sprouts of capitalism in China that had been bred since the middle of the Ming Dynasty developed quite slowly, and Chinese society had become poor and weak.

In Europe, after bourgeois revolutions in politics and the industrial revolutions witnessed in the economy, many countries entered into the silver age of rapid development of capitalism. Due to virtue of their powerful comprehensive national strength, major countries, such as England and France, began to use modern military weapons and conducted colonial invasions in Africa and then Asia, especially India and China. Under the circumstance of invasion and being invaded and colonization and being colonized, though the exchange between European and Asian civilizations still continued, there was a fundamental change compared with before.

From China's perspective, cultural exchange between it and Europe still continued, but under unequal political conditions. Though European missionaries, scholars, and officials came to China one after another, their roles and the purpose and nature of their activities were quite different from the late Ming and early Qing dynasties. The primary purpose of missionaries coming to China was no longer to introduce "Chinese learning" to Europe or "Western learning" to China; instead, they had already become tools of colonialism. On the contrary, during the seventy to eighty years, from the middle of the 19th century to the beginning of the 20th century, Chinese people took the leading role in promoting the exchange of ideology and culture between China and Europe and finally pushed it to the third wave.

Facing the expansion and invasion of foreign big powers, the Chinese people also carried out various forms of resistance in this great moment of historical rethinking. A large number of Chinese scholars, officials, and overseas students such as Gong Zizhen, Lin Zexu, Wei Yuan, Xue Fucheng, Yan Fu, Guo Songtao,

Wang Tao, He Qi, Ma Jianzhong, Feng Guifen, Zheng Guanying, Zhang Zhidong, Kang Youwei, Liang Qichao, Tan Sitong, Gu Hongming, Rong Hong, Zhang Jian, Sheng Xuanhuai, and Zhan Tianyou, either speeded up the translation of classics and masterworks of Western philosophy, economics, politics, law, literature, and natural science or went to Europe or America for field investigation and study, as a way of to carry out China's national salvation. They held many views, such as the need to better communicate between East and West and "achieve mastery through a comprehensive study of the subject," believing that all blend into a harmonious whole and the requirement of learning from the advanced technologies of the West in order to resist the invasion of the Western powers. Among these lines of thinking, the most dominant were "traditional culture is fundamental, yet new techniques can be applied" and "Chinese learning as substance, Western learning for application," raised by Zhang Zhidong and Liang Qichao. The original intention of this viewpoint was to, under the condition of inheriting Chinese historical culture and political orthodoxy, learn from Western ideology and culture and the strong points of Western politics, economy, military, and science and technology in order to seek strategies for national salvation and seek a way for China to get rid of its crisis and become strong and prosperous.

However, the practices of learning and imitating from the West, including the Hundred Days' Reform by Kang Youwei and Liang Qichao, the Westernization movement by Li Hongzhang and Zhang Zhidong, and the so-called "constitutional reform" by the royal family of the Qing Dynasty, ended as a failure. Afterward, Sun Yat-sen, after learning from the West, led the Revolution of 1911, which didn't completely succeed either. Though it overturned the feudal monarchy that had lasted for more than two thousand years and made great contributions to China's national salvation and revolutionary causes, it failed to change the semi-colonial and semi-feudal position of the country in the end. In general, to raise the policy of "Chinese learning as substance, Western learning for application" was not wrong in principle. Any country or civilization should maintain its culture on its basis when learning from other civilizations. The problem is whether "fundamental" is correct or appropriate. When it entered the 19th century, China was still under a feudalist system established on the basis of small-production agriculture, while the European countries at that time had already established a capitalist system in a production mode that was large in scale. The primary reason why China lagged behind and was vulnerable to attacks was that its production mode, social system, and economic and cultural foundation all fell behind. Under such circumstances, it was surely useless and impractical to maintain feudalism as fundamental and merely apply the techniques of the West and graft Western learning. We should also note that the capitalism bred by Chinese society itself remained weak and impossible to develop. It was also impossible to walk the capitalist path of the West. This is why the strategy of "Chinese learning as substance, Western learning for application" raised by some Chinese officials and scholars at that time went bankrupt and why all the reformist measures learned from the West failed.

In the early 20th century, the exchange of ideology and culture between China and Europe, dominated by "introducing Western learning to the East," entered an important turning point. Two great events occurred in the world: the first was the outbreak of the First World War caused by Western powers fighting for their colonies. At the Paris Peace Conference after the war, as a victorious nation in the First World War, China was bellied again, and the conference decided to transfer all the rights and interests of vanquished Germany in Shandong to Japan, which further aggravated the national crisis of the Chinese people; the second was the outbreak of October Revolution in Russia, which showed the entire world that the socialism system could become a reality. Under such an international political background, the famous "May Fourth Movement" occurred in China, marking a new climax in the exchange between China and Europe.

The May Fourth Movement was a political movement in which Chinese people opposed the invasion of powers outwards, the control of feudalism inwards, and the liberation movement of ideology and culture. At that time, many patriotic intellectuals came to the political arena of China and played leading roles in this liberation movement of ideology and culture. They took hold of the scientific spirit and democratic thought of the West as a weapon. They criticized and rethought China's old political system as well as traditional culture, including Confucianism. The purpose was to discover the new world while criticizing the old one and seek a new way toward national salvation. The criticism and rethinking by the New Culture Movement opened a new field of vision for the Chinese people and broke the old and outdated spiritual shackles that constrained and imprisoned people's thoughts. It was instrumental in developing the ideology, politics, and mass conditions as the foundation of the CPC and the beginning of a fresh face in the country's democratic revolution. Of course, while looking back to this ideological and cultural movement and fully affirming its significance and contributions, we should understand that there were some erroneous tendencies. The first was that some intellectuals advocated the total repudiation of Chinese traditional culture dominated by Confucianism, completely ignored the essence of thought of traditional culture and blindly praised all Western thoughts, and even demanded the "total Westernization" of China; the second was that some intellectuals advocated the need to abide by everything in Chinese traditional culture and totally reject all advanced things learned from the West. Such erroneous advocacy had an adverse effect on ideology and culture and left profound historical lessons. After all, such erroneous tendencies were the tributary streams of the New Culture Movement at that time, and the historical contribution the movement made to China to move toward a new and bright road was undoubtedly the mainstream.

It was just those advanced intellectuals represented by Chen Duxiu, Li Dazhao, and Mao Zedong, who were devoted to the New Culture Movement, that came to the conclusion that Marxism-Leninism was the only correct thought suitable for the salvation and revitalization of the Chinese people and the truth which could truly save the nation and the people after research on various ideological trends, including science, democracy, freedom, equality, and caritas, especially after the comparative study between Marxism-Leninism brought by the October Revolution and Western capitalism. Therefore, the CPC that was founded afterward confirmed Marxism-Leninism as its guideline to action. It was under the guidance of Marxism-Leninism that the CPC led the Chinese people to overturn imperialism, feudalism, and bureaucrat capitalism, become victorious in the new democratic revolution, and found a new China based on socialism. And now, under the leadership of the CPC, the Chinese people are fighting and marching on the route where they implemented socialism reform and opening-up, studied the advanced achievements of other countries, including Western capitalist countries, and strenuously constructed socialism with Chinese characteristics to bring about a great rejuvenation of the Chinese nation. It can be said that the future development of China and the civilization of Chinese socialism are bright.

Throughout the development history of Chinese society and Chinese civilization, I think that two basic historical truths can be obtained: the first is that China didn't go through the stage of capitalism development like Western countries and successfully became a socialist society after a short transition to a neo-democratic society from a long-term feudal society, which could be said to be a new pioneering undertaking in the long river in the development of world civilization; the second is that Marxism, as the opposite of capitalism, after being generated from social practice in Western capitalism and transmitted to China, took root and developed in China and guided the Chinese people to create a new socialist civilization. Such socialist civilization also develops and strengthens itself in coexistence with capitalist civilization. Though socialism is executed only in some countries today and is generally in continuous exploration, it has shown its vitality. As a new form of civilization, socialism fully absorbs the achievements, wisdom, and experience accumulated by all earlier civilizations, gets rid of and overcomes their shortcomings, and constantly encounters new practical experiences. It will make greater contributions to human civilization and open up a more glorious future for the progress of human civilization. It can't be forgotten that Marxism was generated in the West and transmitted from the West to the East and all over the world, which was also a great contribution made by Western civilization.

III. Positions and Significance of the World's Various Civilizations and Their Mutual Relations

Through the review and analysis of the exchange between Asian and European civilizations and between Chinese and European civilizations over more than 2,000 years, especially the rough history of ideological and cultural exchange, I think some important points can be obtained to help us understand the historical position and significance of world's various civilizations and their mutual relations.

The first is that all civilizations existing in the long river of human civilization have equal positions, and their significance and contributions should all be acknowledged and respected. There is certainly the basis for the generation and existence of any civilization in the world, as well as its own characteristics and advantages. They are all important members of the big family of world civilizations and should enjoy an equal status with other civilizations. The significance and contribution of any civilization are indispensable in the progress of human civilization since the day it began. Any civilization, regardless of when and where it is generated and exists and which type and form it belongs to, is a component as well as a distinctive and colorful source and branch of the development of human civilization; their occurrence and existence only differ in time, region and the social formation and stage of social development they belong to, and no one is superior to the other. Their significance and contribution only differ in form, not value.

Therefore, we should insist on the following principles in the engagement of civilizations: firstly, be interdependent and harmonious in diversity rather than seek separation and repulsion; secondly, treat equally without discrimination rather than play favorites; thirdly, mutually communicate and learn from each other rather than restrain and infringe. Only in this way can different civilizations truly coexist harmoniously, get along in pace, learn from each other's strong points to offset one's weaknesses, and realize mutual improvement. Only in this way can various civilizations all flourish in the garden of world civilization. This is the common expectation of the world's people, and we should work hard toward it.

The second is that no civilization can exist and develop alone. It should learn, absorb, and refer to the strong points, wisdom, and experience of other civilizations to maintain and strengthen its own vigor and vitality. Is there any civilization in the world that could exist alone, develop alone over time, and maintain a necessary vitality and advantage? No. There was none, there is none, and there will be none. The existence and development of Chinese and European civilizations, Asian and European civilizations, and Eastern and Western civilizations all have proved and will continue to prove this without exception. As mentioned above, after one thousand years in the Dark Middle Ages, Europe finally got rid of its decline and backwardness through the Renaissance, the Protestant Reformation, the Bourgeois Revolution, and the Industrial Revolution, and it embraced capitalism. It saw the revitalization of European civilization, the work of ordinary Europeans, who kept learning and referring to the strong points, wisdom, and experience of Eastern civilization and other civilizations in the world. We can review how Europe learned and referred to Arabic-Islamic civilization and Chinese civilization dominated by Confucianism to promote the improvement and revitalization of European civilization.

During 100 years from AD 830 to AD 930, and also during the Abbasid Dynasty of the Arab Empire, under the advocacy and support of several generations of the Caliph, in the "House of Wisdom" established in Baghdad, a large number of famous Arabic translators and scholars and some Jewish scholars were concentrated there. They translated the historical and cultural classics of ancient Greece and Rome. During translation and research, they also absorbed the achievements of Persia, India, and China in philosophy, mathematics, medicine, theology, literature, politics, and elsewhere. The historical and cultural classics of ancient Greece and Rome they translated included the philosophical works of Aristotle and Plato, the mathematics and works of literature of Euclid, Archimedes, and Ptolemy, the medicine of Hippocrates and Galen, and the literature and music of Pythagoras. Among the translations of the classics were *Metaphysics*, *Ethics*, *Politics*, *The Republic*, *Statesman*, *Laws*, *On State*, *Physics*, *Elements*, *On the Infinite and Finite*, *On Division*, *On the Sphere and Cylinder*, *Almagest*, *On Anatomy*, *Pharmacology*, *The Canon of Medicine*, *Golden Sayings*, and so on. Translators and scholars participating in this translation and research activity included Ibn al-Muqaffa, Abu Yehia, Yahya ibn Masawaih, Hunayn ibn Ishaq, Sabit ibn Qurra, Al-Battani, Al-Khwarizmi, Ibn Matar, Yehia Ibn Addi, and Al-Kindi. This is known as the famous "Hundred-Year Translation Movement." One thousand years later, more and more European scholars translated these translated documents and related research writings from Arabic into Latin. They transmitted them throughout Europe, which promoted the rise of the Renaissance there.

The ideological and cultural achievements obtained by the "Hundred-Year Translation Movement" and the significant influence and historical contributions of Arabic-Islamic civilization to the progress of European civilization are universally recognized by many Western scholars and statesmen. For example, American historian Philip Khuri Hitti pointed out that "the rediscovery, reversion, and supplementation of ancient science and philosophy and its function of linking the past and future should be owed to the Arabic scholars. It was their efforts that made the Renaissance in Western Europe possible." British scholars Thomas Arnold and Alfred Guillaume said in their book *Legacy of Islam* that "looking back to the history, we can say this way that the science of Islam reflects the light of ancient Greece. When the day passes, the brilliance of Islam is like the moon shining on the dark Europe of the Middle Ages. And it is the Islamic civilization that declared and guided the great Renaissance, and we have reasons to say that such civilization is still with us." Hegel said that "the philosophy of Aristotle acquired by the Arabians was transmitted to countries in West Europe and became the source of philosophy. British scholar Robert Briffault said that "what is certain is that there would be no European civilization without Arabians; and without them, Europe would not have played the role surpassing all advanced stages," and "without the influence of Arabic civilization, there wouldn't have been the real Renaissance." British historian Herbert George Wells believed that "the West got rid of the Dark Middle Ages and entered into the civilized age thanks to Islamic culture, and without Islamic culture, European society would have fallen behind for at least 200 years." Former American president Richard Nixon also pointed out in the book *Seize the Moment* that "while Europe was still in the obscuration status of the Middle Ages, Islamic civilization was experiencing its golden age" and "when the giants in the Renaissance period were exploiting people's knowledge boundary forward, the reason why they could see further was because they were standing on the shoulders of Muslim giants."

The influence and significance of Chinese civilization on the progress of European civilization and the contribution to the occurrence of the Enlightenment and Bourgeois Revolution in ideology and culture after the 14th century were analyzed when I mentioned the exchange between Chinese and European civilizations during the late Ming and early Qing dynasties. What I want to discuss now is the significance of scientific and technological achievements in ancient China on Europe's Industrial Revolution and industrialization. As is known to everyone, the four great inventions of papermaking technology, printing, gunpowder, and compass, were among the top scientific and tech-nological achievements in agriculture during ancient China. They were gradually transmitted to European countries via West Asia and had far-reaching influence on the progress of modern economics and politics of Europe, especially the foundation laying and development of industrial civilization. Marx used to call the spreading and application of China's four great inventions the "omen" of "the coming of bourgeois society" in the article "Application of Machine, Natural Force and Science." He thought that, to Europe, the four great inventions "became the means for scientific revitalization and became the strongest lever that created necessary conditions for spiritual development."

Here, I would like to mention a book, *Eastern Origins of Western Civilization*, written by the famous British scholar John Hobson several years ago. In 2009, Chinese scholars translated this book into Chinese and published it in China. I had the honor to read this book, from which I benefited a lot and felt grateful. Mr. Hobson mentioned the contributions of Chinese civilization to European civilization. In the aspect of material civilization, he also stated the significance of the technological achievements of the Song Dynasty on the emergence and devel-opment of industrial Europe. The Industrial Revolution and industrialization of Europe first began in England. Mr. Hobson used some expressions such as "the Chinese origins of the Industrial Revolution in Great Britain," "the Chinese origins of British industrialization," and "China: prototype of British industrialization" in the book to argue the tie between the British Industrial Revolution and the scientific and technological achievements of ancient China. He also quoted Marshall Hodgson's words that European countries were "the unconscious suc-cessors of the industrial revolution in the Song Dynasty of China." On the basis of historical data, Mr. Hobson specifically analyzed the origin between the technological underpinnings of the British Industrial Revolution, such as the steam engine, coke iron-making technology, coal technology, blast furnace, steel-making techniques, and textile machinery, and the industrial achievements of the Song Dynasty of China. He said the British people believed they made these contributions by themselves, but rather, there was an "exogenous" transforma-tion that facilitated Britain's achievements. Britain consciously acquired and absorbed Chinese technologies—both genuine technologies and specific technical knowledge. In this sense, like other "backward countries" or emerging industrialized countries, Britain enjoyed "the advantages of being backward" and was able to absorb and improve "the advanced technologies developed by 'advanced countries.'" British people "had strong imitation ability and were good at imitating, absorbing and improving foreign thoughts." He said, "My central argument is that the British people are not born to be smart inventors, and their ability is more embodied in absorbing and improving inventions and technical ideas of early China." Mr. Hobson also said that we "can't say that the British Industrial Revolution was based only on China, but we can say that the British industrialization was obviously established based on the process of 'exogenous' transformation, and such change could be traced back to many creative inventions in China which were 700 to 2,300 years earlier than the West," and "Without the earlier inventions of China, there wouldn't have been the improvements by the British people. And without the contributions of China, Britain might still be a backward country and dissociate at the continental margins of Europe, which was also backward."

Hobson's viewpoints are based on historical facts. His arguments also prove again that advancement and backwardness exist by comparison. They transform by a unity of opposites and by learning from the advanced. By making use of their own "late-starting advantages," the backward can become advanced, surpass the advanced, and become the leaders themselves. And didn't such historical experience of the development of human civilization prove again that the mutual exchange and reference between different civilizations could produce significant historical influence and powerful material strength?

The third is that the development of different civilizations is unbalanced, and all their development courses are advancing wave upon wave. The history and experience of human civilization have found that different civilizations in the world differ in formation time, development speed, and contributions to world civilization, as well as in the degree and quantity of contributions. That is to say, different civilizations are not generated in the same way, advance side by side, or equate with each other. And it is just because of this that there is a need for mutual exchange and reference and to learn from each other. The so-called advancement wave upon wave means that the development course of any civilization, due to the application of objective conditions, the mistakes in seizing opportunities, and the restriction of various limitations, is not and cannot be plain sailing in a straight line. They may differ in the advancement speed and level of development, which may look like a wave with both crests and troughs in the end.

The unbalanced development and wave-upon-wave advancement of various civilizations is the objective law of the development of things. The historical experience of the development of Eastern civilization, Western civilization, and any other civilization in the world keeps enlightening or warning us. Though one civilization may be in the leading position for some time and has made great contributions to other civilizations and the world civilization, it can't become narcissistic and refuse to make any progress or learn from other civilizations, nor could it think it is supreme and look down upon or reject or strike other civilizations. Such cognition and behavior are to bring about its own destruction.

Such cases did exist in Chinese history. The development of the Chinese economy and culture has been in the front ranks of the world for quite a long time. However, since the middle of the 15th century, after Zheng He's travels West, the political rulers of the Ming Dynasty thought that their national strength and prestige far surpassed all the other countries and gradually adopted a policy of seclusion and refused to absorb the wisdom and strong points of the civilizations of other countries. Thus, the development of China and Chinese civilization began its downhill trend. Although Emperor Kangxi of the early Qing Dynasty was interested in Western culture and had learned some Western knowledge, he and the political rulers of the Qing Dynasty indulged in the arrogant cognition of the "celestial empire." They didn't encourage officials and others to absorb the strong points of European civilization. And the Western knowledge he and some officials had learned was limited to a surface and not an institutional level. In the late Qing Dynasty, the invasion of foreign powers was like crushing dry weeds and smashing rotten wood, and the dangerous situation of the nation was hard to retrieve. This lesson spoke volumes about how any country, region, or civilization that may be dominant must be modest and prudent and keep learning from other countries and civilizations in order to survive and develop.

The famous Western scholar Oswald Spengler thought that "no civilization could play a leading role for long" in the world. The viewpoint of "center theory" that considered itself as the "center" of the world forever is actually unreliable and is just a kind of "phantom generated in the mind." I agree with Mr. Hobson's viewpoint on "Europe-centralism" in his book *Eastern Origins of Western Civilization*. He argued that there used to be such a traditional viewpoint that "the European people expanded outwards and conquered the East and the Middle East, and designed the path of capitalism, and as long as you walked along this path, the whole world will be able to get rid of poverty and misery and enter into modernization." "Such a traditional viewpoint could be called Europe-centralism" and "that is to say, no matter in the past or at present, the West should completely stand at the center of the stage of world history development. But is it really so?" Mr. Hobson thought that "such 'Europe-centralism' was wrong in all aspects."

Historical facts and experience also constantly tell us that there are both high tides and low tides and both crests and troughs in the development course of any civilization, which is a necessary and objective historical phenomenon. It is not horrible that a civilization entered into the low tide and troughs for whatever reasons. It can return to the high tide and crest by drawing lessons from the past and learning from advanced civilizations to overcome its own weaknesses. This is well proven by European civilization, which moved from the disorderly Middle Ages to become a modern capitalist civilization and made great historical contributions to the development of human civilization. It is also well proven by Chinese civilization, which got rid of the position of backwardness and humiliation more than 100 years after the First Opium War and entered a new society of constructing a socialist civilization and is making new historical contributions to the progress of human civilization.

IV. On the Essential Characteristics of Confucian Culture, Its Ideological Value, and Development Prospects

This academic conference, with the theme of "Dialogue between Confucian Culture and European Culture—Decline or Prosperity of Confucianism in an

Age of Globalization," will examine how to understand the characteristics of Confucianism, its value and prospects. I think we all think about these issues, and scholars, politicians, and people of other countries in the world will also notice and consider these issues.

My general view is that the ideological value of Confucianism can not only be used to realize the common development of various countries and regions, maintain world peace, establish a new world order with win-win cooperation as the core, and promote and improve global governance services, but also certainly can play a role of significant influence. This is due to the essential characteristics of Confucianism. After coming into being in China, Confucianism not only existed and developed in China, but also spread to the rest of Asia and the world, and continues to this day. The reason for its enduring vitality is determined by its essential characteristics.

Well, what kind of essential characteristics does Confucianism have? I think it has four: firstly, openness and inclusiveness; secondly, seeking truth from facts; thirdly, pragmatism; and fourthly, advancing with the times.

Because Confucianism has the characteristic of openness and inclusiveness, it can absorb anything from other doctrines, like a sea that refuses no river; it can learn from the strong points of others to make up for its deficiencies while coexisting with other doctrines, and can also constantly enrich and develop itself. When Confucian thoughts represented by Confucius were formed, other schools of thought, such as Taoism, represented by Lao Zi, and Mohism, represented by Mo Zi, also existed. It was just because of modestly learning from the theory of Taoism, Mohism, and other schools and seriously absorbing their ideas that Confucianism became the supreme "famous school" among the Hundred Schools of Thought during the Spring and Autumn and Warring States periods. After it spread to other parts of East Asia, it integrated with local ideology and culture and promoted the formation of the East Asian cultural circle. All of these reflect Confucianism's openness and inclusiveness, which also gives it endless development vigor.

As Confucianism seeks truth from facts, it requires people to "be practical and realistic, and correct the mistake as soon as you know the answer" instead of "clinging to the mistake and covering up your errors." The concept of seeking truth from facts comes from a historical book in China, the *Book of Han · Biography of Hejian Prince Liu De*. Liu De was a person of Confucianism. The *Book of Han* says that he "is true to facts and seeking truth from facts." The spirit of seeking truth from facts in the development of Chinese Confucian culture remains consistent and was pursued by Chinese Confucian scholars of the past dynasties. Here is an example. *On Balance*, Wang Chong, a famous Confucian thinker in the Eastern Han Dynasty, wrote two articles titled "Ask Confucius" and "Refute Mencius." Wang Chong thought that negligence and error in the thoughts of even a sage and founder of Confucianism, such as Confucius and Mencius, should also be queried, the "wrong" should be corrected, and the "fact" should be sought out. He said: "Even if careful and strict sages still cannot fully get facts in writing, let alone hurriedly written articles, how could they completely correct without error?" Through the ages, there are many scholars in the Chinese Confucianism circle, like Wang Chong, who dare to point out and correct the mistakes of Confucian predecessors. This alone justifies that seeking truth from fact is an important characteristic of Confucian culture.

As Confucianism is pragmatic, it requires people to "unite the knowing and doing and practice personally." Pragmatism insists on the application of the moral requirements and the ideas of Confucianism in the personal accomplishment and governance of the state and society, namely, Confucianism advocated by Confucianism masters who insist on "self-cultivation, regulating the family, managing state affairs, and making all peaceful" and "hard work to rejuvenate the nation." During the period of the Western Han Dynasty in China, a famous Confucian thinker, Dong Zhongshu, proposed the policy of "paying supreme tribute to Confucianism while banning all other schools of thought," which was adopted by Emperor Wu of Han. The purpose and essence of implementing this policy was not to exclude nor even abolish other ideas and theories of other schools, but to establish a positive, enterprising, and practical Confucianism as the dominant idea for governing the state and, at the same time, exert strength and advantages over other theories to jointly safeguard national unity, achieve peace, and promote economic and social progress. As the backbone of the

Chinese traditional culture, Confucianism gives full play to its practical functions in governing the state and handling affairs successfully, contributing to the advancement of Chinese civilization and continuously enriching its own ideological value through social practice. This is a magic weapon for Confucianism to maintain vitality.

Because Confucianism has the ability to advance with the times, it can "change at the right time and get rid of the stale and bring forth the fresh." The common pursuit of Confucian scholars and workers of the past dynasties in learning and governing the state is to get rid of obsolete words and expressions, abandon the old and seek the new, reject old conventions, and set routines. Two thousand years after the formation of Confucianism, China experienced many instances of self-renewal and evolution. Firstly, the Confucianism of pre-Qin evolved into the study of Confucian classics of the period of the Han Dynasty; later, the coexistence and blending of Confucianism, Buddhism, and Taoism in the Wei, Jin, Southern and Northern Dynasties as well as the Sui and Tang dynasties evolved into the Neo-Confucianism in the Song and Ming dynasties. After summarizing and drawing lessons, the empty Neo-Confucianism evolved into practical learning in the Qing Dynasty. After the founding of new China, through discarding the dross and selecting the essential, eliminating the false, and retaining the true, China carried forward and developed the thought essence contained in Confucianism and made it serve the development of socialism. Confucianism has become a part of the socialist spiritual civilization. Confucian scholars and workers, as well as all the far-sighted thinkers and politicians of past Chinese dynasties, constantly promoted the creative transformation and innovative development of Confucianism according to current conditions, historical missions, and the need for development and change in social practice. Confucianism can be present in today's world and adapt itself to the organic nature of civilization.

In short, these essential characteristics of Confucianism are very precious. They give permanent and unfading vigor and vitality to Confucianism and lead and drive Confucianism to constantly contribute wisdom and strength to historical and social progress.

Today's world has entered into the era of globalization, and ideological, political, economic, cultural, and social ties between countries and regions are unprecedentedly close, and dialogue and exchange between various civilizations gradually grows; under the push of globalization, human civilization has made great progress, especially in material civilization, which has reached completely unimaginable prosperity compared to the ancient world. However, like all things, globalization has both advantages and disadvantages and is the unity of opposites of pros and cons coexisting. It brings about a lot of deficiencies and problems, such as the widening gap between the rich and the poor, the materialistic pursuit of luxury, the vicious inflation of individualism, poorer ethics, an increasingly tense relationship between humans and nature, and so on. To eliminate and address these drawbacks and challenges, it is not only necessary to apply the various wisdom and strengths created and developed in today's human society but also essential to harness all the wisdom and strengths accumulated and stored throughout the history of various civilizations worldwide. As for Confucian culture with its long history, there is no doubt that we should fully tap its rich thought value and combine it with globalization and modernization to achieve a new and creative Confucianism so as to improve global governance and eliminate the existing shortcomings and difficulties of today's world.

The speech made by Chinese President Mr. Xi Jinping at the 5th Congress of the ICA in September last year made important observations about Confucianism and the thought value contained in Chinese traditional culture based on Confucianism. He pointed out, "China's excellent traditional culture, including Confucianism, holds the key to solving the problems facing the contemporary society, for example, on the thought of natural rule, and theory that man is an integral part of nature, on the thought of the whole world as one community and the world of universal harmony, on the thought of constant self-improvement and great virtue, on the thought of people orientation and reassuring, enriching, and delighting people, on the thought of exercising government by morality and rightness, on the thought of destroying the old and establishing the new and advancing with the times, on the thought of being down-to-earth, and seeking truth from facts, on the thought of pragmatism, unity of knowing and doing, and practicing personally, on the thought of brainstorming and bestowing boons on the people, on the thought of the benevolent loving others and cultivating a person with morality, on the thought of treating people with sincerity and having faith and promoting good will, on the thought of being honest and upright officers, and diligently pursuing public affairs, on the thought of practicing thrift, self-control, and strictly avoiding luxury, on the thought of neutralization, coordinating *yin* and *yang*, seeking common ground while putting aside differences, harmony in diversity and harmonious coexistence, on the thought of being mindful of possible danger in times of peace, of demise in times of survival, and of riot in time of stability, and being prepared for danger in times of safety, and so on. The rich philosophical thought, humanistic spirit, cultivation of thoughts, and moral concepts in Chinese traditional culture can provide ideas to transform the world. It can provide enlightenment for governing the state and managing state affairs and provide some useful inspiration for moral construction." Likewise, distinctive ideological values contained in various kinds of cultures should also be inherited and carried forward in combination with the conditions of today in order to eliminate the disadvantages of globalization and modernization, promote world peace and the common development of various countries, and benefit present and future mankind.

Confucian culture, like the traditional culture of the rest of the world, was inevitably affected by various restrictions and influences in the process of its formation and development, such as age and social systems, and thus inevitably has obsolete content or content that has become dross. This requires people to destroy the old and establish the new instead of indiscriminately copying without any analysis while learning, researching, and applying Confucian culture. Specifically, we should take an attitude of both identifying and discarding the inheritance of Confucianism; secondly, we should clearly know that the purpose of this inheritance is to make the past serve the present and use ancient ideas for today's reference instead of esteeming the past over the present and using the past to attack the present; thirdly, we should closely combine with the new social practices of the times to constantly summarize and draw fresh experience in practice, and to make the ideological essence of Confucian culture realize new transformation, sublimation and development according to the times. All colleagues engaged in Confucian culture should pay attention to implementing these principles.

We have entered the 21st century, a century full of great change. All rational knowledge and practical experience accumulated by humans for thousands of years are still the important foundation for our creative progress in the new century. Only by constantly exploring and using all outstanding ideological and cultural achievements at our disposal, including enlightenment, wisdom, and experience, can we better understand the world, society, and ourselves in order to promote the healthy development of globalization and modernization and better create a stronger human civilization.

The task of the ICA is to tap the very best of its ability to spread to the rest of the world through the work of thinkers, politicians, scholars, and Confucianists from around the globe. The Confucianism of today must be enriched and developed by combining it with the actual conditions of today's world to advance our common.

The ICA will strengthen dialogue and exchange between Confucian organizations and between Confucian culture and other kinds of culture by holding international forums in various countries and regions to better promote Confucianism research, education, dissemination, and application. This international Confucianism forum, held in Venice, Italy, and later held in Bucharest, Romania, is considered the beginning. As an old Chinese saying goes, "All are good at first, but few prove themselves to be so at the last." However, we believe that through positive cooperation between the ICA, Confucianism scholars, and countries from around the world, our work will start well and end well.

Strengthening Research on Asian Values and Eastern Wisdom *

Presentation at the Closing Ceremony of International Confucianism Forum · Beijing International Academic Conference on Asian Civilization Exchange and Mutual Learning

July 11, 2016

The international academic conference on exchanges and mutual learning among Asian civilizations is coming to an end. In the past few days, we have expressed and exchanged opinions. Through academic exchanges and discussions regarding some major issues concerning Asian civilizations, we have achieved numerous accomplishments and achieved great success.

---

* In July 2016, the ICA convened the International Confucianism Forum · Beijing International Academic Seminar on Asian Civilization Exchange and Mutual Learning in Beijing. Dozens of experts and scholars, primarily from the Asian region, attended the conference. This speech, given at the closing ceremony on July 11, 2016, highly affirmed the historical contributions of Asian civilizations. It further explored the nine aspects of the content of Asian values and Eastern wisdom: harmony in diversity and the unity of harmony and integration; seek truth from facts and advance with the times; be industrious and frugal, independent and self-reliant; value the collective and be devoted to public duty; employ both virtue and law in governance like treating both the symptoms and root causes of a disease; live in harmony and peace with neighboring countries; be sincere and maintain mutual respect and trust; combine righteousness with benefit to achieve reciprocity and win-win; be open and inclusive and learn from each other.

I have carefully read the papers, listened to your speeches at the conference and panel discussions, and reaped great benefits. Now, I'd like to share my personal understanding regarding two issues: the historical contributions of Asian civilizations and Asian values and oriental wisdom accumulated through the communication between Asian civilizations. If there is anything improper, your comments would be much appreciated.

I. Historical Contributions of Asian Civilizations

It is known to all that the "Belt and Road Initiative (BRI)," proposed by Xi Jinping, President of the People's Republic of China, has drawn extensive attention globally and has been universally supported by governments and the people of Asia, Africa, and Europe along the "belt and road." President Xi Jinping has also proposed communication between Asian civilizations on different occasions and made an appeal to strengthen the research and application of Asian values and oriental wisdom. The purpose of such strategic proposals and appeals is to promote the construction of the "belt and road" in order to facilitate joint development and the mutual prosperity of each country along it and make positive efforts to build a fair and rational world order of multi-polarization, thus creating a win-win community of shared interests and a common destiny.

As a large continent, Asia comprises 29.4% of the global total land mass and 60% of the world's total population. Its population has now exceeded 4 billion. Throughout the ages, all parts of Asia, East Asia, Southeast Asia, West Asia, and Central Asia, have experienced different changes and periods of history leading to the development of civilization. With their own characteristics and advantages, all of them have made their own contributions to the formation and development of Asian civilizations and played their own roles in the formation and development of the civilizations of the whole world.

The earliest settlement of human beings occurred in Asia. In ancient times, there were many alluvial plains along big rivers in each of the regions of Asia, where ancient agriculture first emerged and developed and where people built their homes, their tribes, their states, and their countries on the basis of an agricultural economy. Thanks to the stable agricultural economy and agricultural life, which was advantageous for the formation and development of civilization, Asia became an important birthplace of human civilizations. It was the first to give birth to several ancient civilizations, including the Mesopotamian civilization in West Asia, the Chinese civilization in East Asia, and the Indian civilization in Southeast. These civilizations had a significant influence on the formation of Greek and Roman civilizations in ancient Europe. American historian Will Durant pointed out that "The ancient Greek civilization was admired by the whole world. However, the truth was that most of it derived from cities in the Near East," and "the Near East was the real creator of Western civilization." Greece's former Prime Minister George Papandreou also said, "Ancient Greece learned a lot from India, Persia, Egypt, and other ancient civilizations. It was like a piece of sponge and continually absorbed new knowledge and advanced experience."

Moreover, during almost 2,000 years, from around the late years before Christ to the mid-19th century, the economic aggregate of Asia, especially of China and India, had always occupied the vast majority of the world's economic aggregate and had always been the most important force in promoting the world's development in economics and science and technology. According to statistics, by 1750, China occupied 32% of the world's economic aggregate, and India occupied 24%, while Britain, France, Prussia, Russia, and Italy occupied 17% in total. In his book *When China Rules the World*, British scholar Martin Jacques wrote, "The degree of marketization, agricultural development, proportion of urbanization, living standards, and economic aggregate of Europe didn't surpass those of China until 1800." And it was also written in *The Times Complete History of the World* that during the whole of the early modern period, "the size of the economy in the East was much larger than that of the West," "the center of the world's industry was Asia, not Europe," "from 1500 to 1750, Asia produced about 80% of the world's products, in other words, 2/3 of the world's population produced 4/5 of the world's products," and "therefore, in almost three centuries after 1500, the Asian economy had the most advanced levels of productivity." The development of Asia's economy, culture, and science and technology, especially of China, India, and the Arabic-Islamic states, had long occupied world-leading positions and provided important conditions and even had a fundamental influence in ideology, culture, and economic technology on the occurrence of the Renaissance and the rise of capitalism and the Industrial Revolution of Europe. At that time, Europe was still in the darkness of the Middle Ages, while the Abbasid in the Arabic region carried out the famous "Hundred-Year Translation Movement" during the 100 years from AD 830 to AD 930. They spread the historical classics of ancient Greece and ancient Rome, which are preserved in the Arabic region. It was with further developments made on them by the Arabs that the number system of India and the ancient civilization of China to Europe lit up the path for the Renaissance in Europe. These contributions made by the Arabic region won universal praise from Western scholars and people of vision. The American historian Philip Khuri Hitti believed that "the Arabic scholars were the medium through which ancient science and philosophy were recovered, supplemented, and transmitted in such a way as to make possible the Renaissance of Western Europe." British scholars Thomas Arnold, Alfred Guillaume, and Herbert George Wells all pointed out that "the brilliance of Islam illuminated the darkness of Europe in the Middle Ages like the moon, and it was the Islamic civilization that declared and guided the Renaissance." And "without the Islamic civilization, European society would lag at least 200 years behind." America's former president Nixon also said that "while Europe was still in the obscuration status of the Middle Ages, Islamic civilization was experiencing its golden age" and "when the giants in the Renaissance period were exploiting people's knowledge boundary forward, the reason why they could see further was because they were standing on the shoulders of Muslim giants." The great contributions of Chinese civilization to the formation of modern European civilization have also been spoken approvingly of by Western scholars and people of vision. The so-called "Chinese culture fever" once occurred for about 100 years, from the late 17th to the late 18th century. French scholar Maurice Robain said, "China was everywhere in the West at the Age of Enlightenment." American scholar L. S. Stavrianos said, "In the 17th century and the beginning of the 18th century, China had much greater influence on Europe than Europe had on China. The Western people were totally fascinated after learning about Chinese history, art, philosophy, and politics." Marx used to call the spreading and application of China's four great inventions the "omen" of "the coming of bourgeois society." In his book *The Eastern Origins of Western Civilization*, British scholar John Hobson wrote that "Britain consciously obtained and absorbed technology from China—

either genuine technology or specific technical expertise." "Without China's early inventions, there wouldn't have been the improvements made by Britain. And without China's contributions, Britain would still be a backward country drifting at the continental margin of the same backward Europe." So, what do all of these indicate? They indicate that the contributions made by Asian civilizations to the emergence and development of modern European civilization were well-grounded. This is a glory that Asian people should treasure and be proud of.

After the Renaissance and Protestant Reformation, and with the success of the Bourgeois Revolution and Industrial Revolution, capitalist civilization was successively established in European countries and developed very quickly. This was the point when the industrial civilization of Europe, which was based on socialized mass production, replaced the previous agricultural civilization, which was based on small production. It was also a point when all human civilizations began to enter a new stage of leap-forward development and when European and Western civilizations began to surpass Asian and Eastern civilizations and take the leading position among the world's civilizations. Marx and Engels highly appreciated the historical contributions of the capitalist civilization to the world's development and progress, first established by Europe and the West. They pointed out that "within less than 100 years since winning the position of ruling class, the bourgeoisie created productivity that was larger than the total productivity created in previous generations." However, the nature of capitalism determined that it would pursue the appreciation of capital and the expansion of the commodity market, investment market, and origins of resources without limit. So, it would inevitably keep expanding throughout the world. For more than 300 years, from the late 16th to mid-20th century, Asia suffered colonial plunder from the Western powers. According to the statistics, of the 48 national independent countries in Asia today, over 40 of them suffered aggression by force from Western powers and became their colonies or semi-colonies within those 300 years. This was a period of humiliation and suffering experienced by Asian countries during modern times. But, they were unwilling to bear such ravage. They carried forward their patriotism of unity, perseveringly fought with the colonizers, and successively won the victory of state independence and national liberation after the Second World War. These national liberation movements, together with the Five Principles of Peaceful Coexistence proposed by Asian and African countries at the Asian-African Conference in 1955, made great historical contributions to winning a long-term peaceful international environment for the development of various countries throughout the world, especially the third world.

Now, the world has entered the development stage of economic globalization dominated by Western developed countries. This, on the one hand, has promoted the unprecedented development of the world economy and science and technology. The world economy and technology are progressing with each passing day, and both the material civilization and spiritual civilization of humans have obtained tremendous advances, especially with the degree of material abundance, far beyond the imagination of those in ancient times. And on the other hand, economic globalization has also brought various problems and drawbacks. In the world's development pattern, the great disparity between developing and developed countries hasn't been fundamentally changed yet and is even worsening. A fair and rational world political and economic order hasn't been established, the democratization of international relations hasn't been realized yet, and hegemonism, power politics, and neo-interventionism still exist. Economic crises occur from time to time in the West, many regions of the world are still in turmoil, security threats like armament competition, terrorism, and network chaos are intertwined, and many developing countries are still faced with crises of independence, sovereignty, and development. Therefore, peace, development, cooperation, and win-win have become the common voice of various countries throughout the world, especially developing countries, and have become the historical trend in modern times as well. China's BRI has drawn extensive attention and won extensive support from countries along the "Belt and Road" and other regions of the world. This fully indicates that this strategy properly reflects the universal demand of the whole world. Many people of vision have pointed out that "the implementation of China's BRI will provide a new scheme and new experience for establishing a new fair and rational world order, forming a new world economic and cultural context of joint development and mutual prosperity and creating a win-win community with a common destiny of human beings. William Jones, an American expert on international issues and the Washington Bureau Chief for the *Executive Intelligence Review*, recently said that China's BRI is of great significance and it gives hope to the world. China is now undertaking that which has never been done by any other country before—they are not developing themselves supported by the suffering of others, but helping them with infrastructure construction and promoting mutual prosperity. What China is doing now is an important basis for the new world economic order, bringing great hope to humanity.

By strengthening the dialogue between Asian civilizations and strengthening research on Asian values and oriental wisdom, we are devoted to better applying them to the construction of the "Belt and Road" and to improving global governance in order to make more contributions to joint development, mutual prosperity and the mutual improvement of various countries and regions throughout the world.

II. Strengthening Research on Asian Values and Oriental Wisdom

Having accumulated thousands of years of social practice, the people of Asian countries and regions have created and accumulated a great many ideas with precious values and wisdom on how to understand and manage the relations between man and nature, man and society, subjects and objects, knowledge and practice, production and livelihood, material and spirit, individual and collective, independence and assistance, different nations, different countries, and reality and future. The Asian countries and regions may convey these precious values and wisdom-contained ideas in different languages and with different forms of expression, yet what they convey tends to share the same, equal, or similar fundamental points. Therefore, these ideas are referred to as Asian values and oriental wisdom commonly owned by people from Asian countries and regions. The values and wisdom are endowed with distinctive Asian and oriental characteristics and colors, each presenting its strong vitality and mass appeal to the world. They are both an ideological treasure to all Asian people and a magnificent exotic flower among all of the values and wisdom in the grand garden of world civilizations, capable of reaching mutual understanding and complementing the values and wisdom of the European civilization, Western civilization, and civilizations from other regions of the world.

In this forum, many experts and scholars have conducted meaningful discussions and delivered some significant ideas on what Asian values and oriental wisdom are, and I am very much inspired. Based on these discussions, ideas, and my own personal understanding, I would like to highlight several vital points regarding the rich connotations of Asian values and oriental wisdom, so let's discuss this further.

The first point is harmony in diversity and the unity of harmony and integration. This is wisdom on how to understand and deal with the differences and similarities between all things, as well as the relations between man and nature and man and society. Its core thinking is man and nature and man and society living in harmony. In the history of China, the idea of harmony in diversity and unity of harmony and integration goes back to ancient times and has taken deep root in people's hearts. It has been demonstrated in theories such as "harmony fosters new things, and similarity does not sustain," "complementary opposites," "unity of man and nature, unity of knowing and doing," "moderation and neutralization, avoiding extremes," "negotiation and dialogues, seeking a common ground while reserving differences." Thinkers in the history of the Korean Peninsula and Japan came up with the theory of "compromise and competition" about "neither similar nor different" and the "theory of man and nature in affinity," which elaborated on the idea of "seeking a common ground while reserving differences" and the "unity of man and nature." When it comes to South Asia and Southeast Asia, we can observe that in India, the *Upanishad* came up with "rahmatmaikyam," the Vaisesika proposed that "harmony and integration is a form of relation," the poet Tagore said "the harmony between man and nature is a great fact," Sukarno proposed "Pancasila" as the philosophical foundation to integrate diversified cultures, and the ASEAN community suggested "negotiation, harmony, and cooperation" as its core values to form a "harmonious entity of different countries." The ideas of "a pluralistic whole," "the unity of harmony and integration," and "the unity of man and nature" are fully demonstrated in these examples. Meanwhile, the

Arabic philosopher Al-Ghazzali introduced the theory that "moderation is best for everything" to elaborate on the idea of avoiding extremes and choosing "the middle way" and "neutralization," and it has become the basic belief that Arabic people abide by in their life and work.

The second point is to seek truth from facts and advance with the times. This is wisdom on how to understand and deal with the relations between subjects and objects, knowing and doing, suggesting that subjects and objects and that knowing and doing must remain consistent and unified. In the history of China, the idea of seeking truth from facts and advancing with the times also goes back to ancient times and is deeply rooted in people's hearts. Chinese scholars in previous generations have advocated theories like "only with practice can you succeed, only by probing can you know the truth," "stay realistic and pragmatic and refrain from the empty talk," "walk the talk, practice what you preach," "change with the times, walk with the times," and "bring forth the new through the old, discard the old and establish the new." These are all demonstrations of the idea—seek truth from facts and advance with the times. The Korean grand master of real learning, Jeong Yak-yong, also clearly presented that "the essence is pragmatic deeds instead of dead letters." An Arabic proverb about the "sampajanna" theory means that we must seek true knowledge, sharing the same thinking with the idea of seeking truth from facts. Radhakrishnan, the Indian "Master of Eastern and Western Comparison Philosophy," suggested that "change is the nature of existence," and the Indian former prime minister Jawaharlal Nehru claimed that "all modern philosophy must answer the questions of today." Their opinions share the same thinking with the idea of advancing with the times, emphasizing that human knowledge must be in accord with the changes of the times and develop with the development of practices.

The third point is to be industrious and frugal, independent and self-reliant. This is wisdom on how to understand and deal with the relations between production and livelihood, accumulation and consumption, and independence and assistance. Chinese ancestors learned the truth a long time ago: Human existence relies on hard work. There were many analects encouraging people and officials to be industrious and thrifty in managing households and countries, to stand on our own feet, and to strive for a life without ceasing. There were sentences like "man's livelihood depends on industrious work, and hard work will always offer food and clothing," "men are born to be hard-working and it's the only way to make achievements," "success comes from thrift and hard work while failure comes from luxury," "achievement is founded on diligence and wasted upon recklessness," "stick to ethics of industry and thrift, frugality cultivates a noble character," "cut expenses and ban luxuries, and it's a nation's urgent business," "as Heaven's movement is ever vigorous, so must a gentleman ceaselessly strive along," and "difficult conditions make a stronger man, a man with unwavering high ambitions." Meanwhile, these ideas have been highly praised in other countries and regions of Asia throughout the ages. The Vietnamese former President, Mr. Hồ Chí Minh, advocated for people in their youth to be diligent, frugal, forbearing, and to uphold the spirit of self-reliance and sacrifice. The Indian Mahayana prescribed the "Vīrya" concept as its creed, teaching people to work hard for the well-being of others. The Arabic scholar Al-Ghazzali stressed that people should develop a plain diet and daily life habits, cultivate a spirit of diligence and thrift from childhood, and avoid the bad practice of loving ease and hating work. In recent history, Asian countries and Asian people have been striving for state independence and national liberation, fighting their way to build up the country after victory. The practice vividly demonstrates that industry and frugality, independence, and self-reliance are the precious spiritual characteristics shared by Asian people.

The fourth point is to value the collective and be devoted to public duty. This is wisdom on how to understand and deal with the relations between individual and family, the individual and society, and the individual and country. The individual and the collective are an interdependent dialectical unity. As a social creature, man lives his life as a part of a social group, and no one can be separated from the collective, the family, the ethnic group, or the country at any time. Ever since ancient times, ancestors from Asian countries and regions have learned the great power of the collective with farming production experiences. They learned that only by cooperation could they overcome the difficulties and challenges resulting from natural and social risks. Therefore, since remote times, they have fostered the notion of valuing the collective. Ancient Chinese books and records contain many explanations like "people's concerted efforts to make a nation stronger," "people working with one aim will move Mount Tai," "collect the public's wisdom and accept favorable suggestions," "people must come first, the world is equally shared by all," "the way of running a state is to enrich the people first," "enrich the people, and it's easy to govern; deprive the people, and it's hard to run," and "the officials should work to comfort, enrich and delight the people." The medieval Arabic thinker Ibn Khaldun pointed out that "people can only live and defend themselves by group living and cooperation." A Kazakstan proverb says, "The history of a land is the history of the people living there." The Indian book *Upanishad* exhorted people to "abandon all selfish desires, and jump out of the circle of personal interests." These ideas tell people to set up a collectivist concept of valuing the collective and being devoted to public duty. Some Asian countries still advocate "people-oriented" and "enrich people first" basic principles to run the country. The people-oriented concept represents the best of collectivism in social politics. The British scholar Martin Jacques said, "Individualism is the core of European values, while in Asia, especially in East Asia, collective identity is more important than personal identity. This value difference determines that the two of them will have totally different social patterns." In brief, the ideology of valuing the collective and putting collectivism as a core concept of values is an outstanding feature and a distinctive advantage of Asian civilizations.

The fifth point is to employ both virtue and law in governance, like treating both the symptoms and root causes of a disease. This is wisdom on how to understand and deal with the relations between the rule of virtue and the rule of law, the treatment of symptoms, and root causes in governing approaches. There is an inalienable relation between the rule of virtue and the rule of law, in which virtue is the basis of law and law is the guarantee of virtue. The rule of law is like treating the symptoms, and the rule of virtue is like treating the root causes, each supplementing the other. This is a widely acknowledged idea in Asian countries. China has been emphasizing the "rule of both virtue and law, with morality guiding and punishment supplementing" and "virtue is the essence of administration, penalty is the manifestation of administration" principles in the governance of the state and society. Today, in the construction of socialism, China sticks to the important governing principle of combining the rule of law with the rule of virtue. In ancient West Asia, the Hebrew legal ideology believed that law is actually "a tool used to execute morality and etiquette attached with a penalty." The ancient Babylonia *Code of Hammurabi* prescribed detailed legal provisions and stressed "establishing benevolent governance across the country" on the other hand. It is clear that they stand for a combination of the rule of law and the rule of virtue.

The sixth point is to live in harmony and peace with neighboring countries. This is wisdom on how to understand and handle state-to-state relations. For thousands of years, conflict and warfare of varying degrees have occurred throughout the countries and regions of Asia. Still, Asian people persist in the principle of "living in peace and harmony with neighboring countries" to deal with state-to-state relationships and always yearn for and cherish a peaceful coexistence with neighbors. In addition, this principle is the mainstream of developing relations among Asian countries. As early as ancient China, the concepts of "Xie He Wan Bang" and "He He Wan Guo" were put forward, and both concepts refer to "all nations living side by side in perfect harmony." Of course, both "Wan Bang" and "Wan Guo" referred to all vassal states within the territory of China at that time. In order to develop a good relationship and partnership with neighboring countries, all political rulers after the Qin and Han dynasties took "benevolence and good-neighborliness" as their guide, believing "a warlike nation is doomed to ruin itself, even if it is a great one" and adhering to emphasize morality and peace. Historically, the so-called "tributary system" has been long implemented by China, namely "paying tribute to a suzerain or emperor" and "returning tribute," which was a way of exchanging with other countries in politics, economy, and culture. Actually, this system presented a state-to-state relationship of "peaceful coexistence and mutual benefit" to a large extent. Historically, when Prince Shōtoku of Japan enacted the *Seventeen-Article Constitution*, he put "harmony is most precious" as the first article. What is more, scholars of the Korean Peninsula put forward the concept of "treating each other with respect and righteousness," scholars of Arab countries proposed "cooperation between cities and countries," Jawaharlal Nehru, former prime minister of India initiated "one world, one family," and the poet Alisher Navoi of Uzbekistan announced that "nothing is better than living in friendship." All of these have embodied the ideology of peaceful diplomacy. It is definitely not by chance that Asian countries first proposed and practiced the Five Principles of Peaceful Coexistence in the 1950s and took it as the criteria for dealing with the relationship between countries all over the world.

The seventh point is to be sincere and maintain mutual respect and trust. This is wisdom on how to understand and deal with the moral behavior relationship between individuals. Since ancient times in China, there have been rites and music culture that "manage a country, maintain social stability, order people's lives, and benefit future generations." In addition, township treaties and family rules were prevalent in Chinese folk society. The whole society regarded sincerity, mutual respect, and trust as basic moral principles to normalize people's behavior and strengthen people's unity and harmony. Many ancient Chinese sayings embody moral principles, such as "respecting god and the people and abiding by the ancients," "to be honest and trustworthy on the basis of mutual understanding and mutual accommodation," "share weal and woe together," "never do to others what you would not have them do to you," "promises must be kept, and actions must be resolute," etc. Besides, sincerity, mutual respect, and trust are also commonly advocated by other Asian countries and regions. The Epic *Mahabharata* chanted by Indian people for thousands of years teaches people to respect their elders, teachers, and others and to be self-disciplined and honest. The Islamic doctrines take integrity as a fundamental rule and measure the morality and belief of a Muslim's behavior by observing whether they have implemented the fundamental rule or not. Asian people also deeply understand that sincerity, as well as mutual respect and trust, should not only become a major concept of mutual interactions among individuals, but also a cardinal principle for the exchanges among nations and countries.

The eighth point is to combine righteousness with benefit to achieve reciprocity and win-win. This is wisdom on how to understand and deal with the relation between moral correctness and material interests among individuals, societies, and countries with different interests. It is not only a cardinal principle for Asian countries and regions to oppose venality, propose justice and benefit, and initiate mutual cooperation and win-win in individual networking, social communication, and national exchange, but also an important aspect with the appealing features of Asian values and oriental wisdom. The old Chinese mottoes "riches and honor attained through immoral means to me are as empty as floating clouds," and the altruism upheld by the Indian Epic *Mahabharata* are striking portrayals of Asian people combining righteousness with benefit to achieve reciprocity and win-win.

The ninth point is to be open and inclusive and to learn from each other. This is wisdom on how to understand and deal with the relationship between different cultures of different nationalities, countries, and regions. It is an objective insight that everything in this world is multifarious and wonderful. Any culture, no matter in which country or nationality it originated, is flowing and open, and this is the objective law of civilization, communication, and development. We learn and exchange with each other to offset our weaknesses, and this is the inevitable route for different cultures to achieve improvement and common progress. Cultures are varied yet equal. History has repeatedly proved that all hegemonic cultures centered on hegemonism, such as "one and only" or "everything belongs to me," ultimately fail and dig their own graves. People in different countries and regions of Asia are always advocating mutual exchange and dialogue between different nationalities, countries, and regions, which is the reason why Asian culture can continuously achieve progress. It is expounded in the Chinese classics that "the tolerance of the empty sea is great," "convince people afar with your culture and virtue and attract them," and "make friends with culture and cultivate your benevolence with your friends." Mohammed, the founder of Islam, encouraged that "we should make an effort to get the knowledge though it is far in China," and it is claimed in Islamic doctrines that "Arabians are not better than non-Arabians, and vice versa." All of these concepts encourage light of openness, inclusiveness, and mutual learning. The famous Hundred-Year Translation Movement of the medieval Arabs epitomizes the outstanding success of learning from each other, including civilizations among different nations and regions.

Finally, besides the nine points listed above, I would like to declare and strengthen some personal opinions further. First, due to limited information and data, some distinctive thoughts in some Asian countries and regions may not be covered, and the statements I have quoted may not be the most representative ones. Second, as the basic elements of Asian values and oriental wisdom, the nine points above exist not only in Asian culture but also in the cultures of the rest of the world, such as Europe, America, Africa, and Oceania, but are just more distinctive and featured in Asian civilizations. Third, the summary on Asian values and oriental wisdom above is only my personal understanding, is my humble attempt, and is just for discussion. I hope that with this modest spur, you can come up with more valuable ideas in the future.

Important Intellectual Wisdom Embedded in Chinese Civilization for Reference in Contemporary National and Global Governance[*]

Speech at the International Confucianism Forum · Lima International Academic Conference

December 10, 2012

Today, we are gathered here in Peru, the birthplace of the ancient Inca civilization, for the "Sino-Latin American Civilization Dialogue" International Academic Conference at the University of San Martin De Porras. The conference is a major event with regard to the exchanges and mutual learning of different civilizations.

---

[*] In December 2016, the ICA, in collaboration with the University of San Martin in Peru and the Sociedad Central De Beneficencia China in Peru, jointly organized the International Confucianism Forum · Lima International Academic Conference. This was the keynote address delivered at the opening ceremony on December 10, 2016. The speech reviewed the history of cultural exchanges between China and Latin America, particularly the increasingly prosperous exchanges and interactions since the 16th-century era of large sailboat trade. It elaborated on the contributions of Sino-Latin civilizations to human civilization and the shared historical destiny and mission of the Chinese and Latin American peoples. Furthermore, it explored the important intellectual wisdom embedded in Chinese civilization for reference in contemporary national and global governance.

Next, I would like to share my personal academic views on the subject of the conference with regard to the following aspects: the history of exchanges between Sino-Latin American civilizations, the contribution of Sino-Latin American civilizations to all of humanity and the common historical destinies and missions of these two peoples, and the important thought and wisdom of Chinese civilization which can be adopted by other countries in global governance.

I. The History of Exchanges between Sino-Latin American Civilizations

Although respectively situated on the east and west sides of the Pacific Ocean, exchanges between Sino-Latin American civilizations have a profound history dating back to ancient times, which can be divided into four stages:

The first stage pre-dates the mid-16th century. Due to the lack of definite written records on exchanges between Sino-Latin American civilizations during this time, research and speculations can only be made according to several archaeological findings and incomplete records from historical classics. The British sinologist Walter Henry Medhurst, French sinologist Digne, American archaeologist James Moriarty, Mexican scholar Paul Kirchhoff, and Chinese scholars Zhang Taiyan and Zhu Qianzhi believed that China and Latin America's population and culture shared the same roots. They put forward three statements to support this view: first, the fact that 30,000 years ago or possibly much earlier, a branch of Asian Mongoloids became the ancestors of the American Indians after their arrival in America across ice bridges along the Bering Strait; second, in ancient China, troops belonging to the Shang Dynasty (around 1600–1046 BC) were defeated by troops of the Zhou Dynasty (1046–256 BC) and then sailed eastward to America; third, in the middle and latter half of the 5th century, a Chinese monk named Hui Shen traveled to America during the Southern and Northern Dynasties (AD 420–589). All of the aforementioned are just speculations that need to be proven with new literature, cultural relics, and historical materials.

The second stage is from the mid-16th century to the early 19th century. According to specific written records, exchanges between Sino-Latin American civilizations during this period were performed mainly via the Maritime Silk Road and the Manila Galleon Trade. The material and cultural interactions during this time led to the writing of a splendid chapter in the history of exchanges between Sino-Latin American civilizations.

In 1565, the Spanish navigator Andrés de Urdaneta and his sailors discovered the channel across the Pacific Ocean from Manila in the Philippines to Acapulco in Mexico. Eight years later, in July 1573, two galleons made their maiden voyage, passing by Manila on route to Acapulco in November, loaded with Chinese goods, including 712 bolts of Chinese silk and 22,300 pieces of porcelain. Since then, the Sino-Latin American economy and trading relationship have been established and thrived via the channel. Businessmen sold Chinese silk, cotton cloth, porcelain, lacquer, gunpowder, and tea to Acapulco, sailing it across the Pacific in galleons that transferred to Manila. Then, those goods would be sold in local markets with two approaches, one down to Peru, Chile, and Argentina by sea along the Pacific coast, the other up to Mexico City, Central America, and the Caribbean region, and then along the land route by mule. Meanwhile, Latin American silver served as the currency of settlement in merchandise trade, and crops such as maize, potato, tomato, sunflower, pumpkin, peanut, and tobacco produced in Latin America were continuously transported to China via the maritime channel.

The Manila Galleon Trade lasted for around 250 years from the mid to latter period of the 16th century up until the early 19th century. During that time, dozens of galleons with hundreds and even thousands of chests of goods voyaged back and forth along the Maritime Silk Road from the southeast coastal region of China to Acapulco, with a transfer in Manila. Such trade greatly facilitated the social and economic development of the Sino-Latin American.

Sino-Latin American trade also promoted exchanges of personnel and culture. Some Chinese businessmen, craftsmen, sailors, and people in other fields came to Mexico and Peru via Manila to do business, work, or travel. It was said that from the late 16th century to the mid-17th century, more than five or six thousand Chinese people migrated to Latin America, bringing along Chinese spiritual and cultural achievements, science and technology, and material products. For example, in the 17th century, the clothes of a Chinese woman who migrated to Puebla City, Mexico, were imitated by local women. This style gained popularity and became a clothing style called the "Chinese Pueblan." Another example is that since the late 16th century, numerous Chinese craftsmen have come to Peru and spread their skills for making fireworks, which has enabled the setting off of fireworks to become a popular form of celebration at festivals.

According to statistics, from 1571 to 1821, the silver transported from Latin America to Manila amounted to 400 million pesos, of which about half went to China. According to the German scholar Andre Gunder Frank, around 3,000 tons of Latin American silver flowed to China from the Galleon Trade in the 18th century, which not only alleviated the pressure on Ming and Qing governments caused by the shortage of silver, but also promoted the economic development of China by transforming the currency from silver ingots to silver dollars and facilitating the commodities circulation and settlement. Crops from Latin America that were planted in China improved the grain production layout and the food structure of China, conducive to increasing grain output, boosting agricultural development, and enriching the food varieties of China, thus relieving the pressures associated with grain supply caused by the sharply increasing population.

The third stage is from the early 19th century to the mid-20th century. Great changes took place in Latin America, China, and the world. In Latin America, although many countries succeeded in achieving national independence against foreign colonial rule in the Latin American War of Independence, their economies remained under the control of new and old colonialists. The new labor force was in desperate need in the plantation and mining industries after the recession and the abolishment of the black slave trade. China became a semi-colonial and semi-feudal country after the First Opium War and the invasion of the Western powers in 1840. They stole China's resources and took China to be the biggest market for selling cheap labor force. The Maritime Silk Road on the Pacific descended into a road for "Coolie Trade." According to incomplete statistics, more than 300 or 400 thousand Chinese laborers were sent to Latin America in the mid-19th century. Just like black slaves, they were sold to plantations, factories, and mines and were humiliated and tormented. Finally, in 1874, the "Coolie Trade" was abolished under the joint fighting of Chinese laborers and Latin American people, allowing contracted Chinese laborers to become free. From then on, they played a positive role in promoting the economic and social development of Latin American countries by working hard with their wisdom and making joint efforts with local people in planting and processing crops, exploiting mines, digging channels and building railways, operating business and manufacture, and spreading and applying Chinese agricultural and manufacturing technologies to local areas. Such contributions are undeniable.

The development of Sino-Latin American cultural exchanges and the enhancement of Sino-Latin American friendly cooperation facilitated the establishment of diplomatic ties between the Qing government and several Latin American countries. In 1875, China established diplomatic relations with Peru, followed by Brazil, Mexico, Panama, and Cuba in the 1910s. After the Revolution of 1911, Brazil and Peru were the first to recognize the government of the Republic of China in 1913. Before 1949, 13 countries had established diplomatic ties with China. Despite the long period of the suspension of Sino-Latin American economic and trade relations due to frequent wars, fluctuations of society, declining economies, and poor livelihood, the exchange of thinking and culture between both sides obtained new fruits. With the efforts of Chinese intellectuals and Latin American progressives in translation and dissemination, China's May Fourth Movement and the Revolution of 1911 against imperialism and feudalism were known by more and more Latin American countries and people, which also exerted a profound influence on the university reforms in Argentina, Mexico, Peru, and Chile.

The fourth stage is from 1949 to the present. After the founding of the People's Republic of China in 1949, some Latin American countries couldn't establish diplomatic ties with China because of the Cold War and the containment policy imposed upon China by the United States. However, the success of China's revolution and economic and cultural development were cared about and supported by Latin America's insightful people. The works of Mao Zedong and books on China's revolution and construction were continuously spread to Latin America. China's independent foreign policy of peace was accepted by the Latin American people, which advocated fighting with power and firmly defending sovereignty and dignity. They were also impressed by China's support for their fight to safeguard sovereignty and national interests. With the efforts of wise people in Latin America, various social organizations for facilitating Sino-Latin American friendly cooperation were successively established in Chile, Mexico, Brazil, Argentina, Bolivia, Uruguay, Peru, Venezuela, Ecuador, and Colombia. Several famous politicians and public figures such as Salvador Allende, the former leader of the Socialist Party of Chile; Lázaro Cárdenas, the former President of Mexico; Che Guevara, a Cuban revolutionary; Ricardo Anaya, the President of the Left-Wing Party of Colombia; Antonio Fernandez Arce, famous Peruvian writer; Pablo Neruda, Chilean writer; and Jorge Amado, Brazilian writer also promoted Sino-Latin American non-governmental communication during their visits to China. At the same time, Chinese economic and cultural delegations were sent by the government and social organizations to Latin America and welcomed by local people. These non-governmental exchanges deepened the understanding and friendship between these two peoples.

In 1959, Cuba succeeded in its revolution. It established diplomatic ties with China, followed by Chile in 1970 and other Latin American countries later, which opened a new chapter for the exchanges of Sino-Latin American civilizations. Up to now, 21 Latin American and Caribbean countries have established diplomatic relations with China. We have conducted more and more friendly cooperation to strengthen mutual understanding and build up a fair and rational international order of politics and economics. In July 2014, President Xi Jinping of China had historical meetings with leaders of Latin American and Caribbean countries in Brasilia during his visits to Brazil, Argentina, Venezuela, and Cuba. Both sides declared that they would build up a comprehensive cooperative partnership on the grounds of equality, mutual benefit, and common development and establish the China-CELAC Forum, so as to lift the Sino-Latin American relationship to a new height. Recently, President Xi Jinping attended the 24th APEC Economic Leaders' Meeting in Lima and signed several bilateral cooperation agreements during his visits to Ecuador, Peru, and Chile. President Xi and other Latin American leaders also proposed to inject new momentum for the comprehensive cooperative partnership by forging the Sino-Latin America community of common destiny. Now, we are glad to see the sound situation where the Sino-Latin American economic and cultural exchanges have become more frequent and profound. In terms of the economy and trade, the volume of Sino-Latin American trade continues to rise. China has become the second largest trade partner of Latin America; Latin America has become the second largest destination of China's foreign investment, just after Asia. Great achievements have been obtained in bilateral cooperation with mutual benefits in energy, resources, infrastructure construction, finance, agriculture, manufacturing, and high technology. Culturally, China has signed several cooperation agreements in culture, education, and science and technology with many Latin American countries. For example, China set up Latin America's first Confucius Institute in Mexico City in February 2006, followed by others in Brazil, Peru, and Chile. In March of this year, the "China-Latin America and Caribbean 2016 Year of Culture Exchange" was launched and involved nearly 30 countries in that area. It has held dozens of cultural exchange activities and enhanced our mutual trust and friendship. We can say that a new "Chinese Economic Culture Fever" is surging in Latin America.

Reviewing the history of exchanges between Sino-Latin American civilizations, three old Chinese sayings come to mind: the first one is, "Distance cannot separate true friends who feel so close even when they are thousands of miles apart." The vast Pacific Ocean and fluctuations in the world cannot stop the development of exchanges between Sino-Latin American civilizations. The second one is "The key to sound relations between states lies in the affinity between their people, which largely stems from mutual understanding." The friendship between the two peoples has been the source of the development of the Sino-Latin American relationship. The history of exchanges between Sino-Latin American civilizations is accompanied by the history of two peoples respecting and understanding each other. The last one is "Those who do not mix with the crowd know nothing." Different cultures enrich themselves through exchanges and mutual learning. As both advantages and disadvantages exist in each civilization and culture, only continuous communication and mutual learning can give full play to each other's advantages while offsetting their weaknesses and realizing common progress, thus promoting and enriching world culture.

II. The Contribution of Sino-Latin American Civilizations to Humanity and the Common Historical Destiny and Mission of These Two Peoples

The major civilizations of the ancient world consisted of the Chinese civilization, Mayan-Aztec-Inca civilization originating from Latin America, Mesopotamian civilization, Egyptian civilization, Indian civilization, and Greco-Roman civilization, which all made a significant contribution to the origination, development, and progress of human civilization. Both China and Latin America have been renowned for their marvelous historical civilizations since ancient times.

The ancient Chinese civilization revolved around Confucianism. It had a great influence not only on East Asia, where the East Asian cultural circle formed, but also on the cultural development of Southeast Asia, South Asia, Central Asia, and West Asia. It can also be said that China held a leading position in the world for more than ten centuries in terms of ideas and thought relating to the natural world and human society, government and society, material progress benefiting from the development of agriculture, industry, trade, science and technology, and comprehensive national strength. For example, by 1750, China accounted for 32% of the global economy, while five European countries, i.e., the United Kingdom, France, Prussia, Russia, and Italy, accounted for only 17% in total. In his book *When China Rules the World*, British scholar Martin Jacques wrote that Europe didn't surpass China in terms of marketization, agricultural development, urbanization, people's life quality, and economic aggregate until 1800. The material and spiritual achievements of Chinese civilization were spread to Africa and Europe a long time ago via the Land and Maritime Silk Roads.

This was especially so during the late Ming Dynasty and the early Qing Dynasty when Columbus discovered the New Continent, and Magellan achieved an almost complete circumnavigation of the globe. With missionaries, scholars, and businessmen introducing Chinese culture to their homeland, a "Chinese culture fever" set in and lasted from the 17th century to the late 18th century in Europe, which promoted the development of Chinese culture in Europe to new heights.

It is remarkable that the Chinese civilization made huge contributions to the cultural and economic development of Europe, such as the Renaissance, the Bourgeois Revolution, and the Industrial Revolution, which was recognized by many Western scholars, thinkers, and politicians. The historical contributions that Chinese civilization has made to the development of civilizations in Asia, Europe, and other regions of the world are something that the Chinese people, as well as people around the world, can take pride in and cherish.

As for Latin America, its civilization, represented by the Mayan-Aztec-Inca civilization, served the same role as the Chinese civilization and others, boosting the economic and social development of Latin America and contributing to the civilization of all of humanity with its strength. Located in the tropics, the ancestors of Latin America took advantage of their unique geographical and natural conditions. They created a grain and agriculture-based civilization with tropical characteristics through long-term practices. They cultivated diversified crops such as maize, potato, sweet potato, tomato, pepper, tobacco, and cocoa, which enriched grain and food varieties, promoted world agriculture, and improved the structure of people's diets, thus playing a vital role in human subsistence. Apart from agriculture, Latin America also obtained outstanding achievements in mathematics, astronomy, and philology. Latin American Indians were the first group to discover and apply the concept of "0" (zero) and use a shell to represent it, dating back to the Christian era. They also created distinctive, concise, and efficient counting and operation methods centuries earlier than the rest of the world. They created a calendar that is more accurate than that of Europe. What's more, considerable accomplishments were made in architecture, sculpture, and metal smelting, as well as in the organization and management of society. Such contributions to the world civilization should be things to be proud of and cherished.

Further major transformations of human civilization took place from the 14th and 15th centuries onwards. Capitalist civilization set in and rapidly developed in European countries after the Renaissance, Protestant Reformation, the Bourgeois Revolution, and the Industrial Revolution, marking the turning of Europe from an agrarian civilization relying on small-scale production to an industrial civilization based on socialized mass production. Since then, this advanced capitalist civilization has taken the place of what was a backward feudal civilization; the European and Western civilizations surpassed those of Asia and the Orient and took the world lead, which allowed human civilization to enter a stage of leap development. Marx and Engels highly regarded the role of capitalism in world progress, "The bourgeoisie, during its rule of scarce one hundred years, has created more massive and more colossal productive forces than have all preceding generations together." However, decided by its nature, the unlimited pursuit of more capital, a larger market for commodities and capital, and larger resource origins are sure to result in global expansion. Since the 16th century, Europe and other Western powers have carried out massive armed aggression and colonial plunder for centuries in Asia, Africa, and Latin America. Against such a global political backdrop, all countries were colonized and invaded by Western powers, including China and Latin American countries, which unprecedentedly upheld the same political views and joined hands under a similar historical experience and destiny. From the perspective of China and Latin American countries, their common destiny was reflected in the following aspects.

First, both China and Latin American countries became colonies, semi-colonies, or dependencies of Western powers. They lost state sovereignty and national independence when they were invaded with humiliation and oppression, which awakened them to ponder the reasons for their miseries.

Second, many patriots and heroes in China and Latin America led their people to unite as one and fight back against Western powers, which mirrored the determination and confidence of the Chinese and Latin American people to defend state sovereignty and realize national independence.

Third, during the fight against the foreign invasion, the Chinese and Latin American people were not alone. They cared for and supported each other and received help from other countries, jointly composing a great epic of anti-colonialism. In the second half of the 19th century, many Chinese people were committed to the upsurge in fighting against invaders and for national independence, with Latin American people, for example, the armed uprising of over a thousand Chinese laborers in Cuba from 1868 to 1878, and the Chinese people's support in the Second War of Liberation of Cuba led by their national hero José Martí. These demonstrated that Chinese people there viewed the independence and liberation of Latin America as their own mission and were willing to fight for it with their own lives. On the square of Havana, the capital of Cuba, there is a cylindrical monument with the inscription of José Martí's comrade-in-arms Gonzalo General, "No hubo un chino cubano desertor. No hubo un chino cubano traidor." (There were no Cuban Chinese deserters. There were no Cuban Chinese traitors.) Likewise, Latin American people also provided strong support to Chinese people in our long-time struggle to repel invasions and achieve national independence. The founder of the Peruvian Aprista Party, Víctor Raúl Haya de la Torre, once supported and praised China's Democratic Revolution led by Sun Yat-sen, saying, "The revolution weakened the foreign cultural invasion while strengthening the Chinese culture, and learned the necessary knowledge to withstand imperialism." Young Costa Rican students expressed support and expectation for China's May Fourth Movement in 1919 as well. From these, we can see that although separated by the vast Pacific Ocean, China and Latin America stood on the same side in wars against colonial invasions. Time and space cannot disrupt our mutual support in just wars.

Fourth, the Chinese and Latin American people finally realized state independence and national liberation and repelled colonialists through an arduous struggle, from which two people learned the following historical truth. First, justice is bound to win. Second, we should cherish and maintain the hard-won success of justice, which was the result of tremendous national sacrifice. Third, the contradiction and conflict between justice and injustice will remain for a long time. Having understood these truths, after achieving independence, China and Latin America joined hands with other regions that realized independence and liberation, such as the whole of Asia and Africa, to fight neocolonialism, hegemony, and power politics and make efforts to maintain the results of national liberation movements and global peace and justice by advocating new norms of dealing with international relations such as the Five Principles of Peaceful Coexistence. That's part of the contribution to the relatively peaceful international environment after the Second World War. In brief, maintaining world peace and justice is the common political mission of all developing countries, including China and Latin America, for now and in the future.

Fifth, we have deeply understood the truth that lagging behind leaves one vulnerable to attacks from our previous struggle. The productivity of a country could be seriously impeded by backward modes of production, the economy, and political-administrative systems, which lead to low productivity and poverty. Therefore, we should carry out economic and political reforms that are appropriate for our national conditions and development requirements to realize the progress of productivity and the modernization of our countries and society, which is the historical mission for people in China, Latin America, and all developing countries after getting state independence and national liberation. Nowadays, China and many Latin American countries have gained tremendous progress in economic and social development compared to the past. However, we still have a long way to go to achieve complete success. Chinese and Latin American people should set an example of mutual learning and support as well as friendly cooperation to realize the common mission of developing countries and common prosperity with equality and mutual benefits for the whole world.

III. Important Intellectual Wisdom Embedded in Chinese Civilization for Reference in Contemporary National and Global Governance

Today's world is currently at the stage of economic globalization. Dominated by Western developed countries, economic globalization has allowed unprecedented economic, scientific, and technological development worldwide. Every passing day is marked by new advancements in the economic and technological fields. Human civilization has made great progress on both material and spiritual levels, especially regarding the material abundance it now produces, which would have been completely unimaginable in the ancient world; \on the other hand, it also brings problems and disadvantages under the great influence of neoliberalism. In the development pattern of the world, a wide gap still remains between the developed countries and a vast number of developing countries;

a fair and reasonable political and economic order still hasn't been established, the democratization of international relations still hasn't been realized, and hegemonism, power politics, neo-colonialism, and neo-interventionism are rife. International economic crises keep on happening occasionally, and internal disparities persist between the rich and the poor in developed countries, which fuels increasingly acute political and social crises; many parts of the world are in turmoil. Arms races, terrorism, online lawlessness, and other security threats have grown intertwined. Regional conflicts and wars continue to take place, and many developing countries also face crises and trials as regards their independence, sovereignty, and development. Therefore, it has become a common wish of the popular masses all around the world, especially in developing countries, and a global historical trend nowadays that we should adhere to the principle of peace, development, and win-win cooperation to strengthen and improve global economic and political governance, for progress and the promotion of the development of all countries. The wide attention and support that China's BRI has received from concerned countries and other parts of the world fully reflect the general requests of the international community. Many insightful people around the world have pointed out that the implementation of this initiative proposed by China will provide new solutions and experience in establishing a fair and rational new international order, forming a new world economy and cultural context favoring common development and common prosperity, and creating a community of common destiny through win-win cooperation. William Jones, an American expert on international issues and the current Bureau Chief for the *Executive Intelligence Review*, declared that China's BRI is of great significance and gives hope to the world. China is now undertaking that which has never been done by any other country before—they are not developing themselves supported by the suffering of others, but helping them with infrastructure construction and promoting mutual prosperity. What China is doing now is an important basis for the new world economic order, bringing great hope to humanity.

In order to promote the continuous progress of human society and realize common ideals of peace, development, and win-win cooperation for people worldwide, we have to work together to strengthen and improve the management of respective countries as well as global economic and political governance, so as to build a fairer, brighter and more beautiful planet and world in which to live. To this end, we must make full use of human civilization, including the rich ideological wisdom accumulated by all kinds of historical and rational civilizations, and give full play to its role as a source of guidance and inspiration and as a reference in strengthening and improving current national and global governance. This is also the purpose of the international academic conference "Sino-Latin American Civilization Dialogue" held in Lima this time. I will now briefly introduce the thoughts and wisdom born within Chinese culture that are relevant to current national and global governance. I will discuss six main aspects.

First, harmony will only be reached by seeking common ground while preserving differences and by remaining tolerant and all-embracing. This aspect stresses the wisdom there is in recognizing and handling the similarities and differences between things. Many ancient Chinese thinkers have proved insightful in this matter. For example, before Confucius, a man called Shi Bo once said, "It takes different things in harmony to create the world; on the other hand, the world will no longer develop if everything is consistent." Confucius said, "The gentleman aims at harmony and not at uniformity. The mean man aims at uniformity and not at harmony." Mencius said, "It is the law of nature that things differ in thousands of ways." These words reflect the philosophy that everything in the world is part of a whole composed of mutually contradicting elements. They are both opposed and united and can be converted into each other under given conditions, thus producing new things. If things on all sides are exactly and absolutely the same, mutual conversion will never happen, and things will always remain the same without new things ever coming along. In other words, "harmony" and "common ground" are different. "Harmony" doesn't mean absolutely the same, but the coexistence of different things. The idea of "reaching harmony by seeking common ground while preserving differences" is the philosophy of the "unity of opposites," which is the basic law of the development of all things in the universe and the fundamental dialectics of human history and civilization. We advocate and embrace dialogue and exchange, mutual learning and development, as well as common prosperity between different civilizations, which is precisely the philosophical foundation of the idea and wisdom of "reaching harmony by seeking common ground while preserving differences."

By being tolerant and all-embracing, we believe in the notion that the sea is only immense because it accommodates countless rivers with the broadest tolerance. The civilization of a country or a region can only continue to develop and produce brilliant achievements if it stays broad-minded and apt at learning from useful features of other civilizations. All civilizations develop and are passed on in a flowing and open environment. Only by preserving an open and inclusive attitude and constantly absorbing external nutrients can a civilization enrich and develop itself while maintaining its advantages, enhancing vitality, and flourishing sustainably. This is the objective law of the development of all civilizations.

The social systems and values of different countries in the world today are not the same, and the same goes for their civilizational characteristics. However, difference means diversity, which also involves integration and unification. Only through mutual respect, equal treatment, and mutual learning can different civilizations turn the world in which we live into a better place, which is implied in the old Chinese saying, "Each nation should promote its own beautiful cultural traditions while remaining inclusive and continuing to learn from all the others." If a civilization keeps indulging in self-admiration, regards itself as supreme, and even goes so far as to despise or suppress other civilizations and engage in cultural hegemony—seeing itself as "the one and only"—this attitude will ultimately backfire and cause that civilization to wither and decline. China promotes the common prosperity of different countries and establishes a benefit-sharing community of common destiny through the implementation of the BRI, which is a vivid expression of the ideological wisdom of reaching harmony by seeking common ground while preserving differences, as well as being tolerant and all-embracing" in international socio-economic development and political governance.

Second, we should retain a spirit of independence, perseverance, and tenacity. This is about the wisdom of understanding and dealing with the subjective and objective relationships between oneself and others. Preserving a spirit of independence, perseverance, and tenacity enables a nation or a country to maintain its self-esteem, self-confidence, and self-reliance, to pursue its own theoretical guidance, social system, and development path, and, therefore, to construct a strong and affluent country. Naturally, emphasizing independence, perseverance, and tenacity does not mean rejecting others, along with external support and cooperation. It should be interpreted as meaning that while accepting foreign aid, a country or nation should remain mostly self-reliant and always develop using its own strength and position. By doing so, it can be truly self-reliant and avoid becoming the vassal of external forces. Encouraged by a spirit of independence, perseverance, and tenacity, since modern times, the Chinese nation and the Chinese people have continuously realized and maintained the unity and prosperity of ancient China while making economic and social headways and staying loyal to the great cause of saving, rejuvenating and strengthening the Chinese nation.

In a poem, the famous Chilean poet Pablo Neruda wrote, "I love even the roots of my little cold country," "There I would want to die," and "There I would want to be born." Mexico's famous poet Octavio Paz also said that a nation without history and without roots is sad, just like a child without a mother feels lonely. In these words, the two Latin American poets expressed their sincere love for their country and their self-confidence, which also implies their respect for—and agreement with—the spirit of independence, perseverance, and tenacity. This also shows that the people of China and Latin America share the same feeling and that we all know that the spirit of independence, perseverance, and tenacity is the "root" of every country and nation, the one thanks to which we exist and flourish! We should not only champion this spirit and persist in it in every country's development and governance, but also fully respect and safeguard the right of each country to think and handle affairs in economic and political governance around the world.

Third, one should not impose on others what he himself does not desire. This concerns the wisdom of understanding and dealing with the moral relationship between men, countries, and nations, which is regarded as a source of wise words and noble deeds in China. It means that you should not impose on others the things you do not want to have forced onto you, not even things you like, believe in, or pursue. In dealing with the relationships between men, countries, and nations, we should always put ourselves in other people's shoes, treat other people as we would treat ourselves, and always stay ready to help others fulfill their goals as we would fulfill our own. This wisdom was written into the French *Declaration of the Rights of Man and of the Citizen* as early as the end of the 18th century. It was praised by the French Enlightenment thinker Voltaire as "the purest moral principle," to the extent that it ought to become "everyone's motto." It has also been hailed by the international community as the "golden rule" for dealing with relations among nations, and it is engraved on the walls of the lobby of the United Nations Headquarters.

Throughout history, those who believe in the law of the jungle, class oppression, ethnic discrimination, power politics, and all manners of hegemonism have strongly rejected this moral law in thought and politics. They, on the contrary, advocate the logic of "imposing on others what one does not desire." However, there has been much evidence, at various stages in human history, proving that the hegemonic violation of the golden rule of "not doing unto others what you don't want others to do unto you" will harm others and themselves. The cases are too numerous to mention. In today's state and global governance, the spirit and the principle of "not imposing on others what one does not desire" should be widely advocated and applied to promote equality, mutual assistance, and unity among all the countries and people of the world, thereby truly forming a just and reasonable international political and economic order.

Fourth, we should "cross the river together" and coexist peacefully. This concerns the wisdom of understanding and dealing with the equal political relations between men, countries, and nations. "Crossing the river together" and coexisting peacefully means that regardless of wealth, size, or strength, men, countries, and nations should advocate equal treatment, mutual trust, and assistance and live in harmony. We should not bully those who are poor, small, or weak just because we are rich, big, or strong. In ancient Chinese texts, sayings such as "It is a nation's treasure to be benevolent to the neighbors," "Relatives and neighbors always wish the best for one another," or "Belligerence will bring the decline of any country, no matter how strong" have all expressed the pursuit of mutual assistance and peaceful coexistence.

In today's world, there are different types of countries and ethnic groups. Different countries exhibit different social systems, degrees of development, scales, and gradations of national strength; ethnic groups display differences in terms of population, economic and cultural development, religious beliefs, and customs. Therefore, it is of the utmost importance to safeguard the peace and stability of the world and to promote the common prosperity and progress of all nations by always upholding the principle that all countries, regardless of their strength and size, should treat each other as equals and coexist peacefully. Both Chinese and Latin Americans have long experienced the pain of foreign aggression and colonialism and are greatly aware that peace is precious. We should, as always, pursue a peaceful foreign policy, handle international relations on the basis of mutual assistance and peaceful coexistence, and continue to contribute our wisdom and strength to peace and development in the world. President Xi Jinping said, "We do not accept the logic of 'a strong nation is bound to seek hegemony,' and are willing to live and develop in harmony with the people around the world while achieving, safeguarding, and sharing peace."

Fifth, we should seek truth from facts and advance with the times. This is about the wisdom of understanding and dealing with the relationships between subjectivity and objectivity, as well as cognition and practice, while advocating the unity of subjectivity and objectivity as well as that of cognition and practice. By seeking truth from facts, one should integrate theory with reality, proceed from reality, and unify subjectivity, objectivity, cognition, and practice. One should also test in practice all policies, measures, and solutions governing state and society, adhere to truth that coheres with objective reality and laws, and amend erroneous ideas that are contrary to objective reality and laws. Only thus may progress, as well as economic and social development, be achieved continuously. This idea is derived from the Chinese historical work known as *Book of Han · Biography of Hejian Prince Liu De*, in which Liu De was described as "being true to facts and seeking truth from facts." The spirit of seeking truth from facts is in line with the development of Chinese civilization. Ancient sayings such as "being truth-seeking and pragmatic, and eschewing empty talk" or "to preserve consistency between words and deeds, and practice what one preaches" embody the spirit of the Chinese, intellectuals, and commoners alike, which is that of seeking truth from facts.

Likewise, advancing with the times is the essence and the fundamental embodiment of the spirit of seeking truth from facts. As objective reality and social practice keep constantly moving forward, people's understanding, as well as policies, measures, and solutions, should change and develop correspondingly, for fear of falling out of touch with actual reality and practice and losing sight of realism. In Chinese history, the idea of advancing with the times is also long-standing and deep-rooted. Many ideas prescribed in Chinese historical books, such as "change and sail with the times," "get rid of the stale and bring forth the fresh," or "if you can one day renovate yourself, do so from day to day and let there be daily renovation," embody such wisdom.

Today, the development of the world is under rapid progress, and new things emerge continuously. The rise of a new era of scientific and technological revolution, along with the industrial revolution, has brought to light many new issues of national and global governance. To solve these new issues, it is necessary and meaningful to creatively use the wisdom of seeking truth from facts, advancing with the times, and learning from it. On the contrary, if a nation remains complacent and conservative, finding new solutions and the road to a bright future is out of the question.

Sixth, we should pursue harmony between men and nature while practicing thrift and self-preservation. This concerns the wisdom of understanding and dealing with the relationship between men and nature, as well as between thrift and luxury. Pursuing harmony between men and nature while practicing thrift and self-preservation means that men and nature should maintain a coordinated and balanced state. In order to achieve this, people should live frugal and simple lives and avoid luxury so as to avoid placing an excessive strain on nature and destroying the balance of nature itself and that between men and nature. Humans are a part of nature and should obey the laws of nature to achieve harmony with it; on the other hand, it means that human beings should not be helpless when facing nature. Through subjective initiative, humans can not only understand nature, but also grasp the laws of nature in order to make use of natural resources for human society. Nevertheless, the above use should be reasonable, orderly, and frugal. Any abuse or waste of natural resources will be punished by nature itself. Sayings in Chinese traditional culture such as "Thrift is the highest virtue, and extravagance is the worst evil," "Countries and households all thrive through thrift and decay through extravagance," and other well-known proverbs have all expressed and stressed the extreme importance of cherishing and preserving natural resources, and of pursuing harmony between men and nature by forsaking extravagance in governing the country.

With the rapid development of economic globalization, human society has achieved unprecedented achievements in civilization. But at the same time, the deterioration of global resources and the ecological environment has also reached an unprecedented level. The time has come to ask ourselves. Has the relationship between mankind and nature lost all balance? Are we claiming too much from nature? What kind of consequences will humans suffer due to the serious damage we inflict on the natural world in which we live, if we never curb the pursuit of our material desires? Scientists, thinkers, and politicians who care about the fate of the earth should feel highly concerned and answer these questions seriously. There is no doubt that seriously bearing in mind and actively putting into practice the ideas of harmony between men and nature, as well as thrift and self-preservation, is essential to answer and solve these problems.

Dear friends, my colleagues from the ICA and I traveled a long way to Latin America with an open mind to learn from the Latin American civilization and from our friends here. We believe we will return with fruitful results through this learning.

As participants in this conference in Lima, Peru, we cannot help but think of the important position held by Peruvian people in the history of Sino-Latin American relations. The first Chinese immigrants reached the port of Callao in 1849. There are 3 million Chinese in Peru, accounting for almost one-tenth of the population. With the help and support of the local people of Peru, they are well integrated within Peruvian life and the local industries and have established profound friendships with Peruvian people. In the meantime, many Peruvian people have come all the way to China. They are committed to the friendly economic and trade exchanges between the two countries, thus contributing to the development of bilateral relations. In his speech in front of the Congress of Peru recently, President Xi Jinping mentioned Peruvian Sinologist and translator Mr. Guillermo Danino Ribatto, who taught Spanish at Nanjing University and the University of International Business and Economics from 1979 to 1991 and wrote several books, including *A Report from China*, *Selected Poems of Li Bai*, and *Encyclopedia of Chinese Culture*. He also played in 25 Chinese movies, including *Decisive Engagement* and *The Chongqing Talks*, which were well-received by Chinese spectators. We believe that this close friendship between our two peoples will grow even further with time.

Mutual Learning on the Ancient Silk Road and Cooperative Construction on Today's Belt and Road[*]

Speech at International Confucianism Forum · International Academic Conference in Colombo

December 1, 2017

Today, we have come to Sri Lanka, reputed as a pearl of the Indian Ocean, and get together in beautiful Colombo for an international seminar themed on historical contact along the Maritime Silk Road and mutual learning and reference among Asian, African, and European civilizations, which is of great significance.

---

[*] From December 1 to 2, 2017, the ICA and the University of Kelaniya in Sri Lanka jointly hosted the International Confucianism Forum · International Academic Conference in Colombo, the capital city of Sri Lanka. More than 40 scholars from 15 countries, including China, Sri Lanka, Singapore, Malaysia, Indonesia, Vietnam, India, Bangladesh, Iran, Egypt, Ethiopia, Morocco, Portugal, Peru, and others in East Asia, South Asia, West Asia, North Africa, South Europe, and Latin America, along the Maritime Silk Road, engaged in in-depth discussions on the theme of "Historical Interactions of the Maritime Silk Road and Mutual Learning of Asian, African, and European Civilizations." This was the keynote speech delivered at the opening ceremony on December 1, 2017. The speech summarized the historical characteristics of exchanges and mutual learning among different civilizations and countries along the ancient Silk Road over thousands of years. It highlighted the historical experiences of exchange and mutual learning among different civilizations and countries left by the ancient Silk Road. The speech introduced the international community's background, purpose, and enthusiastic response to China's proposal of the BRI. It discussed the historical connection between the exchanges along the ancient Silk Road and the 21st-century BRI.

With her long history, Sri Lanka is an important stop of the ancient Maritime Silk Road and deserves the name Oriental Crossroads. The friendly contact between the peoples of China and Sri Lanka enjoys a long history. In the 5th century AD, monk Faxian of the Eastern Jin Dynasty came here to study Buddhist sutras. In the early 15th century, navigator Zheng He of the Ming Dynasty made seven westward voyages and passed here many times. After the People's Republic of China was founded, the friendly contact between the two peoples left us with many good tales and moving stories of mutual help between them.

The main purpose of this seminar is to study and summarize the historical experience of economic, political, and cultural contact along the ancient Silk Road and mutual learning among different civilizations to serve the promotion of BRI being implemented, enhancement of exchange and mutual learning among different civilizations and building a community with a shared future for mankind.

Next, I want to make an academic speech on two aspects around the theme of this seminar, namely, exchange and mutual learning among different civilizations, countries, and regions along the ancient Silk Road and the new pattern of international cooperative construction along today's Belt and Road. I would like to consult all experts and scholars present.

I. On Exchange and Mutual Learning among Different Civilizations, Countries, and Regions along the Ancient Silk Road

The ancient Silk Road included the Land Silk Road and the Maritime Silk Road. The Land Silk Road generally consisted of northern, middle, and southern routes. The northern route started from East Asia, past Central Asia, and through the Southern Russian Prairie into Europe. The middle route started from East Asia and passed Central Asia and the Asia Minor Peninsula into Europe. The southern route started from East Asia, past West Asia and North Africa, and into Europe. The Maritime Silk Road included two routes: one started from Northeast Asia past Southeast Asia, South Asia, West Asia, and East Africa into Europe, passing the East China Sea, South China Sea, the Pacific Ocean, the Indian Ocean, the Mediterranean, and the Atlantic Ocean. The other route started from East Asia through Southeast Asia, mainly the Philippines, to reach Latin America, that is, the trans-Pacific Manila Sailboat Sea Route opened in the 16th century.

Since ancient times, the ancient Silk Road has been the main passage linking the East and West and crossing through many countries and regions of Asia, Africa, Europe, and Latin America. For thousands of years, it has made indelible historical contributions to the realization and development of exchange and mutual learning among countries and regions along it and different civilizations of the East and West, as well as for the promotion of their respective development and common progress.

1. *The historical features of the exchange and mutual learning among different civilizations, countries, and regions along the ancient Silk Road*

The exchange and mutual learning along the ancient Silk Road is like a rich and colorful historical scroll. Its historical features are also diverse. I selected the important ones and summarized them into the following seven points.

First, the ancient Silk Road is a road of exchange and mutual learning crossing through the East and West, gradually formed and developed among countries and regions along it that went from the near to the distant and combined the near and distant.

The ancient Silk Road was not opened and accomplished in one action. It experienced a long process of formation and development. It gradually developed from small-scale and non-continual economic and cultural exchanges among countries of local areas to large-scale continuous exchanges among many countries and regions along it. On the Land Silk Road, Zhang Qian's travel to the Western countries during China's Han Dynasty was the first trip that opened the east part of the ancient Silk Road from East Asia to Central and West Asia; then, the Persian Royal Road built by the Persian Empire located at the junction of Asia, Africa, and Europe made its own contribution for opening the middle part of the ancient Silk Road from Central Asia to the east bank of the Mediterranean Sea. The passage from Europe to Central Asia established by Alexander's eastward expedition laid an important foundation for the opening of the western part of the ancient Silk Road. In short, the gradual completion of the Silk Road that connected Asia, Africa, and Europe was like a flowing artery on the earth that connected the ancient Chinese, Indian, Persian, Mesopotamian, Egyptian, Greek, and Roman civilizations as an important bridge for the exchange and mutual learning of Eastern and Western civilizations.

Second, the ancient Silk Road was a road for comprehensive exchange and mutual learning among countries and regions along it, with economy and trade as its mainline and combined and promoted fields including economy, politics, culture, religion, military affairs, and diplomacy.

The exchange among countries and regions along the ancient Silk Road mostly started with the exchange in economy and trade as a mainline. It started from there to promote exchanges in culture and religion and then extended to exchanges in politics, military affairs, and diplomacy. Finally, all these elements were combined and promoted. Because of this, teams of merchants and entrepreneurs engaged in economic and trade exchange became the main force for the exchange and mutual learning along the ancient Silk Road. Scholars, monks, officials, and envoys who streamed on the ancient Silk Road also had important roles in exchange and mutual reference. They jointly put on many vivid and dramatic historical plays to promote exchange and mutual learning in material, spiritual, and political civilizations among different countries and regions. Seen from the mainline of economic and trade exchange, what was exchanged in large amounts were economic crops and material products from countries and regions along it, which played an important role and influence on the economic and social development of various countries and regions. The role and influence created by the exchange in the achievements of science and technology were particularly important and profound. For example, British scientist and philosopher Francis Bacon once said, when referring to the role and influence of the westward spread of the four great inventions of China, that China's inventions "changed the outlook and state of things of the whole world" that no country, religious sect or celebrity could "yield stronger force or influence on the undertaking of humankind."

Third, the ancient Silk Road was a road of exchange and mutual learning among countries and regions based on non-governmental forces and was guided and monitored by governments.

On the ancient Silk Road, merchants from countries and regions along it could often be seen to spontaneously organize huge caravans for transport over a long distance, enter towns and cities along the road, and operate in teams or individually or in cooperation with local merchants. Besides the foundational force of spontaneous non-governmental exchange and mutual reference, governments of countries along the road provided material conveniences, such as roads, post houses, trading venues, and ports for the smoothness of the Silk Road, or security guarantee measures such as observation posts, patrol stations, and public security kiosks, or political direction systems with rules, organizations, and agencies by dispatching emissaries and officials to coordinate exchange affairs among different countries and regions and resolve disputes and conflicts. For example, China is located at the eastern end of the Silk Road, and as early as during the reign of Emperor Wu of the Western Han Dynasty, the imperial court recruited a large number of local merchants and encouraged them to do business in the countries of the Western Regions using commodities allocated by the government. By the Sui Dynasty, to publicize and promote the Silk Road trade, international frontier trades were held irregularly. The Tang Dynasty established the Court of State Ceremonial and Office of Guest Service, and the Song Dynasty established the Maritime Trade Supervisorate to administrate affairs concerning exchange and mutual learning along the Silk Road. Europe was located at the western end of the Silk Road, and a large number of missionaries and scholars were sent to the East in the 16th and 17th centuries in order to promote exchanges and mutual learning with the East. In January 1685, French King Louis XIV personally signed a letter of appointment and allocated 9,200 pounds as an annuity to subsidize Jesuits for missionary and cultural exchange activities in China. In a word, wide non-governmental exchange and governmental guidance and supervision were the two cornerstones for mutual learning along the ancient Silk Road that lasted continuously.

Fourth, the ancient Silk Road was a road of exchange and mutual learning among countries and regions along it that was dominated by big countries and actively joined by other countries.

The ancient Silk Road was a product of active participation and joint promotion by countries and regions along it. Meanwhile, it was also a product centered around the big leaders in different periods fusing various civilizations. Countries and regions along the Silk Road all made their respective historical contribution to its formation and development. At the same time, the cradles of ancient civilizations such as China, India, Persia, Babylon, Egypt, Assyria, Greece, and Rome played leading and dominant roles in the forming and developing process. The strong economic, political, and cultural power of China's unified dynasties and its influence promoted the prosperity of the whole Silk Road. It particularly guaranteed the thoroughfare and security of the eastern and middle parts of the Silk Road. The ancient Persian Empire, Alexander Empire, Assyrian Empire, Roman Empire, and Arabian Empire successively led and dominated the exchange and mutual learning activities in the middle and western parts of the Silk Road and radiated it to Asian and African countries along the Mediterranean and all the way to West Europe. The contribution of these big countries in leading, dominating, and maintaining the development and prosperity of the ancient Silk Road shall not go unnoticed.

Fifth, the ancient Silk Road was a road of exchange of mutual learning among countries and regions along it after jointly overcoming the destruction and difficulty brought by the chaos caused by wars and realizing the mainstream of peaceful contact.

The exchange and mutual learning along the ancient Silk Road did not go smoothly and peacefully. Many land and sea conflicts and warfare took place in Asia, Europe, and Africa. For example, the Greco-Persian War, Alexander's Crusade, the Punic Wars, the war between Han and Hun, the Battle of Talas, An Lushan Rebellion, the Crusades, the westward expedition of the Mongol Empire, the Thirty Years' War in Europe, and the colonial wars the Western powers launched against Africa, Asia, and Latin America all brought various impacts and harms to the Silk Road. Although these wars sometimes objectively played certain promoting roles, expanding and developing the exchange and mutual learning along the Silk Road, their negative influence far exceeded their objective positive influence. For example, the nine eastward expeditions of the Crusades lasted over 200 years. Although they helped the West understand the East, opened the trading gate to the East, promoted the development of Western cities, and resulted in a world favoring the generation of seeds of capitalism and promotion of Europe to openness from darkness and isolation, the lives taken in the East and Europe, the colossal material loss and the harms and destruction to the exchange and mutual learning along the Silk Road during the two centuries or so were disastrous. When the Crusaders took Constantinople, an important stop along the Silk Road, killing and plunder of the city lasted a week, with all gold and silver and art treasures looted, and this once prosperous ancient city of civilization was turned into a wasteland, which was sufficient evidence of their destructiveness. However, generally speaking, the destruction of these wars could not extinguish the belief of various peoples along the Silk Road to exchange with and learn from each other. With joint efforts, the various destructions, hindrances, and difficulties brought by wars could finally be overcome. After wars and chaos, the Silk Road would present a brand-new prosperous scene with endless streams of exchanging teams flooding the road. In a comprehensive review of the developing history of the Silk Road, the pursuit and maintenance of peace were always the bottom color of the ancient Silk Road, and peaceful contact and mutual learning were the mainstream of the ancient Silk Road.

Sixth, the ancient Silk Road was a road of exchange and mutual learning among countries and regions along it, during which land and sea routes were alternately used, with each being primary and secondary during different historical stages.

During a long period, the land route and sea route of the ancient Silk Road coexisted and were used alternately. According to China's historical records, during the 900 years between AD 138, when Zhang Qian traveled to Western countries, and AD 755, when An Lushan Rebellion took place, the land and sea silk roads were used side by side, but generally on-land exchange was primary. In general, after the rebellion with the Land Silk Road being hindered during the Five Dynasties due to the increase of warfare in Central Asia, the Maritime Silk Road gradually became the leading role in the exchange and mutual learning among Asian, African, and European countries and between the East and the West. Especially after the Song Dynasty and throughout the Yuan and Ming dynasties, the exchange and mutual learning along the Maritime Silk Road reached their prime time. Zheng He's western voyages in the early Ming Dynasty were a notable mark. During the 28 years from 1405 to 1433, Zheng He led twenty thousand people and scores of large ships for the great feat of seven sea voyages from the East China Sea through the South China Sea, the Pacific, and the Indian Ocean all the way to the Mediterranean. On his way, he passed Southeast Asian countries, Sri Lanka, India, Iraq, Saudi Arabia of West Asia, and Somali, Kenya, Ethiopia, and Egypt in Northeastern Africa, over 30 countries in total. This feat not only made an important contribution to economic and cultural exchange between the East and West, it initiated a maritime navigation era as well as, as remarked by Australian scholar Anthony Reid, a new era of trade in Southeast Asia that merged into the global trade tide. During the seven voyages, over a thousand envoys from countries along the road assembled in the capital city of the Ming Dynasty, which was an unprecedented grand occasion.

Seventh, the ancient Silk Road was a great road on which the peoples of countries and regions along it jointly strove to make great historical contributions in promoting mutual learning between the Eastern and Western civilizations to develop the whole human civilization.

Things in the world differ in thousands of ways. Any civilization is mobile and open no matter the social soil of the country or nation it was born into. This is an objective law for a civilization to spread and develop. Learning from and referring to each other and making the best of both worlds are the only roads to the common progress of different civilizations. It was through exchange and mutual learning that the people along the ancient Silk Road made a great historical contribution to the development and progress of human civilization. On the great historical contribution of the ancient Silk Road in the history of human development and world civilization, Director of the Oxford Center for Byzantine Research Peter Frankopan said that the ancient Silk Road was never only a trading passage that linked the East and the West. It was a great road that ran throughout two thousand years of human civilization and world history. The Silk Road is not at the edge of the world; on the contrary, it has been the center of the world and will influence the present world.

The formation and development of the ancient Silk Road that went through Asia, Africa, Europe, and America and exchange and mutual learning between the Eastern and Western civilizations and its land or sea routes from the East to West mainly took place in the juncture of Asia, Africa, and Europe along the

Mediterranean and the eastern and southern parts of Asia. Since ancient times, the juncture of the three continents, namely, western Asia, eastern and northern Africa, and southern Europe along the Mediterranean extending to southern and eastern Asia, was the origin of the most famous ancient civilizations in the world, including Egypt, Mesopotamia, Greece, Rome, India, and China, and also the origin of world's major religions Judaism, Christianity, Islam, and Buddhism. It was also a rich region where ancient agriculture, handicraft, animal husbandry, commerce, science and technology, and modern industry appeared earliest and prospered. It is also a central region in which various conflicts, reforms, and innovations of the ancient world were assembled and developed, as well as a central region in which the economic and political order of the ancient world was formed and operated earliest. Therefore, for the ancient Silk Road to form a passage of exchange linking the East and West of the ancient world in such a region accorded with the objective reality, process, and law of the development of world history and progress of human civilization, so it was an inevitable product of history. Scholar Jean-Pierre Lehmann said in a recent article that Great Eurasia, located around the Mediterranean, was a spot where civilizations prospered, and history was made, a history of exchange and transformation. This Eurasian society exchanged commodities, science, and thoughts For thousands of years and referred to each other. Arabian thought influenced the Renaissance, Confucianism influenced the Enlightenment, and India invented "0." Today, the Eurasian region is still filled with exciting potential, and here is also a melting pot of geopolitics. This quote from Lehmann is worth contemplating.

2. *The historical tales of mutual learning among civilizations, countries, and regions spread on the ancient Silk Road*

In the long history of the ancient Silk Road, there have been many historical tales of mutual learning among different civilizations, countries, and regions, which are still eulogized today. Here, I'd like to elaborate on three colorful stories full of profound significance.

First, the famous Hundred-Year Translation Movement was carried out by the Abbasid of Arabia from the first half of the 9th century to the first half of the 10th century AD. The large volumes of historical and cultural classics of

ancient Greece, Rome, Persia, India, and China were translated into Arabic and Latin and generated a major influence in promoting the Renaissance in Europe.

The so-called Hundred-Year Translation Movement refers to the large-scale organized translation activity carried out under the advocacy and support of several caliphs of the Abbasid Dynasty of the Arabian Empire during the hundred years from the first half of the 9th century to the first half of the 10th century AD. At that time, the "House of Wisdom" established in Baghdad assembled a great number of famous Arabian translators and scholars, as well as some Jewish scholars who translated ancient Greek and Roman historical and cultural classics they had collected and preserved for a long time into Arabic. Meanwhile, in their translation and research, they absorbed the achievements of Persia, India, and China in science, philosophy, mathematics, medicine, theology, literature, and politics. The ancient Greek and Roman classics included philosophical works by Aristotle and Plato, mathematical and astronomical works by Euclid, Archimedes, and Ptolemy, medical works by Hippocrates and Galen and literary and musical works by Pythagoras, and so on. After the Hundred-Year Translation Movement, a large amount of ancient Greek and Roman historical culture was preserved and gained new development. Then, after the joint efforts of Arabian scholars and other scholars, they were translated into many European languages, especially Latin, and re-transmitted to Europe in the late period of the Dark Middle Ages to provide rich ideological and cultural nourishment for the Renaissance. Besides, they also exerted an important influence on Europe's modernization, like the Protestant Reformation and the Bourgeois Revolution. British scholar Robert Bradford said, "What we can be sure about is, without Arabians, modern European civilization would not have appeared at all," "but for the influence of Arabian civilization, real Renaissance would not have happened in the 15th century." In his book *Seize the Moment*, Former US President Nixon also said that "while Europe was still in the obscuration status of the Middle Ages, Islamic civilization was experiencing its golden age" and "when the giants in the Renaissance period were exploiting people's knowledge boundary forward, the reason why they could see further was because they were standing on the shoulders of Muslim giants."

Second, mutual learning between Chinese and European civilizations from the 16th to 18th centuries exerted an important influence on the development and progress of both sides.

From the 16th to 18th centuries, China was situated between the end of the Ming Dynasty and the beginning of the Qing Dynasty, while Europe was experiencing a social transformation period from the feudal society of the Middle Ages to the modern capitalist society. In order to meet the demand of newborn capitalism to develop the market externally and expand the place of origin of raw materials, European countries successively dispatched Jesuit missionaries to China and the East, which objectively facilitated an unprecedented exchange and mutual learning between Chinese and Western civilizations.

Matteo Ricci was an important trailblazer in this exchange and mutual learning between China and Europe. After Ricci and other Italian Jesuits, Jesuits from France, Germany, Britain, Belgium, Spain, and Portugal also came to China. They translated a large number of Chinese historical and cultural classics. They wrote substantial records about China, including classics introducing China's history, geography, and social institutions, as well as philosophy, ethics, literature and art, astronomy, medicine, and biology to spread to European society. This is what historians called the "Western spreading of Chinese knowledge." Through such spreading, a centennial heat of Chinese culture was expedited in Europe between the 17th and 18th centuries. At that time, a batch of European thinkers, such as Voltaire, Leibniz, Holbach, Quesnay, and Goethe, all gave a high appraisal of China's history and culture. They regarded Chinese Confucian thought as a gift from heaven. They thought the enlightenment work they were engaged in was not isolated because, in China, over 2,000 years before, "Confucius meditated on the same thought in the same way and carried out the same battle." So they proposed loudly to "transplant China's spirit" to Europe. German mathematician and Enlightenment thinker Leibniz said, "The greatest civilizations of humankind, that is, European countries and China on the coast of Far East at the two ends of the Eurasian continent, are now joined together." "Before, none of us believed in the existence of a nation with sounder ethics and more progressive ways to build lives than ours. Now, we are awakened by oriental China." French Enlightenment thinker Voltaire said, "China is the only country in the world that combines politics with moral principles." "The princes and merchants of Europe discovered the East to pursue wealth while philosophy found a new spirit and material world in the East." "The East has given the West many things." French physiocratic thinker Quesnay said, "China is not a desirable but unreachable object of admiration; instead, she is an imitable example."

Then, what influence did the westward spreading of Chinese history and culture generate on European Enlightenment thinkers and the progress of European history? It can be said that, as a non-Christian country, China's oriental civilization, which stressed naturalism and human rationality, played an enlightening role to the thinkers in Europe. To Enlightenment thinkers who objected to the theological rule in the Middle Ages of Europe, it was tantamount to a sharp ideological weapon. The moral principles of Confucianism and other Chinese schools and doctrines that stressed education also encouraged the Enlightenment, which pursued rationality and wisdom and opposed ignorance and fanaticism. "Rule of a wise monarch," "moral politics," and government of great unity in Chinese history were also praised and borrowed by Enlightenment scholars to boost their reform and construction of a capitalist society. During the formation of various concrete doctrines of Enlightenment, Enlightenment scholars also absorbed rich ideological nourishment from China's history and culture. For example, Leibniz's monadism and binary arithmetic were to some extent enlightened by ancient Chinese *The Book of Changes* and *liqi* cosmology of neo-Confucianism of the Song Dynasty. The ideological foundation of deism, followed by Voltaire, also absorbed the Confucian ethics of doing unto others as you would be done. Quesnay's basic physiocratic theory absorbed elements of China's traditional agriculture-first thought, and so on. In short, elements of naïve dialectics in China's ancient philosophical thinking, ethic ideology in Confucianism, *liqi* cosmology in neo-Confucianism in the Song Dynasty, and political and legal systems and economic thoughts of successive dynasties of China, as the ideological nourishment of European Enlightenment met the need of European Bourgeois Revolution and promoted the process of the Bourgeois Revolution after transformation by Enlightenment thinkers by combining them with the reality of Europe. So, when people appraise the historical contribution of the Enlightenment in Europe, they shall not forget the historical contribution of ancient Chinese civilization.

On the role and influence of China's scientific achievements, like four great inventions in Europe on Britain that first carried out the Industrial Revolution and the whole European Industrial Revolution, In his book *The Eastern Origins of Western Civilization*, British scholar John Hobson made such pertinent description, "we can't say that the British Industrial Revolution was based only on China, but we can say that British industrialization was obviously established based on the process of 'exogenous' transformation, and such change could be traced back to many creative inventions in China which were 700 to 2,300 years earlier than the West," and "Without the earlier inventions of China, there wouldn't have been the improvements by the British people. And without the contributions of China, Britain might still be a backward country and dissociate at the continental margins of Europe, which was also backward."

During the exchange and mutual learning between China and Europe for over 100 years between the 17th and 18th centuries, China also learned, absorbed, and borrowed quite some progressive thinking, development experience, and advanced technology from Europe's ideological culture, economy, and science and technology. With the assistance of Chinese scholars, Jesuit missionaries from Europe taught Western learning to Chinese officials, scholars, and religious people by translating classics of European history and culture into Chinese and compiling Chinese writings introducing European history, thinking, culture, and science and technology, passed on and applied latest knowledge and achievements of science and technology of Europe in China, promoted the process of eastward spreading of Western learning and opened the horizon of Chinese at that time, especially scholars. Compared with the centennial heat of Chinese culture in Europe, the spreading of Western learning did not lead to the heat of European culture in China, but its influence was also profound. If moving from "virtual" to "real" was a new cultural trend appearing in the European Renaissance, then, in China's late Ming Dynasty and early Qing Dynasty between the 17th and 18th centuries, there also appeared a new cultural trend that moved from "virtual" to "real," that was, to substitute practical knowledge for Neo-Confucianism that gave empty talks of mind. One of the founders of practical knowledge, Xu

Guangqi, was a Chinese scholar who had close contact with Jesuits like Matteo Ricci and was deeply influenced by Western learning. Far-sighted personages like Xu Guangqi, Li Zhizao, Yang Tingjun, Gu Yanwu, Huang Zongxi, Wang Fuzhi, Song Yingxing, and Fang Yizhi made definite declaration that the purpose of their advocating Western learning was to remedy the fault of empty talks since the Song and Ming dynasties. They sharply denounced that empty talks brought no benefits to the state and households, were irrelevant to state affairs, and could not improve people's livelihood. Some of their works, such as *Nongzheng Quanshu* (Agricultural Administration Book), *Tiangong Kaiwu* (Exploitation of the Works of Nature), and *Wuli Xiaoshi* (Small Encyclopedia of the Principle of Things), absorbed some of the Western cultural knowledge and achievements of science and technology. The advanced Chinese intellectuals they represented had "shown a kind of new trend of thought that broke national one-sidedness and insularity" in some views, while this just "happened after the exchange between Chinese and Western civilizations." In a word, the latest knowledge and achievements of science and technology brought from Europe by the eastward spreading of Western learning played an important expediting role in the gestation of China's seeds of capitalism and the generation of China's modern science, technology, and industry. The modern political thinking of Europe cast a beam of light in the garden of China's ideological culture, still ruled by feudal autocracy, and made ideological pavement for the later rise of Western thinking in China that advocated science and democracy.

Third, the eastward spreading of Marxism, generated in Western civilization, at the turn of the 20th century played an important guiding role in China's revolution and construction and national emancipation of many countries of Asia and Africa.

The greatest event in the early 20th century was the happening and victory of the Russian October Revolution. It turned the imagination of Marxism on establishing a socialist society from theory to reality. It not only opened a new era of human history and the development of human civilization, but also raised the curtain for Marxism, a scientific truth generated in the West to be spread and applied in the East and the whole world.

In China, a group of advanced intellectuals represented by Chen Duxiu, Li Dazhao, and Mao Zedong studied various trends of thought brought by Western learning, including science, democracy, liberty, equality, and fraternity, and finally chose the road of Marxism. This was not an accidental choice but a correct choice made by summarizing the experience and lessons in national salvation in China in modern times, especially after making sound comparisons between Marxism sent by the Russian October Revolution and Western capitalist thought. Because only the revolutionary thought of Marxism conformed with China's reality could completely change the semi-colonial and semi-feudal state and enable the Chinese nation to move to rejuvenation. Under the guidance of Marxism, Chinese Communists led Chinese people to overthrow the rule of imperialism, feudalism, and bureaucratic capitalism, gained the victory of the new-democratic revolution, and founded a socialist New China.

Meanwhile, the spread of Marxism and the influence of the world socialist revolution also prompted the outbreak of national emancipation movements in many countries in Asia, Africa, and Latin America, which gave heavy blows to the colonial rule of capitalism and imperialism. After long struggles, many countries in Asia, Africa, and Latin America successively got rid of the shackles of colonialism after the Second World War and gained national independence and victory in national emancipation.

Dialectics of history is just so amazing. As the opposite of capitalism, after Marxism was generated in the social practice of Western capitalism and spread to the East following the Russian socialist revolution, it rooted, bloomed, and bore fruits in China and some other countries and guided people of China and other countries to create a brand new socialist civilization before Western capitalist countries. After the influence of Marxism and the socialist revolutions of Russia and China spread to Asia, Africa, and Latin America, it combined with the reality there and guided many colonial and semi-colonial countries long subordinate to the West to gain victories of national emancipation and independence. It should not be forgotten that this was also a huge contribution of Western civilization to human beings. It was also a chapter of great tales of human society in exchange and mutual reference history.

3. The historical experience left by the ancient Silk Road about exchange and mutual learning among different civilizations, countries, and regions

China has an old saying, "By reflecting on the past and turning back to look into the future, one can know both the past and today." Seriously summarizing and absorbing our predecessors' experience would bring benefits to the practice of contemporaries and our descendants. Then, what historical experience has exchange and mutual learning among different civilizations, countries, and regions along the ancient Silk Road left us? Here, I would like to address the following four points.

First, peace must be prized so that all states can enjoy peace.

"Peace is to be prized most," "All states can enjoy peace," "Take virtue as our neighbors," and "harmonious states." all came from ancient classics before China's Qin Dynasty. Their implication was to advocate peaceful coexistence among states, and harmony and peacefulness are prized in approaching all matters. "Harmonious states" came from *The Book of Documents* of China's Western Zhou Dynasty and "All states can enjoy peace" from *Yi Zhuan* (Commentary on *The Book of Changes*) of China's Warring States Period. At that time, China was still a slave society in transition to feudalism and surrounded by fiefdoms and foreign tribal states in great numbers. People hoped to enjoy peace instead of encountering it on the battlefield. However, subjective will cannot replace objective reality. Between the Western Zhou Dynasty and the Spring and Autumn and Warring States periods of the Eastern Zhou Dynasty, warfare among tribal states and vassal states never stopped, resulting in the displacement of people, the split of the country, and turmoil in society. This was described in historical books as "there were no righteous wars in the Spring and Autumn Period." It was by summarizing this lesson that Confucian and his disciples proposed and advocated "Peace is to be prized most," "Take virtue as our neighbors," and "All within the four seas are brothers." After Qin Shi Huang unified China, China gradually took "prizing peace most" and realized peace for all states as a principle in approaching political diplomacy with neighboring states and even distant states. It was because all dynasties of China persisted in such a principle that China could keep kind and peaceful relations with her neighboring countries and even distant countries for a long time. Such an external environment was an important historical reason for China to become one of the main founders of Eastern civilization.

Of course, the idea of promoting peace and peaceful coexistence is not unique to China. It is also the common will and idea of all humankind. In the first half of the 17th century, the Thirty Years' War broke out in Europe at the west end of the Silk Road. After this war, European countries recalled the painful experience and signed the Pease of Westphalia in 1648, establishing multiple international criteria for nation-states to coexist in peace, including mutual respect for sovereignty and territorial integrity. Thereby, a relatively peaceful situation for development was re-implemented and ensured for Europe for quite a period after that. The once powerful Roman Empire split, leading to the perishing of the Western Roman Empire in AD 476, and the arrogant Mongol Empire at the eastern end of the Silk Road that launched expeditions on the Eurasian continent also went to split and decline as a result of military hegemony. Their historical lessons explained the historical truth in approaching nation-to-nation relations from the opposite side, "By prizing peace, all nations can enjoy peace."

Second, only by learning from others' strong points to offset one's weak points can latecomers surpass the old-timers.

The development of the world and the progress of human civilization are always imbalanced. There are always some of the countries or civilizations that are at the forefront and some that are lagging behind. But nothing is inalterable. The advanced is not destined to be advanced forever, nor is the backward destined to be backward forever. The advanced and backward can transmute into each other. China has an old saying, "Haughtiness yields loss, as modesty brings gain," meaning conceit makes one lag behind, and modesty helps one to make progress. You are ahead of other people by making brilliant achievements. But if you conceitedly think of yourself as number one in the world, indulge in self-admiration, and even lord it over everyone, refusing to learn from others, one day, you will become a laggard. On the contrary, when you are lagging behind others temporarily, as long as you learn with an open mind and are good at learning from others' strong points, you will turn from a laggard into a precursor. Many clear proofs can be found for such positive and negative transformations in the history of exchange and mutual learning along the ancient Silk Road.

Europe used to experience a thousand years of the Dark Middle Ages. At that time, the development level of Europe far lagged behind China, India, and Arabian countries in the East. But European people were unwilling to lag behind. Through the Renaissance, Protestant Reformation, Bourgeois Revolution, and Industrial Revolution, they finally got rid of the state of decline, chaos, and backwardness and created an advanced capitalist civilization ahead of the rest of the world. So Europe surpassed the old-timers from the ranks of latecomers. This was first the result of the joint awakening and efforts by the people of European countries. Still, it was also inseparable from their efforts in learning and borrowing from the strong points, wisdom, and experience of Eastern civilization and other civilizations of the world.

It is known that China used to stand at the forefront of the East of the world and even the whole world with her comprehensive national power for as long as a dozen centuries. However, when Europe entered the era of building advanced capitalist civilization, the feudal rulers of China were still conceited and blind to the rest of the world. Instead of learning from the advanced stuff in the civilization of Western capitalism, they stubbornly held on to their feudalistic system, which was established in small production mode and a small-peasant economy. Finally, they became losers, left behind the trend of the times. But in the early 20th century, when Marxism generated in European civilization spread to China, under its guidance, Chinese Communists led the Chinese people to seriously summarize the historical lesson that when you were backward, you would get beaten and seriously learn the advanced achievements made by all countries and nations in the world, and then built on the soil of China a thriving and brand-new socialist civilization increasingly demonstrating its superiority. The Chinese people firmly believe that if they continue their efforts along the road of socialism with Chinese characteristics, they will surely bring China back to the center of the world stage with the great rejuvenation of the Chinese nation. This again vividly proves that through learning and endeavor, latecomers are more than able to surpass the old-timers.

Third, only through mutual benefit and reciprocity can we cooperate with and help each other.

Ancient Chinese thinker Laozi had a famous saying, "The more that he expends for others, the more does he possess of his own; the more that he gives to others, the more does he have himself." That is to say, people, countries, and regions can only cooperate through mutual benefit and reciprocity and create a win-win situation. This is a correct understanding and a fundamental point concluded by summarizing the experience of social intercourse. Undoubtedly, such understanding and points went throughout all countries, regions, and civilizations along the ancient Silk Road. Otherwise, the Silk Road would not have extended for thousands of years as a passage for the exchange of needed products and mutual reference.

Here, taking the Eastern trading system in the form of "tribute" advocated by ancient China and the comprehensive exchange system in economy, politics, and culture as an example, we can fully explain the extreme importance of adherence to mutual benefit and reciprocity to the promotion of cooperation, common development and progress in interaction among countries and regions.

The so-called "tribute" trading system and the comprehensive exchange system based on it was a mutually beneficial and cooperative trading system and comprehensive exchange system formed among countries and regions of ancient Northeast Asia and Southeast Asia, with China as the leading country and center of the exchange and other countries of Northeast Asia and Southeast Asia as participating countries and partners. In this system, as the leading country and exchange center, the Central Court of China conferred ceremonial titles to neighboring countries participating in the exchange, and according to such titles, the participating countries delivered to the Chinese court at regular or irregular intervals featured products of their countries, the so-called "tribute." When the diplomatic corps of the participating countries went to China with the "tribute," they would conduct various trading activities with the Chinese side on their way. After the corps presented their tribute to the Chinese court, according to rules, the latter would grant the corps and tributary countries with China's material and cultural products, the so-called "return tribute" or "tribute grant." Besides, the two sides would conduct exchange and mutual learning activities in politics, culture, and diplomacy. Such a "tribute" system was not only conducted between China and neighboring countries of Northeast Asia and Southeast Asia, but also in other big countries of Northeast Asia and Southeast Asia, such as between Japan and her neighboring island countries, between Java and small countries of South Sea Islands and between Vietnam and small countries of Indo-China Peninsula.

Such a "tribute" trading system and its comprehensive exchange system was a special kind of system for exchange and mutual reference, a system of international relations, and an international economic and political order formed and long practiced in Northeast Asia and Southeast Asia at the east end of the ancient Silk Road. Superficially, there seemed to be a divide between superior and inferior, principal and subordinate, and hierarchical order in such a system and order, but it was not so. In such a "tribute" system, China and neighboring countries of Northeast Asia and Southeast Asia were equal, mutually benefiting, and cooperative. In most cases, the tributary countries would gain more benefits from China's "return tribute" and other exchange and mutual learning activities. For example, the copper coins used in ancient Japan always depended on the "return tribute" and "special grant" from China. Japanese scholar Takeshi Hamashita pointed out, "Tribute relationship was a system featured by multiple character-istics. The basic feature of tribute was an activity conducted in commercial trade. That is to say, tribute relationship led to the formation of a trade network." Another Japanese scholar Nishijima Sadao also pointed out: "Title conferment by Chinese dynasties to her neighboring countries became a medium of political cohesion. The 'title conferment system' of such political cohesion was a form promoting the formation of the international order and international political scene of East Asia." American scholar John King Fairbank said that the tribute system "or the world order of China was a whole set of thinking and practice." Peter Nolan, Director of the University's Centre of Development Studies, University of Cambridge, made it clearer, "What tribute sought was peace and security"; "Tribute system could absolutely not be explained as an idea of conquest or comprehensive dominance"; "It could never be thought that only the Chinese court profited from the tribute. The gifts returned by the Empire were usually of higher value than the tribute articles." Such tribute relationship "was based on morals and so was mutually benefitting." In short, such a comprehensive exchange and mutual learning system in the special form of "tribute" not only benefited China, but also benefited countries of Northeast Asia and Southeast Asia and brought peace, stability, interest, and order to Northeast Asian and Southeast Asian regions. This is also an important reason that since ancient times, the Northeast Asian and Southeast Asian regions have formed a brilliant civilization full of developing vitality and innovative wisdom.

Fourth, only by reform and innovation can we advance with the times.

Thousand-year vicissitudes on the ancient Silk Road witnessed the disappearance of some civilizations and the rebirth of others. The Dark Middle Ages of Europe used to be an atmosphere of political oppression. After some advanced European intellectuals led European people to launch the Renaissance with strong revolutionary passion and pioneering spirit, the political, economic, and cultural situation of Europe turned on a new look. Renaissance was a dazzling movement of ideological emancipation as well as a movement of reform and innovation. As French Enlightenment thinker Voltaire said, "The major significance of Renaissance was innovation." It dealt a heavy blow to the theocracy of the Catholic Church, liberated people from the shackles of Christian theology, and awakened people's optimistic and aggressive spirit to strive for their happiness in this life. It was under the guidance of such spirit that the European bourgeoisie created the capitalist system, which destroyed rigid scholasticism, advocated scientific approaches and experimental scientific spirit, and laid the foundation for the great development of natural science in Europe. It cleared the way for the progress of the ideological culture of Europe, drew a political blueprint for the bourgeoisie to construct a capitalist society, and promoted the formation of nation-states and the development of capitalist civilization in Europe. In a word, this historic reform brought a rebirth to Europe on the foundation of a new system, new order, and new civilization.

The Meiji Restoration in Japan, conducted in the late 1860s, was also a movement of reform and innovation. At that time, Japan was impacted by Western capitalist industrial civilization, and people's thoughts and socioeconomic life were plunged into a state of confusion. After Emperor Meiji came to power in 1868, politically, Japan carried out modern reform to a constitutional monarchy. Economically, Japan implemented social development based on industry, encouraged learning from the technology of Europe and America, and invigorated the tide of industrialization. In terms of social life, Japan advocated measures including civilization, enlightenment, and vigorous development of education. The Meiji Restoration was an important turning point in Japanese history. It turned Japan into the first Asian country to be industrialized and modernized and gradually got into the ranks of world powers.

In brief, only by reform and innovation can we advance with the times; this historical experience repeatedly proven and left behind by the ancient Silk Road, like other historical experiences repeatedly proven and left, is precious historical enlightenment, wisdom, and truth for us to remember forever and apply creatively in combination with the new reality of development and new conditions of times.

II. On the New Pattern of International Cooperative Construction on Today's Belt and Road

Reflection and summarization of the historical exchange experience and mutual learning among different civilizations, countries, and regions on the ancient Silk Road can provide an important and beneficial mirror and revelation for today's Belt and Road construction.

1. The presentation of BRI and the warm response it evoked in the international community

The initiative for international cooperative construction of the Belt and Road, or Silk Road Economic Belt and 21st Century Marine Silk Road, was presented by Chinese President Xi Jinping when he visited Kazakhstan in September 2013 and Indonesia in October of the same year.

After the initiative was presented, it was widely responded to and supported by countries and regions of Asia, Africa, and Europe along the Belt and Road as well as other countries and regions in the world. Now, it has smoothly entered the stage of comprehensive implementation. Over 100 countries and international organizations have participated in it, and a large number of projects of international cooperation have started successively. A connectivity infrastructure network has preliminarily been formed, industrial cooperation along the line has formed a good momentum, policy coordination among various countries is being strengthened, and international exchange in all fields is deepening. On November 17, 2016, the 71st UN General Assembly took BRI into its resolution for the first time, which was unanimously approved by 193 members. In May 2017, the Belt and Road Forum for International Cooperation was held in Beijing, where 33 heads of state, chiefs of government, and principals of important international organizations attended. A total of 1,600 friends from over 140 countries and 80 international organizations attended as formal representatives. These all reflected the earnest expectation and wide support of the international community for promoting Belt and Road construction.

Once BRI for the new pattern of international cooperative construction was presented, it was praised and highly appraised by many media, politicians, scholars, and far-sighted personages in the world. A German website on diplomatic policy published an article to make a general description of the BRI, stating that the New Silk Road had been formally called the Belt and Road and was the major economic and strategic program in the world. One route of the Belt and Road is a land route that passes Central Asia, Russia, Iran, and Turkey to Europe. The other is a sea route that passes the South China Sea, the Strait of Malacca, the Indian Ocean to East Africa, and past the Suez Canal into the Mediterranean to Europe. Now, many countries have participated in the Belt and Road program, accounting for one-third of the global economic aggregate, covering 4.4 billion people or half of the global population. The Belt and Road will bring economic prosperity to the participating countries. A Spanish website also published a signed article that made a general analysis of the Belt and Road that this modern Silk Road was composed of the Silk Road Economic Belt and 21st Century Maritime Silk Road, including several corridors respectively: China–Mongolia–Russia, China–Central Asia–West Asia, China–Southeast Asia, China–Pakistan, and China–Bangladesh–India–Burma. The main content of the initiative is to stress policy coordination, infrastructure facilities and equipment connectivity, elimination of trade barriers, financial integration, and close social contact of various countries. Although the main objects of the initiative are Asia, Europe, and Africa, it also welcomes active participation by countries in Latin America. This initiative has the potential to change the economic territory of the world and is also a brand-new mode of globalization. UN Secretary-General António Guterres said that China's BRI as an important platform has provided a new train of thought for promoting international cooperation and played a core leading role. It is far-sighted in that it helps connectivity among countries, causes the peoples of different countries to join hands so that a community of human destiny can jointly face and endeavor to solve global challenges, and provides a Chinese option for the world. Russian President Putin indicated at the Road and Belt Forum this May, "China's initiative is timely and beneficial. It is not only China's initiative but also an initiative of everyone present at the forum. The imbalance of world economic development and the crisis of the old mode of globalization have brought negative impacts on international relations and security. Generally speaking, the logic of the old mode cannot solve contemporary problems, and new thought is needed. Belt and Road construction is the prototype of a new mode of globalization and international cooperation." Kazakhstan President Nazarbayev said, "The Belt and Road initiative is a timely solution to the political, economic, and humanitarian crisis the world is facing in this century, and its successful implementation will bring substantial benefit to the world people." Former French Prime Minister Raffarin pointed out, "China has set an example for the international community by promoting multilateral cooperation through ways such as the BRI. China's long-term goal and her comprehension of the era's needs are beneficial to the development of the world. In a world marked with innovation, I think China has a wonderful trump card, that is, the long and profound Chinese civilization. The BRI presented by China is a great plan that needs innovation, construction, and sharing. The voice China has sent to the world is a voice of balance, a voice of multilateral cooperation, and naturally a voice of progress." Czech President Zeman thought the BRI was a pioneering undertaking, a major initiative in modern history. Chile President Bachelet thought the BRI was rooted in the ancient Silk Road. It can help the connectivity of Asia, Africa, Europe, and South America, open new markets, promote investment and tourism, help various countries deepen their understanding of each other, and promote a fair, accommodating, and peaceful world. Former Egyptian Premier Essam Sharaf said, "The globalization we need must be one with a foundation of cultural ideology. It must be able to raise the living quality of all people. It must be able to make people understand and live peacefully with each other instead of being hostile to each other. The BRI is a response to the needs of today's world. Its important principle is to seek common points while reserving differences. This is the important foundation of cultural ideology." Former Indian diplomat Mukul Sanwal said, "The BRI presented by China reflects the trend of today's world and has built a new mode for globalized cooperation." Peter Maurer, President of the International Committee of the Red Cross, indicated that the BRI had provided a new channel for the realization of a community with a shared future for mankind. It is a feasible initiative that can make the world better. Peter Nolan, Director of the University's Centre of Development Studies, University of Cambridge, thought that China had found the road for her own development and was looking for a road for the sustainable development of the whole world. The Belt and Road construction is not a threat to the West but a true opportunity for cooperation. This is what the Chinese call a win-win situation. American futurist John Naisbitt thought that the BRI had become a direction for global development. Its most unusual point is to benefit all countries and people of all countries instead of only benefiting a small part of the population. African countries have developed their infrastructure under the support of China and benefited from it. This is more effective than copying the democratic system of the West. South African scholar Cobus van Staden said that the BRI was a new exposition for globalization, and its connotation far exceeded an initiative for development. This construction plan will bring development to East Africa, which is badly needed, and bring a different future to the whole African continent. Compared with the relationship between Africa and the West, this is at least a different kind of future. UAE scholar Jamil Matar said that China's BRI was like a mission from the East. It is not mixed with colonialism or political interference. This mission from the East is to serve and take care of the interests of most people in the world. So, a new era and a cooperative mode totally different than the past will possibly start. According to Russian scholar Grigory Trofimchuk, the BRI is a long-term, superb, and mutually beneficial conception. Its purpose is to borrow the historical symbol of the ancient Silk Road, hold high the banner of peaceful development, actively develop economic partnerships with countries along the line, and jointly build a community with shared interests, destiny, and responsibilities that are politically mutually trusting, economically integrated and culturally accommodating. Pakistani scholar Muhammad Zamir Asadi thought the BRI would create new opportunities for the international community as a "new form of globalization." Indonesian scholar Bambang Suryo said that the Belt and Road construction was the best public product provided to the world. It contains the Chinese wisdom of "prizing peace," "common development," and "harmonious coexistence." It will surely generate a profound influence on the world. The BRI reflects the revival of the Eastern civilization and is of great significance to the promotion of equal exchange between the Eastern and Western civilizations. Canadian Indian scholar Amitav Acharya pointed out that the Belt and Road construction would lead to globalization in a new mode. This new pattern of globalization will differ from the past one, which focused only on trade. Instead, it will pay more attention to investment, infrastructure, and common development. Globalization of investment and infrastructure more suits developing countries. It differs from Western-led globalization. Countries of the Eastern world, including China, will give more respect to sovereignty and follow the principle of non-interference. The "world system" they propose to establish is a world order for all countries to realize harmony while keeping their differences.

The discussions made by the media, politicians, scholars, and far-sighted personages have made a relatively comprehensive appraisal of the history of the BRI and its purport, prospect, and profound influence. These discussions fully show that the BRI has widely formed some important consensus in the international community. First, the BRI did not appear out of nothing. It inherited the good tradition of the historical contact on the Silk Road and adapted itself to the needs of the development of today's world. By summarizing the historical experience of mutual learning on the Silk Road and the realistic experience of today's international contact, we can say that it has creatively opened a new road for realizing a new pattern of international cooperation. Second, the BRI follows the development trend of globalization and tries to overcome the drawbacks of past economic globalization. It has provided new channels, modes, and governing principles for the healthy development of economic globalization. Third, the Belt and Road construction will not only benefit the initiating country or the countries and regions along it but will drive and promote all countries in the world. All countries, Eastern or Western, Southern or Northern, developing or developed, can benefit from it so that various countries of the world can live together in peace, treat each other equally, benefit each other, and develop together. Fourth, the development achievements made in the Belt and Road construction will not only be enjoyed by a small part of the social population, but efforts will be made to benefit the vast masses of people of all countries and regions to help the gradual narrowing of the gap between the rich and poor among members of society. This is also to, within the scope of the world, provide a brand-new option for an unprecedented exploration and experiment for building a community with a shared future for mankind. Fifth, the BRI complies with the development trend of today's world and reflects the interests and will of people of all countries of the world, so it has a limitless bright future. Sixth, the wisdom and value reflected by the BRI not only belong to China or the East but also to the West, the whole world, and all mankind. So, all sections of the international community should cherish and protect it. We should do what we can to positively participate in it, provide support for it, and make our own contributions.

2. The global governance concept reflected and followed by the BRI

A core concept, essential requirement, and basic principle throughout Belt and Road construction is joint discussion, joint construction, and benefit sharing. This is also the governance concept to be followed in global economic governance. This clearly answers and solves the important questions of how to conduct Belt and Road international cooperative construction, who is to construct, and for whom to construct.

The joint discussion is that for the infrastructure and various projects of economic development in the cooperative construction, the decision is not to be made by any party in the cooperation. All parties' opinions of the cooperation are to be fully listened to, their will is to be respected, and their interests are to be concerned. Each party is to be consulted as much as possible to pool their wisdom before making a decision. During the discussion, special attention must be given to make sure that all the cooperative projects comply with the actual situation and needs of the countries and regions in which they are located. Only in this way can we properly and reliably implement the cooperative projects and help real connectivity and mutual benefit.

The joint construction is that for the projects to be jointly constructed and developed, all parties in the cooperation should be based on the spirit of those who have money give money, those who have manpower give manpower, those who have plans give their plan, and those who have technology give their technology, make sure that concerted efforts are made for their same aim. During the construction, all parties should be clear that they will not only share their opportunities for development but also jointly meet challenges and overcome difficulties, dissolve their conflicts, and bear risks. Only in this way can the joint construction be successful.

The benefit sharing means that all interests formed and all achievements gained in the projects of cooperative construction shall be shared by all parties of the cooperation based on the principle of fairness and justice so that all parties benefit. All parties involved in the cooperation are equal partners, and no one should bully the weak by being strong so that interests and achievements are unreasonably and unfairly shared. If so, the principle of Belt and Road construction is violated, and the cooperation can't succeed.

In a word, the Belt and Road construction is not a "solo" by one country or one party but a "symphony" participated by various countries and parties. It is not a Belt and Road for one country or one party to enjoy the benefits alone, but a Belt and Road for all countries and all parties to share the interests. In a word, the essence of the BRI is in "joint." The purpose of a win-win situation is finally reached through joint discussion, joint construction, and benefit sharing. This is the biggest difference between the international cooperative construction of the Belt and Road and the unfair and unreasonable cooperative mechanisms existing in past international intercourse.

It can be firmly believed that in Belt and Road construction, as long as we adhere to the common wishes and needs of people of various countries in pursuit of peace and development, adhere to the guidance of the spirit of peaceful cooperation, openness and inclusiveness, learning from and referring to each other and mutual benefit, adhere to the goal of cooperation for building a community with a shared future and interests for mankind, follow the law that all countries big or small, strong or weak, are equal and mutually benefiting and are to jointly discuss plans for development, jointly construct platforms for development and share the achievements of development, we will fundamentally distinguish ourselves from the such "zero-sum game rules" as "jungle law" and "winner gets all" long existing in international social intercourse and it will surely help the establishment of a new international political and economic order that is fairer and more reasonable as well as help the opening of a new situation for world development and human progress. The BRI we all talk about has provided a new option and mode for promoting the development of today's world and improving international contact and global economic governance. It is new in its joint discussion, joint construction, and benefit sharing.

3. *The conception of BRI and a community with a shared future for mankind is a creative inheritance, application, and development of the ancient oriental wisdom and historical wisdom of the whole human society, such as "the whole world as one community" and "one world, one family"*

When presenting the initiative for building the Belt and Road, Chinese President Xi Jinping also proposed building a community with a shared future for mankind. At the 19th CPC National Congress just convened, General Secretary Xi Jinping again appealed that people of all countries should make concerted efforts "to build a community with a shared future for mankind, to build an open, inclusive, clean, and beautiful world that enjoys lasting peace, universal security, and common prosperity." The core requirement of the proposal for building a community with a shared future for mankind is to ask for peace instead of war, for development instead of poverty, for cooperation instead of confrontation, and for a win-win instead of a win-lose situation. This conception was also presented on the basis of complying with historical trends, responding to the requirements of the times, reflecting the common wishes of people of the world, and condensing the consensus of far-sighted personages of all countries. It has indicated the direction for improving global governance and building a new international order that is fairer and more reasonable.

Man only has one earth, and all countries live in one world. Today's world is in a period of great development, reform, and adjustment. With the deepened development of political multi-polarization and economic globalization of the world and continuous promotion of cultural diversification and social infor-matization, economic, political, cultural, and social associations between various countries and regions are unprecedentedly close, and dialogues and exchanges between different cultures are getting increasingly frequent. Peace, development, cooperation, and win-win situations represent popular sentiment and the general trend. Meanwhile, the uncertainty and instability facing the world are increasing. The economic recovery caused by the economic crisis is going slow, polarization between the rich and poor is getting increasingly serious, all kinds of frictions, conflicts, and local wars happen now and then, and global challenges such as terrorism, network security, population explosion, moral decline, transnational crimes, resource shortage, environmental destruction, and major infectious diseases are getting increasingly prominent. Hence, the noble undertaking of promoting peace and development for mankind still has a long way to go. In the face of the intricate international situation and unprecedented challenges, no country can stand alone, and no country can cope alone. Only by making concerted efforts, keeping exploring and utilizing the excellent ideological and cultural achievements man has accumulated and is creating, especially the enlightenment, wisdom, and experience contained in them, jointly building a community with a shared future for mankind, can people of all countries effectively answer and dissolve the challenges and problems so as to start a beautiful future for world development and human progress.

For China to develop the proposal for building a community with a shared future for mankind, she is supported by her long and deep cultural deposits. Long ago, Chinese culture formed an important ideological concept and ideal for a good society: "the whole world as one community" and "a world of great harmony." China's ancient classic "Li Yun" in *The Book of Rites* of the pre-Qin period said, "The supreme political ideal is that the whole world is one community." "For the world to be one community is great harmony." The so-called "the whole world as one community" means that the world is not one of one person, family, or nation but a world owned by all people, all nations, and all countries. Based on the purport of "the whole world as one community," Chinese scholars of the past also came up with an important political thought, that is, the people-centered doctrine that regarded people as a basis. The so-called people-centered doctrine advocates that social, economic, political, and cultural affairs and state governance must be subordinate to and serve the common interests of all people and give peace, wealth, and happiness to people. Jia Yi, a famous political commentator of the Western Han Dynasty, once said that administrators should "take it as a merit to bring wealth and happiness to people and take it as a sin to impoverish people and cause people to suffer." Of course, historical facts had once and again shown that in the feudal society in which the minority ruled the majority, the rulers did not and would impossibly implement the thought of "the whole world as one community," neither did they, or would they carry out the people-centered doctrine and neither did they or would they bring peace, wealth, or happiness to people. But the advanced political concepts and the ideal for a better society, such as "the world as a community," "a world of great harmony," and "people-centered doctrine" that reflected the progressive law of social development, people's character and democracy have been inherited as the essence of the traditional Chinese culture by Chinese people with lofty ideas in their incessant pursuit and long practice and struggle.

The ideological concepts of "the whole world as one community" and "a world of great harmony" are not unique to Chinese culture and civilization. They are also proposed and advocated by the culture and civilization of many countries and regions of the world. From Aristotle, who proposed "man should live in harmony with each other," to the cosmopolitanism advocated by European Enlightenment scholars in the 18th century, and then to the "one world, one family" advocated by former Indian Prime Minister Nehru; from the view of "compromise and competition" proposed by thinkers of ancient Korean Peninsula, to "golden mean" proposed by Arabian philosophical thoughts. From China's advocacy of the Five Principles of Peaceful Coexistence in dealing with international relations together with India and Burma to the establishment of the

European Community and European Union, and then to the establishment of the African Union, CELAC, and ASEAN, the ideological concepts of "the whole world as one community" and "a world of great harmony" are reflected from different perspectives, in different levels and degrees. Thus, it can be seen that the ideological concepts of "the whole world as one community" and "a world of great harmony" are the common historical wisdom and ideological essence created by people of all countries and regions of the world in promoting the development of human society.

If this historical wisdom and essence provided important historical revelation and basis for the generation of the BRI and the conception of building a community with a shared future for mankind, then the strong wishes of peoples of all countries of the world for maintaining lasting peace, practicing cooperation, promoting common development and common prosperity and the trend of times formed under today's new international situation are the important realistic basis and impetus for the generation of this initiative and conception. The historical experiences of social development and human progress have repeatedly proven that any inevitable products of history, once they are generated, will keep blazing their way ahead with invincible momentum and force until they reach the other side of success and victory. This is independent of man's will. Suffice it to say that the great feat of building the Belt and Road and a community with a shared future for mankind marks the start and advent of a new era for the development of today's world and human progress.

Three Economic Globalizations of Human Society and the Construction of a Community with a Shared Future for Mankind[*]

Keynote Speech at the International Confucianism
Forum · International Academic Conference in Rabat

November 14, 2018

---

[*] From November 14 to 16, 2018, the ICA, in collaboration with Beijing International Studies University and the Salé Law, Economics, and Social Sciences School of Mohammed V University in Morocco, jointly organized the International Confucianism Forum · International Academic Conference in Rabat, the capital of Morocco. More than 40 experts and scholars from 23 countries, including China, Morocco, Egypt, France, Portugal, Italy, Ethiopia, Sudan, Cameroon, Algeria, Vietnam, Spain, Croatia, Singapore, Israel, the UAE, Tunisia, Togo, Kenya, Nigeria, Liberia, Chad, and Senegal, participated in discussions on the theme of "Building the 'Belt and Road' and Constructing a Community with a Shared Future for Mankind." This keynote speech was delivered at the opening ceremony on November 14, 2018. The speech focused on three key issues: the historical exchanges between China and countries in West Asia, North Africa, and South Europe; the evolution and development of economic globalization; and the historical inevitability of building a community with a shared future for mankind. For the first time, economic globalization was divided into three historical stages, introducing the concept of "three economic globalization" and providing a comprehensive discussion of their main historical trajectories. The speech also elaborated that building a community with a shared future for mankind is a historical inevitability for global development and human civilization progress, emphasizing the basic principles that should be adhered to in constructing such a community.

Today, I, together with my colleagues of the ICA, travel a long way to arrive at this picturesque "Garden in North Africa" Morocco with great joy and modesty to learn and attend this conference with all of you on the "'Belt and Road' and Constructing a Community with a Shared Future for Mankind," which is an event with significant meaning. It has been the first international academic conference held in Africa since the foundation of ICA, with the participation of all excellent experts and scholars here in various research fields. I believe such a gathering of old and new friends and the discussion of events throughout the world, either ancient or modern, is quite a pleasant occasion.

Morocco is an important country on the African continent, and Moroccan people are close friends of Chinese people as brothers. Since ancient times, the Chinese and Moroccan people have established friendships and left many beautiful and precious historical memories. Morocco was the first country in the world to import and consume green tea from China and one of Africa's first countries to apply Chinese papermaking technology. In the early 9th century AD, Chinese papermaking began to be introduced to Egypt and Morocco. After the 10th century, Fez, the capital of Morocco, became a main papermaking center besides China and developed as the base for introducing papermaking into the Iberian Peninsula and then to Europe in the middle of the 12th century. The history of interactions between China and Morocco has lasted for more than 1,000 years. In the middle of the 8th century, a scholar named Du Huan of the Tang Dynasty, after traveling through Central Asia, West Asia, North Africa, and East Africa, wrote a book called *Jing Xing Ji* (The Travel Book), in which there were records about Morocco (then called Molin, the neighboring country). In the mid-14th century, the scholars of China and Morocco, Wang Dayuan and Ibn Battuta, realized "mutual visits," which became a much-told story by the people of China and Morocco. Since modern times, similar historical experiences have enhanced the mutual connection, understanding, and support between the people of the two countries. When the late King of Morocco, Hassan II, talked about the victory of the Battle of Dien Bien Phu, in which China played a significant supporting role, he said, "There would be no independence of Morocco without the Battle of Dien Bien in Vietnam." In other words, the battle plunged a European colonizer who was then unable to cover Morocco, Algeria, and Tunisia in North Africa, which objectively helped the three countries gain independence as soon as possible. China's late Prime Minister Zhou Enlai spoke highly of it, saying that King Hassan II deserved to be a strategist who considered Morocco's independence in terms of the changes in the global situation. The above histories have not only witnessed the millennium friendship between China and Morocco or even Africa but also provided profound and useful historical enlightenment for future generations.

Next, I would like to share my personal opinions from the perspective of academic discussion on three points, which are historical interactions between China and the countries and regions of West Asia, North Africa, and South Europe, the Silk Road witnessing the evolution and development of economic globalization, and the development of a community with a shared future for mankind being the historical inevitability of the world development and human civilization progress.

I. Historical Interactions between China and the Countries and Regions of West Asia, North Africa, and South Europe

Morocco is located at the joint of the three continents of Asia, Africa, and Europe and adheres to the gateway to the Atlantic Ocean from the Mediterranean Sea, which are important junctions and channels of the ancient Maritime and Land Silk Roads. Many events and stories in the progress of human civilization have occurred in this area. Here, the two oldest civilizations in the world were born: Mesopotamian and Egyptian civilizations. There used to be numberless business caravans and various armies in this place. Still, most famously, it has always been an important area where several great civilizations in the world complement each other and learn from each other. The ancient Silk Road was created by people from all nations along the line to achieve mutual exchanges. It does not belong to any specific country or region but the shared wealth created by various countries and regions. The spirits of mutual learning and benefit, as well as peace, friendship, and cooperation left by the ancient Silk Road, are especially worthy of our cherishing.

China is the eastern starting point of the ancient Silk Road and has made great efforts and unique contributions to the opening of the road. The interactions between China and countries and regions of West Asia, North Africa, and South Europe have left many precious memories in history.

—During the period of Emperor Wu in the Western Han Dynasty, Zhang Qian was sent to the Western Regions in 139 BC and opened the easternmost section of the Silk Road after much pain and suffering. He once reached Uzbekistan and Afghanistan in Central Asia.

—During the governance of Emperor He in the Eastern Han Dynasty, Ban Chao, who took the mission to the Western Regions, dispatched his deputy Gan Ying in AD 97 to the capital city of Daqin, which becomes Rome in Italy today and arrived in Seleucid that is the region of Iraq today. When he looked far into Daqin alongside the West Sea, the native told him that the West Sea (the Persian Gulf) had strong wind and rain that could prevent passengers from passing through for three months or even longer, so he returned without going toward Roma. In the Han Dynasty, the Silk Road to the West, which took almost 300 years to be built, left a colorful page in the human civilization communication history book.

—On the western part of the ancient Silk Road, the ancestors in the regions of West Asia, North Africa, and South Europe have kept forging ahead. They excavated the canal connecting the Red Sea and the Mediterranean Sea, explored the sailing route from the Red Sea into the Indian Ocean, and opened up the business road to the East via West Asia. According to the *Book of the Later Han*, in AD 166, under the governance of Emperor Huan of the Eastern Han Dynasty, there were messengers from Daqin, namely, the Roman Empire, arriving at the capital of the Eastern Han Dynasty. After six decades, messengers from Daqin arrived at the capital of Wu in the Three Kingdoms Period and met with the Lord Sun Quan.

—In the Tang Dynasty, China directly bordered the Arab Empire that governed West Asia, North Africa, and South Europe with continuous exchanges at that time. That is the period when Islam was introduced to China. In the early Tang Dynasty, Persia in West Asia is now known as Iran. Some people sent the Nestorian faction of Western Christianity to China, which was called *Jingjiao* (Luminous Religion) in Chinese historical records. "Daqin Jingjiao Liuxing

Zhongguo Bei" (Stele to the Propagation in China of the *Jingjiao* of Daqin), which is now preserved in Shaanxi, records the spread of *Jingjiao* in China for more than 100 years since AD 635. Of course, interactions among countries and regions in history have not always been filled with the fragrance of roses. In AD 751, the armies of the Tang Dynasty and the Arab Empire were involved in a famous battle in Talas of Central Asia, today's Zhambyl in Kazakhstan. Due to the failure of the Tang army, many craftsmen in the papermaking and textile industries and some scholars were captured. The Arab Empire gathered them in Samarkand of Uzbekistan, and by the establishment of paper-making and textile mills, Chinese papermaking and silk weaving have gradually spread from Central Asia to Iraq and Syria in West Asia, Egypt and Morocco in North Africa, Portugal, Spain, and Italy in South Europe, and finally throughout Europe. The above-mentioned Du Huan, who was then a captured scholar in the Talas Battle, has traveled westward from Uzbekistan to Iran, Iraq, Syria, Saudi Arabia, and Israel in West Asia, and then Egypt, Morocco, Ethiopia, and other countries in North Africa, and finally returned to China in AD 763 via the Maritime Silk Road, which has spent 13 years before and after. His *Jing Xing Ji* is a narrative of what he saw and heard in the countries and regions he has traveled to, which can be the first written narrative in history that Chinese scholars have experienced in the regions of West Asia, North Africa, and South Europe.

—In the Song Dynasty, many merchants, scholars, and envoys in West Asia, North Africa, and South Europe went to China for business, study, and visits, and there are written records about it. During the 200 years between AD 968 and 1168, the Arabic Empire sent messengers to China 48 times.

—The overseas communications in the Yuan Dynasty were even more prosperous. There were over 200 trades for Chinese merchant ships along the Maritime Silk Road. A scholar named Wang Dayuan of the Yuan Dynasty traveled through Southeast Asia, South Asia, and West Asia to North Africa via the Maritime Silk Road, once from AD 1330 to 1334, and another from AD 1337 to 1339. For the first time, he reached Mecca in Saudi Arabia, Aden in Yemen, Basra in Iraq, Damietta in Egypt, etc., with the most distant Tangier in Morocco, as well as Oceania for the second time. His travel log *Daoyi Zhilüe* (A Brief Account of Island Barbarians) involves 222 names of countries and sites and a detailed narrative on landscapes, customs, and products of 99 among them. Several years after his second travel, Moroccan scholar Ibn Battuta, born in Tangier, visited China, passing through West Asia, South Asia, and Southeast Asia in AD 1345. He left his footprints in Guangzhou, Quanzhou, Hangzhou, and Beijing and stayed in China for a year. In 1354, *The Travel Note of Ibn Battuta*, which was recorded by others in terms of his narratives, became a well-known masterpiece across the Arab world. In this book, there are descriptions of Chinese culture and the costumes of the day, as well as praise for the vast territory and abundant resources of China and the wisdom of Chinese people. *Daoyi Zhilüe* and *The Travel Note of Ibn Battuta* are rare companion pieces in the history of the interactions between China and Arabia and China and Africa, respectively, and exerted great influence on the promotion of mutual understanding between the countries and regions.

—Zheng He, in the Ming Dynasty, made his maritime voyages seven times, lasting for 28 years (AD 1405–1433) during the golden age of the economic, political, and cultural communication between China and regions of West Asia, North Africa, and South Europe, which again demonstrated China's sincere goodwill of sharing peace with nations all over the world. After over 100 years of Zheng He's voyages, that is, the era of geographical discovery in the late 15th and early 16th centuries, an envoy named Tomé Pires from Portugal in South Europe traveled via the similar route of Zheng He's voyages and arrived in China in 1517. He wrote *An Account of the Orient: From Red Sea to China* according to his experiences, which became precious material for the research on the history of the East and West exchange, together with the records of Zheng He's flotilla.

Over time, Mediterranean countries and regions have become the key areas to strengthen the economic, political, cultural, and social ties as well as economic and technological cooperation among the three continents of Asia, Africa, and Europe, and additionally to implement the new international cooperation of the BRI. Since China proposed the initiative in 2013, 103 countries and international organizations have signed 118 cooperative construction agreements with China, expanding from Asian-European continent to Africa, Latin America, the Caribbean, and the South Pacific; China's import and export volume with countries along the road has exceeded US$5.5 trillion, and non-financial direct investment to those countries was more than US$80 billion; the number of economic and trade cooperation zones jointly built by China and the countries along the road has reached 82. This alone has added 244,000 jobs to the countries. Among them, the African continent accounts for a considerable proportion of the new international cooperation in the BRI. Since President Xi Jinping proposed the implementation of "10 Major China-Africa Cooperation Plans" at the Johannesburg Summit of the China-Africa Cooperation Forum in 2015, the projects that Chinese enterprises have built and are building in Africa will help Africa to add about 30,000 kilometers of highway mileage, an annual port capacity of 85 million tons, more than 9 million tons of clean water treatment capacity per day, nearly 20,000 megawatts of power generation capacity and over 30,000 kilometers of power transmission and transformation lines, as well as nearly 900,000 jobs created for African countries. *The Economist* once called Africa "a desperate continent" in 2000, but today's Africa is burning up hope for a vibrant development. Many leaders of African countries and African people are full of good prospects for the future development and prosperity of Africa. As President of Djibouti Ismaïl Omar Guelleh said, "Westerners have been here for more than 100 years, but our country is still in poverty. Chinese talents have been here for three years, and our country has undergone such a big change, which shows us the hope." The General Secretary of Kenya's ruling Party, Raphael Tuju, also claimed that China's achievements had no precedent in human history, which brought hope to the African people and made them feel light at the end of the tunnel.

It is entirely convincing that people of the countries and regions in West Asia, North Africa, and South Europe of the Asian-African-European area along the Mediterranean will make great contributions to the new international cooperation construction of the BRI, the improvement of global governance, the establishment of a new international political, and economic order more fair and reasonable, and the development of a community with a shared future for mankind.

II. The Silk Road Witnessed the Evolution and Development of Economic Globalization

In a quite long period in history, from Zhang Qian's departure to the Western Regions, which opened the eastern section of the Land Silk Road, to the opening of the entire line of the Land Silk Road and the gradual opening of the Maritime Silk Road, due to the limitations of the transportation conditions and communication techniques as well as the obstacles caused by war factors and other human factors, the passage between the East and the West, whether on land or at sea, was basically piecewise or progressive. That is to say, in general, one road segment was dominated by one or several countries, and another road segment was dominated by another or several other countries. The whole road was composed of several such road segments. Associated with this is that the economic, political, cultural, and social interactions and connections, as well as exchanges and mutual learning of different civilizations between the various countries and various regions along the Land and Maritime Silk Roads, also generally carried out in a segmented manner from the near to the distant. Therefore, the scope and extent of their interactions and exchanges were naturally very unbalanced. Under this circumstance, no country or region could have a systematic and complete understanding of the economic, political, cultural, and social aspects of the Asian, Australian, African, and European countries and regions radiated by the entire Land or Maritime Silk Road. As for North and South America, people in Asia, Australia, Africa, and Europe did not even know their existence then. In short, this is very different from the contact situation between countries and regions after economic globalization. However, under the difficult conditions before economic globalization, people from Asian, Australian, African, and European countries and regions overcame various difficulties and risks. They insisted on mutual interaction and mutual learning through the Land or Maritime Silk Road, which was very valuable. The historical contributions made by the ancestors of these different countries and regions are always worthy of admiration.

The era of economic globalization should start after Europe entered the stage of capitalist development and started the capitalist industrial civilization. The opening of new sea routes and the great geographical discovery are important signs of the beginning of economic globalization.

The rise of the Renaissance in Europe in the 14th century AD marked the beginning of the European people's gradual liberation from the medieval feudal theology of the millennium. It provided an ideological and political basis for opening the way to capitalist society. Later, in the 16th and 17th centuries, after the European Protestant Reformations and the outbreak of the Netherland Revolution and the British Revolution, the Bourgeois Revolution culminated throughout Europe. European countries entered the development stage of capitalism and began the Industrial Revolution. Columbus discovered the New World of the Americas by sea voyage. Vasco da Gama bypassed the Cape of Good Hope at the southern end of Africa and sailed eastward to India. Magellan sailed around the world. The opening of these new sea routes and the great geographical discoveries are the product of the rapid development of European industrial technology. The development of European capitalist social productivity, especially industrial productivity, requires a broad market. In this context, Europeans went to Africa, Australia, and Asia in the South and East of the world, as well as to the newly discovered North and South America to find and open up commodity markets, capital markets, and places of raw materials. As Marx and Engels said, "The need to continuously expand the market for products drove the bourgeoisie to run around the world. It must be settled everywhere and developed everywhere to build connections. The bourgeoisie opened up the world market and made the production and consumption of all countries worldwide." In this way, the era of economic globalization witnessed by the Silk Road arrived.

More than 500 years from the end of the 15th century, marked by the opening of new sea routes and the great geographical discovery, economic globalization has generally gone through three historical stages, namely three rounds of economic globalization with different characteristics. The first round of economic globalization lasted for 400 years, from the end of the 15th century to the outbreak of the First World War at the beginning of the 20th century. The second round of economic globalization lasted for more than 70 years, from the First World War in the early 20th century to the Second World War, to the upheaval in East Europe and the collapse of the Soviet Union in the late 20th century. The third round of economic globalization has lasted for nearly 30 years, from the upheaval in East Europe and the collapse of the Soviet Union in the late 20th century to now.

1. The first round of economic globalization

The historical period for this round is a period in which Western capitalist-imperialist powers colonized the people of Asian, African, and Latin American countries and regions from the perspective of the international political and economic order and its basic characteristics. The main historical trajectory of this economic globalization is summarized in the following aspects.

First, the great geographical discovery, especially the discovery of the New World of the Americas, enabled people to have a relatively complete understanding of the complete picture of countries and regions of the world, which greatly broadened people's horizons and had an inestimable far-reaching significance. It should be said that this is the historical product and major achievements that Europe has brought due to its development toward capitalist civilization.

Second, immediately before and during the European countries exerted colonization of the Asian, African, and Latin American countries, European businessmen, entrepreneurs, missionaries, and scholars brought advanced science and technology, ideas, and culture to the countries of these continents, which played an enlightening and helping role for these countries to develop from the ancient society to the modern society.

Third, the colonial rule of the Western and Northern countries represented by Europe over the Eastern and Southern countries for hundreds of years, including sovereignty violations, political oppression, military aggression, economic plunder, and cultural infiltration, caused deep suffering to the people of the colonized countries. As a result, these countries were long in economic demise, political turmoil, cultural decline, and poor livelihood, which seriously hindered their development and progress. Due to colonial rule, the colonial countries became increasingly rich, and the colonized countries became increasingly poor. This caused a huge development gap between the West and the East and between the North and the South, a great imbalance in global economic and political development, and the world's extreme unrest. This provoked the people of the colonized countries to continue the struggle against aggression, oppression, and colonization.

Fourth, the jungle law developed and promoted by the Western colonialists caused an extremely unfair economic and political order in the international community characterized by an increasing gap between countries in economic strength and comprehensive strength.

Fifth, in Western countries, because the basic contradictions of capitalism (socialization of production and private possession of means of production) are irreconcilable, the wealth from colonies and semi-colonies is only enjoyed by a few wealthy bourgeoisie. At the same time, workers did not get many benefits and suffered more and more serious exploitation. Therefore, a huge gap between the rich and the poor has also formed in Western countries, which is the root cause of the ongoing economic and political crisis in Western capitalist countries.

Sixth, among the Western countries, the competition for raw materials, markets, labor force, and colonies not only caused the division of markets and spheres of influence, but also caused successive conflicts and wars between them. While Spain captured huge sums of money from the American colonies as capital to become a country that led to economic globalization in the 16th century, the Netherlands led the economic globalization of the 17th century by profiting from the Thirty Years' War in Europe. The United Kingdom established its leading and hegemonic position in the economic globalization of the 19th century after plundering many colonies and leading the sixth anti-French alliance in 1815 to win the battle against Napoleon.

Seventh, it is precisely because of the intensification of various contradictions accumulated over several centuries of colonial rule that a total outbreak finally formed. This total outbreak was manifested not only in the world war launched by Western capitalist countries, but also in the rise of the European socialist movement, the general awakening of the colonial and semi-colonial people, and the struggle for national independence and national liberation. The occurrence of the First World War in 1914–1918 and the success of the October Revolution in Russia in 1917 were important signs. At this point, the first round of economic globalization came to an end.

2. *The second round of economic globalization*

The historical period for this round of economic globalization is a period in which the East and the West were in opposition to each other, the markets of the East and the West separated from each other, and the two superpowers of the East and the West strived for hegemony from the perspective of the international political and economic order and its basic characteristics.

The main historical trajectory of this economic globalization can be summarized in the following aspects.

First, during the First World War, the socialist revolution in Russia broke out and won under the guidance of Marxism-Leninism in 1917. This was the product of the development of the European socialist movement, which greatly shocked the entire capitalist world. Especially after the Second World War, launched by several Western fascist countries, a large number of socialist countries were born in the East and West of the world. The socialist countries headed by the Soviet Union and the capitalist countries headed by the United States formed two camps in which the East and the West opposed each other. The world market was divided into Eastern and Western markets, which were separated from each other.

Second, since the two world wars weakened the power of Western capitalist countries, under the encouragement and support of the revolutionary victory of the Soviet Union, China, and other socialist countries, colonial and semi-colonial countries of Asia, Africa, and Latin America set off a climax of fight against Western imperialism and colonialism and struggle for national independence and national liberation. In the more than 20 years after the Second World War, most of the colonial and semi-colonial countries of Asia, Africa, and Latin America achieved national independence and national liberation, thus achieving the political preconditions for developing national economy and culture. Among them, some countries have joined the Western market, some have joined the Eastern market, and some have joined both the Western and Eastern markets. Socialist countries, including China, were liberated from colonial and semi-colonial rule. Together with the vast number of Asian, African, and Latin American countries, they worked hard to develop their economy and culture after gaining independence and liberation and made important contributions to the development of the world economy and culture.

Thirdly, the socialist countries and the vast number of developing countries that gained independence and liberation in Asia, Africa, and Latin America supported and learned from each other and formed a powerful force fighting for and defending world peace. Therefore, in the decades after the end of the Second

World War, although some local wars occasionally occurred in the world, this powerful force effectively prevented the outbreak of a new world war. It thus provided important political and security guarantees for the development of the world economy, science and technology, and culture.

Fourthly, the emergence and development of socialist countries, the rise and progress of the vast number of Asian, African, and Latin American developing countries that have gained national independence and liberation, and the struggle of workers and other progressive forces in the Western countries promoted the governments of the Western countries to learn from the principles or policies of the socialist countries and adopt measures to increase social welfare and other improvements in people's livelihood of the working people. This is also conducive to the alleviation of internal contradictions, the promotion of social stability, and the promotion of economic and technological development in Western countries.

Fifthly, the camp confrontation and market division between the East and the West, especially the complicated world political and economic situation caused by the scramble of the two superpowers (the United States and the Soviet Union) for supremacy, brought many unfavorable serious influences and constraints on the common development of the countries of the world and the progress of human civilization. With the drastic changes in East Europe and the disintegration of the Soviet Union, the second round of economic globalization came to an end.

3. *The third round of economic globalization*

This round of economic globalization is a period in which some Western powers severely weakened their economic strength and overall national strength due to the implementation of neoliberalism while emerging economies of developing countries grew stronger from the perspective of the international political and economic order and its basic characteristics.

The main historical trajectory of this economic globalization can be summarized from the following aspects.

First, due to the drastic changes in East Europe and the disintegration of the Soviet Union, the political and economic situation of the camp confrontation and market division between the East and the West, and the scramble of two superpowers (the United States and the Soviet Union) for supremacy changed, which objectively provided favorable political and economic conditions for all countries and regions in the East and the West and the South and the North to achieve their respective development and progress in the global unified market via mutual competition and cooperation.

Second, some countries in the West did not correctly estimate the political and economic situation in the world. They thought that after the upheaval in East Europe and the disintegration of the Soviet Union, socialist forces would disappear in this world, and capitalist forces would dominate the world forever. The idea that the capitalist liberal democratic system has become "the ultimate form of the human government and all countries will approach it in various forms" proposed by Francis Fukuyama in *The End of History* is the concentrated representation of this political thought. In particular, after the collapse of the Soviet Union, the United States, as the only superpower in the world, relied on its own super strength to continue to pursue hegemonism and power politics in politics, interfere in the internal affairs of other countries, provoke ethnic conflicts, and create local wars. Moreover, the United States economically promoted neo-liberalism centered on operational liberalization and worked with other Western powers to dominate economic globalization. The key to neoliberalism is to promote privatization, advocate market-only theory and oppose government intervention and regulation of the market, reduce the social welfare of the people, limit the rights and functions of trade unions, continue to pursue the "jungle law" and "zero-sum game" in the market competition, attach various economic and political conditions to economic and technological cooperation, and so on. Through their various multinational corporations, they promoted this neoliberal economic model to developing countries in Latin America, Asia, and Africa in order to control the finance, investment, industry, resources, and product sales markets of developing countries and thus obtain huge monopoly profits and limit the economic development and social progress of developing countries. As a result, consecutive financial and economic crises occurred in some developing countries in Latin America and other regions. However, the neoliberalism pursued by Western states is also a double-edged sword. Western multinational companies transferred huge amounts of capital, industry, and services to developing countries to make huge profits, which had a serious impact on their domestic development, such as the hollowing out of industries, especially some real economies, the rising unemployment rate of workers, and the sharply increasing gap between the rich and the poor. As a result, the financial and economic crisis that began with the subprime mortgage crisis in the United States in 2007 almost swept the whole world. Shortly after the outbreak of this economic crisis, in the autumn of 2011, from the United States to Europe, a series of "occupation" movements of the public took place, which was actually a manifestation of the development of the economic crisis into a social and political crisis. This economic and social-political crisis was the most profound in the West since the Second World War. It broke out from the core powers of the West and had an extraordinary historical influence. Its occurrence not only marks the unprecedented sharpness and seriousness of the internal contradictions of the Western capitalist system, but also marks the failure of the neoliberalism economic model. Moreover, it marks that the theory that capitalism is the final form of the human social system is wrong.

Third, in stark contrast to the economic and political situation in Western countries, after 40 years of reform and opening-up and modernization, China has opened up a correct path of building socialism with Chinese characteristics and formed a unique Chinese development model. The basic features of this development model are as follows. In terms of politics, under the leadership of the CPC, the socialist democratic system in which the people are the masters of the country is politically implemented. In terms of economy, the basic economic system in which public ownership is the mainstay and diverse forms of ownership develop side by side is implemented, and the socialist market economic system combines planning and market and plays the role of the guidance and regulation of the state and the decisive role of the market in resource allocation is implemented. In terms of external relations, opening to the outside world on the basis of independence and self-reliance is implemented. The use of domestic markets and resources is combined with foreign markets and resources, and the "bring in" is combined with "going out." Moreover, China not only actively learns foreign advanced technology, advanced management experience, and all useful things, but also insists on equal treatment, mutual benefit, and win-win cooperation in various economic and technological areas. Because the CPC closely relies on the diligence and wisdom of the Chinese people, adheres to the path of socialism with

Chinese characteristics, and adheres to the development model that conforms to China's national conditions, after 40 years of reform and opening-up, China has grown rapidly and created a development miracle that has attracted worldwide attention. China's economic aggregate has climbed to second place in the world. The Chinese people are confidently moving forward toward the realization of the great rejuvenation of the Chinese nation and the grand goal of building China into a great socialist power. Instead of disappearing from the world because of the drastic changes in East Europe and the disintegration of the Soviet Union, the world socialist forces represented by China are full of new vitality and are becoming a pivotal political, economic, and cultural force that promotes world development and human civilization. This fact also fully demonstrates that the theory of "the end of history" that the human social system will end up in the capitalist system is completely untenable. It is worth mentioning that even Francis Fukuyama, the proposer of "the end of history" theory, has to admit that Western democracy is in recession and that China and Russia "have become more confident and stronger" while the free and democratic countries in the United States and Europe are losing their appeal.

Fourth, in addition to China, a number of emerging economies have emerged in developing countries, such as Russia, India, South Africa, and Brazil. The common experience of their development is to actively participate in economic globalization. They fully used the favorable conditions provided by economic globalization to promote their own economic and social development and did not blindly copy the neoliberalism model. Instead, they proceeded from their own national conditions. They took their own road of developing the national economy, thus making important achievements in the growth of economic power and overall national strength. China and these emerging economies support each other and cooperate to promote common development through the Shanghai Cooperation Organization, the Eurasian Economic Union, the BRICS, and other forms of cooperative organization. They have made important contributions to supporting the development of a vast number of developing countries, presiding over fairness and justice in the international community and the international order, opposing hegemonic power politics, and maintaining world and regional peace. These emerging economies are becoming an important force for maintaining the multilateral trade and multilateral economic and technological cooperation system in economic globalization and have brought new experiences and hope for improving global governance and establishing a more just and rational international economic and political order.

Fifth, some Western powers did not learn from the economic, social, and political crisis that occurred in 2008 and the serious consequences of neoliberalism and hegemonism, and did not make a correct analysis of and learn from the growth of China and other emerging economies. On the contrary, they believe that the development of China and other emerging economies is realized by grabbing the wealth from the Western powers through economic globalization and snatching their market and technology patents. In this context, they provoke trade frictions, ignore the multilateral cooperation systems and rules in economic globalization, and engage in unilateralism, protectionism, and national egoism. It is obviously unwise to adopt this kind of bullying practice against economic globalization. It is not conducive to improving his own economic, social, and political situation and could not prevent the development of China and other developing countries or reverse the trend of economic globalization. In the end, it will only promote the vast number of developing countries and all countries that abide by the principles of fairness and justice of the international community to explore and open up a new way of economic globalization more firmly.

Looking back at the historical process and trajectory of the three rounds of economic globalization, we can and should get the following basic lessons.

First, the course and facts of economic globalization fully demonstrate that it is not feasible to engage in colonialism of other countries and nations in the world, and the history of colonialism is gone forever. The sovereignty and territorial integrity of any country and nation must be respected. All countries, big or small, strong or weak, rich or poor, should be equal. Any country should not bully small, weak, and poor countries and should not commit any form of aggression, plunder, and oppression against other countries and nations.

Second, the history and facts of economic globalization also fully demonstrate that it is not feasible to engage in hegemonism and power politics against other countries and nations. The hegemony exerted by one or two superpowers will surely become a thing of the past. Any form of hegemony, in the end, will harm both other countries and the hegemonic country. A new type of international relations characterized by mutual respect, fairness, justice, and win-win cooperation should be established between countries, the West and the East or the North and the South. This is the only correct way for coexistence between different countries and nations.

Third, the course and facts of economic globalization have fully demonstrated that it is not feasible to engage in unilateralism against economic globalization and to engage in protectionism and isolationism in today's world. Today, The world is in a period of great development, great change, and great adjustment. World multi-polarization, economic globalization, society informatization, and cultural diversification are objective, inevitable, and irreversible trends that do not depend on people's will. Countries and regions and all mankind face many common challenges. No country can cope with these challenges alone, and no country can exist like an isolated island.

Fourth, the course and facts of economic globalization have fully demonstrated that the promotion of neoliberalism in today's world, its use as the dominant idea of economic globalization, and its economic cooperation model are not feasible. The unprecedented profound economic and socio-political crisis, the vicious competition in the market and the hollowing out of the industry, and the serious aggravation of polarization between the rich and the poor caused by neoliberalism have made it come to a dead end. To promote the healthy development of economic globalization, we must explore and select new guiding ideologies and new modes of cooperation that can truly reflect the principles of fairness and reasonableness. This has become an inevitable requirement of history and the common will and aspiration of all countries and peoples pursuing development and progress in the world today.

By summarizing and drawing on the basic historical experiences and lessons of the three rounds of economic globalization and scientifically analyzing the current development situation of the world economy and politics, the main features of the trend of the times and the challenges faced by mankind, Chinese President Xi Jinping proposed the important idea of "building a community with a shared future for mankind" in 2013. This provides a Chinese program full of Chinese wisdom for promoting the common development of all countries in the world, the new progress in human civilization, the improvement of global governance, the establishment of a more just and rational international economic and political order, and the realization and development of new economic globalization.

III. Building a Community with a Shared Future for Mankind: The Historical Necessity of World Development and the Progress of Human Civilization

President Xi Jinping advocated the important idea of building a community with a shared future for mankind in the world at a number of international occasions and conferences after he successively proposed the new international cooperation and construction initiative of constructing the "Silk Road Economic Belt" and the "21st Century Maritime Silk Road," which is now known as the "Belt and Road" in September and October 2013. The construction of the "Belt and Road" is closely related to the construction of a community with a shared future for mankind, and their spiritual essence is consistent. It can be said that whether it is to promote the new international cooperation construction of the BRI or to improve global governance, establish a more just and rational international political and economic order, and achieve new economic globalization, they all serve the building of a community with a shared future for mankind. The proposition of this major proposition and important idea has pointed out the correct direction for the future development of the world and established a bright future for the future progress of human civilization.

Next, I would like to talk about some understandings and views around the issue of building a community with a shared future for mankind.

First, the proposal to build a community with a shared future for mankind has been widely recognized and supported by the international community.

After President Xi Jinping advocated building a community with a shared future for mankind, the people of all countries and regions, especially those who pay close attention to the development of the world and the destiny of mankind, including some political leaders, political party leaders, experts and scholars, and heads of relevant media and international organizations in many countries expressed their appreciation and made comments. The views and comments are summarized as follows. First, it is a strong voice of the times that China advocates building a community with a shared future for mankind in the context that some big powers make the utmost effort to promote egotism, unilateralism, and hegemonic politics. It will guide and inspire the people of all countries to work together to build an equal, open, peaceful, and prosperous world, which will benefit not only the Chinese people but also the people of the world. This is China's outstanding contribution to the world today. Second, the concept of building a community with a shared future for mankind reveals the objective laws that various countries are interdependent and the destiny of humanity is closely linked, conforms to the trend of the times of peace, development, cooperation, and win-win and accurately grasps the development trend of the world and human society. It will profoundly affect the future and destiny of human society and will surely point the way forward for the development of human society. Thirdly, in the context that the current international community faces many challenges, such as terror, power, war, disparity between the rich and the poor, and environmental pollution, and no effective solutions have been found, President Xi Jinping proposed to build a community with a shared future for mankind and work together to build a better world. It will surely provide an effective solution that meets the interests of all parties in order to solve the challenges faced by mankind. Moreover, this is another new option beyond the capitalist system that cannot solve these challenges. It is in line with Marxist purposes of liberating and benefiting all mankind and will surely receive the support of the people of the world. Fourthly, China's idea of building a community with a shared future for mankind is a new global view that advocates countries of different social systems, ideologies, historical civilizations, and levels of development to seek common ground while reserving differences and seeking inclusive development. This fully demonstrates the broad mind and mission of the CPC and the Chinese people. This also fully demonstrates that this concept completely abandons the Cold War mentality and is completely demarcated from the hegemonism, the jungle law, and the zero-sum game, which will strongly promote the establishment of a new international political and economic order and the realization of the new economic globalization. Therefore, building a community with a shared future for mankind should be the common goal and common ideal of the people of all countries. Since it quickly gained wide consensus in the international community, the United Nations wrote it into the UN resolution on February 10, 2017, put it into the Security Council resolution on March 17, 2017, and put it into the UN Human Rights Council resolution on March 23, 2017. It can be firmly believed that the idea of building a community with a shared future for mankind will continue to bloom its ideological light, and its era and historical value will be eternal.

Second, building a community with a shared future for mankind is the creative use and development of Chinese historical wisdom such as "the whole world as one community," "a world of great harmony" "Harmony is most precious," and "The whole world is at peace."

The ancient Chinese sages put forward the philosophy of "harmony in diversity" very early. In the early years of the Zhou Dynasty in China around 3,000 years ago, there was a man named Shi Bo who proposed the ideas of "Everything being derived from the state of harmony" and "Harmony generates and sameness stops/stifles vitality" that reflected "harmony in diversity." At the end of the Spring and Autumn Period in China, Confucianism, founded by Confucius, inherited this idea. "Harmony in diversity" means that different things are in unity and symbiotic with each other. They are opposite and unified. They compete and fight against each other and learn from each other to enhance advantage and avoid disadvantage and promote the mutual transformation of things, so that new things can be produced and developed and society can develop and progress. "Harmony generates and sameness stops/stifles vitality" means that if unity is composed of the same things, and the things always remain the same without unification of opposites, mutual contradictions and struggles, and mutual learning, then it is impossible to achieve the transformation of things or produce and develop new things. As a result, the development of things will stop, and the progress of society will stop. This does not conform to the development laws of worldly things and society. Therefore, the idea of "harmony in diversity" is an important and basic philosophical thought that reflects the law of the development of things and society.

In ancient China, Chinese ancestors, especially the rulers and governors of the country, knew very early on how to apply the philosophy of "harmony in diversity" to the governance of the state and society and use it to deal with the social relations within the country and the relations between different countries. Thus, the political thoughts of "All under heaven are equal," "A world of universal harmony," "people-oriented," "Harmony is most precious," "All nations live side by side in perfect harmony," and "The whole world is at peace" were formed. These ideas were expressed and recorded in the historical books of the period before the Qin Dynasty in China.

The chapter "Li Yun" in *The Book of Rites*, which is one of the "Five Classics" of Confucian classics, states, "The supreme political ideal is that the whole world is one community," "For the world to be one community is great harmony." That is to say, "the world" comprises many different people, families, communities, nations, and countries. It is not individually owned by a family, community, nation, or country but jointly owned by all people, families, communities, nations, and countries. The thoughts of "the whole world as one community" and "a world of great harmony" are based on the "people-oriented" political ideology. The thought of "the whole world as one community" means that the whole world shall serve people. It will be meaningless without the people of the world. If the people of the world cannot settle down, get rich, and share happiness together, then there will be no "world of great harmony." All kinds of different people, families, communities, nations, and countries should respect each other, contain each other, and treat each other as equals. If they encounter differences, disputes, and struggles, they should coordinate with each other, seek common ground while reserving differences, and properly handle them. The differences shall not result in secession, and the struggle shall not result in breaking. Whether in the social relationship within a country or in the international relationship between different countries, only by following the above fundamental thoughts, can we achieve mutual harmony, stability, and tranquility and open up the way for common development, progress, and prosperity.

The gist of the fundamental thoughts such as "Harmony is most precious," "All nations live side by side in perfect harmony," and "The whole world is at peace," used in ancient China to deal with state-to-state relations, is to advocate peaceful coexistence between nations and pursue harmony. The thought of "Harmony is most precious" stems from *The Analects of Confucius*. The thought of "All nations live side by side in perfect harmony" stems from *The Book of Documents* in the

Western Zhou Dynasty. The thought of "The whole world is at peace" stems from *Yi Zhuan* in the Warring States Period. During the Spring and Autumn and Warring States periods, China was in transition from a slave society to a feudal society. The surrounding and domestic attached tribal states and vassal states were everywhere. People hoped that they would not meet on the battlefield and that the world could be peaceful. However, the subjective will cannot replace the objective reality. During the Spring and Autumn and Warring States periods from the Western Zhou Dynasty to the Eastern Zhou Dynasty, the wars between the various attached tribal states and vassal states were frequent, causing the displacement of the people, the national secession, and the social unrest. As stated in Chinese historical records, there was no war of justice in the Spring and Autumn Period. Confucius and his disciples, as well as other pre-Qin thinkers, summed up this lesson, proposed and advocated the thoughts of "harmony is most precious," "getting along with virtuous people," and "all the people of the world are brothers." After Qin Shi Huang unified China, he gradually took the thoughts of "Harmony is most precious" and "The whole world is at peace" as China's principle of dealing with diplomatic relations with neighboring and distant countries. In this context, in general, China and its neighboring and distant countries were able to maintain friendly relations of good neighborliness and peaceful exchanges for a long time. Such an external environment was also an important historical condition for China to become one of the main creators of Eastern civilization.

Of course, the facts of history have repeatedly shown that in the feudal society in which a few people ruled the majority for a long time in the history of China, the rulers did not and could not truly implement the political thoughts of "the whole world as one community" "a world of great harmony," "people-oriented," "Harmony is most precious," "All nations live side by side in perfect harmony," and "The whole world is at peace." In this context, it was impossible to truly realize "people-oriented" and "the whole world as one community" in the country and fully realize "Harmony is most precious" and "The whole world is at peace" in the international society. However, these thoughts reflect the historical truths of the laws governing the development of human society and embody the advanced political thoughts and beautiful social ideals of affinity to the people and democracy. As the essence of Chinese traditional culture, these thoughts are passed down through the constant pursuit of the Chinese people and the working people who are committed to social progress.

Ever since the foundation of the CPC, its overarching guideline of "serving the people heart and soul," as well as the diplomatic Five Principles of Peaceful Coexistence, have never been shaken in the almost a-hundred-year-long revolution, development, and reform together with the whole Chinese nation. The recently proposed idea that domestically, to put people first, push forward the building of socialism with Chinese characteristics and realize rejuvenation as well as common prosperity, and meanwhile internationally, to practice the BRI and build a community with a shared future for mankind on the basis of extensive consultation, joint contribution, and shared benefits are all demonstration and evolution for the old wisdom like "put people at the core," "the whole world as one community" "a world of great harmony," "harmony is a priority," "universal peace," and all the efforts made by CPC are also embodiment of those advanced thoughts and lofty dreams in the current world and society.

Thoughts like "the whole world as one community" and "a world of great harmony" are advocated by civilizations of numerous countries. From Aristotle's saying, "Man should live in harmony with each other," the concept of "cosmopolitanism" introduced by European Enlightenment scholars, former Indian President Nehru's "one world, one family," to various kinds of communities following the Second World War, all display such ideas from different perspectives, layers, and degrees. Old wisdom for building a community with a shared future for mankind cannot merely be found in Confucianism and Chinese traditional culture but also in civilizations worldwide. All parties, especially historians around the globe, shall work hard to tap the deep reservoirs of wisdom and shed new light on it to consolidate a common theoretical and political foundation for the community with a shared future.

Third, basic principles shall be adhered to in building a community with a shared future for mankind.

Building a community with a shared future is a groundbreaking feat in human history and an ideal pursued by people of all countries. There is no way to fulfill such an aspiration in one stroke, and it calls for an enduring endeavor by all people. A thousand-mile journey starts with single steps. So which principles shall be followed to secure sound progress of such a grand undertaking? When taking an overview of human history and drawing lessons from different times, especially from colonialism, multiple economic crises, two world wars, cold wars, hegemonism, and neoliberalism periods after the first economic globalization, deliberation shall be conducted by specialists from various countries and regions to forge consensus as for what principals need to be abided by. Following are some primary ideas as food for thought.

Universal development and prosperity. This is out of the fundamental target and development roadmap for building a community with a shared future for mankind.

The truth is that there are inevitable disparities among countries of various kinds. The major difference, however, lies in social systems, namely capitalist, socialist, and others, which gives rise to ideological divisions. The second is the misunderstandings caused by various ethnic groups and religious beliefs. The third is the giant gap in development level, national income, and livelihood between the mostly developed northern area and developing nations in the South. To realize universal development and prosperity calls for equality, inclusiveness, coexistence, mutual support, and win-win cooperation regardless of social systems, ethnic groups or religions, level of economic development, and joining hands for a shared target. On the other hand, hegemonism, imposing power, unilateralism, nation egoism, jungle law, zero-sum game, and obstacles of any form that sabotages common economic and political development shall be objected to and eliminated. Universal development and prosperity hinge not only on the direction in forging a community with a shared future for mankind, but on the constant progress of human society and civilization as well.

Equal exchanges and mutual learning. Building a community with a shared future for mankind needs to draw wisdom from various civilizations. In this process, countries and regions will surely take part in their own political, cultural, and value perspectives stemming from specific civilizations and give play to the practical role of their respective historical civilizations. In the meantime, the inheritance and progress of all the good traditions as well as wisdom are exactly what a community of shared future needs. Civilizations of various countries and regions can be categorized from various angles. For instance, Mesopotamian,

Egyptian, Chinese, Indian, Greece, and Roman civilizations are all ancient cultures; when put into regions, civilizations can then be classified as Asian, African, European, American, and Oceanic ones; as for social systems, primitive, slave, feudal, capitalist, and socialist cultures can be listed. All civilizations are the results of history with their unique characters and strengths, and each, as part of the world treasure house, shall be respected equally. All civilizations impose indispensable effects on human beings' advances from the day they were shaped. Any civilization, regardless of its originating period, region, type, or form, composes the whole splendid and colorful human civilization. There are only differences in the timing, region, and social background for the generation and existence of a civilization, but it doesn't mean which one is better or worse. The contributions made by various cultures are equally important. Meanwhile, it is undeniable that every culture has its strengths and weaknesses. No culture is perfect or useless, so it is unwise to "bully" others out of high arrogance. Above all, the following principles shall be obeyed for better relations among various civilizations: first, to be interdependent rather than repellent to each other; second, to treat other cultures with equal respect rather than be highly discriminatory and show great egoism; third, to learn from each other rather than refuse or even try to replace it. Only in this way can civilizations of all kinds co-exist in harmony, realize common progress, make all flowers blossom together, give advantage to their merits, and thus do good for the construction of a community with a shared future for mankind. This is also the target of the community, and it is predictable that the day when the community is shaped will also witness an all-time high cultural peak.

The balance of justice and interests as well as mutual benefit. It is necessary to strike a balance between righteousness and benefit to build a community with a shared future for mankind.

For any country, any nation in this world, no matter how the state condition is or what development road it takes, to make constant progress all calls for a balance between justice and benefit, and we shall always put justice first. One should never forget the moral standards for getting benefits. The so-called "morality" can be extended to social morality, faith, justice, and friendship, which are social ethical codes in safeguarding public warfare, whereas the so-called "benefit" covers individuals and groups and can be general or specific. Lessons from both history and reality all show that only by combining morality and benefit in a dialectic way and putting morality in a priority position can economic development and social prosperity be boosted. Adam Smith's two masterpieces, *An Inquiry into the Nature and Causes of the Wealth of Nations* and *The Theory of Moral Sentiments*, illuminate the importance of the market on economic development and morality in society, respectively, which echo the coordination between morality and benefit as well. History and reality tell us that without a balance of benefit and morality, a total free of capital on the market will lead to economic chaos, tremendously jeopardizing individuals, groups, and even countries. A country or nation seeking benefit regardless of morality or giving rein to the market without constraint from ethics, laws, or government will eventually collapse. A society laying little emphasis on morality, loyalty, honesty, justice, or ethics but only pursuing personal good or small profit instead of public warfare or other nations' benefit will subject itself to a place of moral bankruptcy and social and economic instability. Can such a society reach economic development? Can there be a sound market? Can people's personal and general benefits be protected? The answer is absolute no. Above all, an appropriate concept of morality and benefit is key to a country's economic prospects and social stability.

By the same token, such a concept can be essential in maintaining relations among countries as a guideline. Countries, be they large or small, strong or weak, shall balance morality and benefit while always putting morality first, and only by doing this can there be respect, trust, and support among each other rather than bullying or treachery. This is also a guideline ensuring mutual benefit when dealing with different countries of various stakeholders. No matter whether trade, economic, technical, or other cooperation, one shall always take into consideration others' benefit and strive for common progress. It is advisable to shoulder risks proactively in a crisis. All parties enjoy achievement and development while sharing responsibilities, which should always be followed in relations with countries and regions. Instead, the jungle law, zero-sum game, and winner-takes-all are arrogant and should be discarded. Under current conditions where countries and regions are closely interlinked, it is especially evident that "loss affects all," so no single country can have prosperity by undermining others nor remain stable when others are still in turbulence. A community with a shared future for mankind has always been established on the basis of a community with shared benefits. Thus, the principle of balancing morality and benefit shall be the sole "way" of treating relations among countries and regions and is also the only measure in forming, developing, and safeguarding the community with a shared future for mankind.

Stick to the extensive consultation, joint contribution, shared benefits, and all-win principle. This requirement is proposed as it is necessary to properly exert and gather global power for common contribution and improve global governance to create a community with a shared future for mankind.

As there were many international construction projects called "cooperation" and global economic and political governance projects, what was the typical case for them? Most of them were controlled by a few powerful nations and developed countries. It was not a case of equality and mutual trust as these powerful nations and developed countries granted a lot of economic and political privileges for themselves and imposed a number of economic and political conditions upon counterparties. The counterparties acted under their command and served for them, even purely as their enslaved laborers. They got the most results from the "cooperation." Maybe they have "bestowed" you something, which in turn was taken back in a certain way. You could only be their low-cost resource suppliers or enslaved laborers. The so-called "cooperation" was what colonialism, hegemonism, great-power chauvinism, etc., did. As a result, strong countries became stronger and stronger, weak countries became weaker and weaker, rich countries became richer and richer, and poor countries became poorer and poorer. This is very common in today's international society. Extensive developing countries have received, and now can't stand, the pain and humiliation. To govern the globe in this way will get worse and worse, and it will not allow progress.

It is clear that the "extensive consultation, joint contribution, and shared benefits" principle proposed by China's President Xi Jinping, who is currently working on a new international cooperation way of BRI, and a new global governance view proposed on such basis are completely in contrast to the above unfair case. The new international cooperation way and the new global governance view are the fundamental methods and construction principles that should be consistently followed to create a community with a shared future for mankind.

Once proposed, it was widely recognized and supported by many countries and regions all over the world, including many Western developed countries. We believe the new international cooperation way and the new global governance view could stand the test of history.

The referred "extensive consultation" means that neither of the cooperating parties has the final say over an infrastructure or other economic project under cooperation. Still, both parties should be listened to and respected, and decisions should be made through consultation for both parties' interests. During the consultation, the parties should ensure that the cooperation project is suitable to the actual situation and needs of the country or region where the project is located. Only in this way could the development and implementation of the cooperation project be stable and reliable to realize the goal of partnerships for mutual benefits. The referred "joint contribution" means that the cooperating parties will exert their respective financial, labor, strategic, and technical strengths to jointly contribute to the cooperation project in the same boat. During contribution, the cooperating parties are required not only to share opportunities for development but to work together to overcome challenges and difficulties, resolve contradictions, and share risks. Only in this way could the contribution succeed. The referred "shared benefits" means that all the benefits and results from the cooperation project should be shared in a fair and impartial manner among the cooperating parties in proportion to their contributions so that the cooperating parties reasonably obtain what they deserve. The cooperating parties are equal partners and cannot play the bully. Otherwise, there would be unreasonable and unfair allocation of benefits and results, finally leading to unsuccessful cooperation.

"Extensive consultation, joint contribution, shared benefits, and all win" can be shorted as "shared governance and all win." "Consultation" and "contribution" can be referred to as shared governance, and "shared benefits" substantially mean "all win." All these terms highlight "con-" or "shared," which is the essence and key to describing the new way and new global governance view for creating a community with a shared future for mankind. The word "new" clings to the "con-" or "shared." The way and view containing the spirits of the "con-" or "shared" conforms to the requirement of historical materialism. Under basic principles of historical materialism, in the long run, a country should be determined and governed based on the common will and wishes of the people of the country. Thus, the world should be determined and governed based on the common will and wishes of the people of the world. Global governance should involve all joint powers and forces from all countries over the world, including North, South, East, and West. This is also reflected by President Xi Jinping's speech before the National Congress of Brazil on July 16, 2014. He said that "a nation's affairs should be handled by the people of the nation, and the world's destiny should be controlled by the people of all nations, and the world's affairs handled by the governments and people of all nations through consultation." In conclusion, this way and view, described as contribution, shared benefits, and all win, or as shared governance and all win, is historically materialistic and democratic. History will prove that global governance will be improved consistently as long as people apply such way a view, and the creation of a community with a shared future for mankind will move ahead from a success phase to a new success phase.

Stick to the "peaceful coexistence and tranquil world" principle. This requirement is proposed as it is necessary to correctly develop safe relations with other countries and regions over the world and establish a peaceful and tranquil international environment for creating a community with a shared future for mankind.

The growth of a nation, a region, or the whole world and the creation of a common community with a shared future for mankind can't be done without a peaceful and tranquil international environment. Otherwise, nothing will be accomplished. Peace and development remain the underlying trends of our times. Indeed, they are the call of the times. To remain peaceful and developing is the common will and universal desire of the people all over the world and has become an irresistible trend of the times. Peace is a prerequisite for development, and development is a source of strength for maintaining peace. They are dialectical unity and complement each other. Peaceful coexistence as a basic principle in dealing with international relations was initially developed by China, India, Myanmar, etc., in the 1950s. The Five Principles of Peaceful Coexistence adopted at the Bandung Conference of developing and non-aligned countries have long been the general rules of the international community. It can be expected that a world of lasting peace and universal security will come. Thus, a peaceful and safe international environment will be provided for creating a community with a shared future for mankind with joint efforts made by all people over the world as long as we stick to the "peaceful coexistence and tranquil world" principle.

As proven by historical and empirical analysis, to stick to the "peaceful coexistence and tranquil world" principle in the international community, properly handle international relations, and create a world of lasting peace and universal security, all people over the world should work together as follows. First, we should truly learn from past wars and make it a common view of all countries and regions. From the Peloponnesian War in the 5th century BC, through the Thirty Years' War in Europe in the first half of the 17th century, then to the two world wars in the 20th century, further to the more than 40 years Cold War between East and West, the lessons we have learned were painful and profound. These hot wars and cold wars bring disaster and destruction to the world and all regions therein. All these repeatedly prove that national peace makes the world safe and that national fighting makes the world chaotic. Experience, if not forgotten, is a guide for the future. The militaristic practice of a nation is harmful not only to other nations and the world but also to its own people. In deeply learning historical lessons from the past wars and maintaining a hard-earned peaceful world, all nations all over the world should make a concerted effort to confront and solve various conventional and unconventional threats and take preventive measures at the very beginning. To make the concepts, i.e., hostility into friendship and swords into plowshares, rooted in mind is the only way to create a tranquil world. Second, All nations and regions should abandon any hot war or cold war desire and build a common, synthetic, cooperative, and sustainable new security concept. Among nations, there should be partnerships that choose dialogue over confrontation and partnership over alliance, new international relations of being partners without mutual threat, and mutual relations in each nation or region should respect others' core interests and big concerns. Any conflict, contradiction, or dispute should be resolved through mutual consultation to prevent deterioration and the occurrence of clash and war. We should keep in mind that in no case is a nation's or region's safety built on the turmoil of any other nation or region. The Confucian doctrine that "do unto others as you would be done" and that "the man of humanity wishing to be successful himself, seeks to help others to be successful; wishing to develop himself, seeks to help others to develop" told the truth long before. Third, we should respect the sovereignty of other countries and never interfere in their internal affairs. The principle of sovereign equality underpins the UN Charter. The principle of sovereignty not only means that all countries' sovereignty and territorial integrity are inviolable but also that their internal affairs are not subject to interference. It also means that all countries' right to independently choose social systems and development paths should be upheld and that all countries' endeavors to promote economic and social development and improve their people's lives should be respected. The principle of sovereign equality did not suddenly fall down but was deprived of past experiences in which other countries' sovereignty was violated, and other countries' internal affairs were interfered with. Thus, it should be cherished. The peaceful coexistence and universal safety will be realized only if each country respects others' sovereignty and does not interfere with others' internal affairs. Fourth, we should strictly fight against various forms of hegemonism, power politics, great-power chauvinism, and national egoism. No countries, especially great, strong, and rich, can prac-tice or permit hegemonism, power politics, chauvinism, or egoism. The historical facts repeatedly prove that hegemonism, power politics, and great-power coex-istence, like colonialism, ignore the principle of sovereignty equality, follow the principles of allowing the big ones to bully the small and the rich to suppress the poor, the strong bully the weak, and embrace the jungle law and the zero-sum game. The logic of national egoism is to seek one's own benefits regardless of impact on others and place one's profits on others' damage and sorrow. In short, hegemonism, power politics, great-power chauvinism, and national egoism are the ideological and political roots of conflicts and wars among manufacturing countries and regions, even in the world. It is impossible to establish a world of lasting peace and universal security and make the construction of a community with a shared future for mankind meaningful if we do not fight against them and strive to eliminate these bad thoughts.

Fourth, it is necessary to realize new economic globalization to create a community with a shared future for mankind.

There have been three times of economic globalization in the progress of human society, and economic globalization is and will continue. It has become the historical and inexorable trend of the world's economic development and thus is irreversible. The creation of a community with a shared future for mankind is accompanied necessarily by economic globalization. A community with a shared future for mankind is built on a community with shared benefits, and the two communities are closely linked. In turn, the creation of a community with shared benefits for mankind is on the foundation of the creation of a community with shared economic benefits. Therefore, economic globalization is an indispensable global economic platform and the only approach to creating communities with shared benefits and a shared future for mankind.

However, it should be noted that regarding the three times of economic globalization we have experienced, notwithstanding major contributions to the world's economic development, there are a lot of problems, challenges, and shortcomings. Economic globalization might be unsustainable if we continue the old-fashioned running mode, operating path, or thinking way, except that we hasten to research and present solutions to the problems, take countermeasures against the challenges, and revolutionarily remove the shortcomings. It does not mean that economic globalization will be suspended or will end. Actually, economic globalization will never suspend or end. This means that if the problems, challenges, and shortcomings existing in economic globalization are not solved, it will not move ahead in a correct and sound direction. Thus, the new economic globalization will never appear.

Here, I would like to make a few remarks on evil practices in economic globalization. What are evil practices that deviate economic globalization from a sound development direction? For short, the dominant running mode is lagged, the operating path is deviated, and there are serious errors in the rules and thoughts. Firstly, why do we consider the dominant running mode of economic globalization lagged? Up to now, economic globalization has always been led by one or a few Western great powers, i.e., developed capitalist countries. We should recognize that they have played contributing and positive roles in facilitating and promoting economic globalization. However, at present, with the same dominant mode, extensive developing countries and other countries that exercise different social systems do not actually participate in or jointly lead economic globalization. This does not conform to the principle of democracy in international relations. In addition, we should note that it is very difficult to prevent and avoid errors of any kind in making running decisions, determining running rules and procedures, and selecting advanced thoughts as guidelines unless all countries and regions over the world work together in certain consulting and brainstorming manner to jointly lead the economic globalization. Secondly, why do we consider the operating path of economic globalization deviated? In the operating path of economic globalization, some countries have always practiced protectionism and egoism in trade contacts and economic & technical partnerships. For example, in recent years, some Western countries, under the banner of "self-priority," disregarded trade liberalization and multilateral trading regimes, multilateral economic and technical cooperation systems, and other operating rules of economic globalization and did unilateralism, protectionism, and egoism vigorously. It has developed into a case where it has existed for a long time but has become even more violent now. This has become a serious barrier to normal operation and sound development of economic globalization at present. Thirdly, why do we say there are serious errors in the rules and thoughts? Over hundreds of years since economic globalization commenced initially, the jungle law, win or lose, winner-takes-all, and other thoughts have dominated. As human society has entered the 21st century, it is the trend of the times that all the countries seek common development and prosperity. Isn't the case where some great Western powers continue such "rules" and "thoughts" a serious error in the times? It is the dominance of the "rules" and "thoughts" that leads to huge development and wealth gaps between developed and developing countries and thus has a strong impact on the stable and common development of the world. Now, it is the time to replace such old-fashioned "rules" and "thoughts" with new ones. Only if all the countries over the world jointly confront the problems and challenges existing in economic globalization, particularly the shortcomings, draw lessons from the past, jointly seek solutions and countermeasures against the problems, challenges, and shortcomings, and jointly determine the new mode, new patch, new rules, and new thoughts for the economic globalization, the economic globalization will be enabled to get rid of current difficulties and dilemmas and turn to new economic globalization of a more democratic, fair, and reasonable style.

On October 11, Enrique Encasodecasco, a professor at Universidad CEU San Pablo, issued an article titled "Toward New Globalization" on a Spain-based international website. It states that economic globalization has entered a transition period, and "it is very difficult to accurately forecast where it will go," "but it will certainly deviate from the current form with which we are familiar."

What I have talked about above is basically the same as what Prof. Enrique Encasodecasco explained in his article. We can expect that among people who hold such opinions and views, whether they are from the East or the West, the South or the North of the world, and whether they are politicians, scholars, or others on all sides, more and more people are reaching a consensus on expecting the arrival of a new economic globalization, and that such expectation is becoming the common will and voice of people in regions and countries around the world.

Similarly, by drawing lessons from the past on economic globalization and by meeting the requirements of the trend of the times on peace, development, cooperation, and mutual benefit, the new economic globalization or the fourth economic globalization that we want to achieve in the future should have many new features, and a new pattern is formed; it should be an economic globalization which countries around the world not only participate in but also play their active roles; an economic globalization under which we continue to adhere to and uphold, and keep improving, making innovations in and developing the rules and systems that have been fully proved correct and effective through practice such as trade liberalization, multilateral trade cooperation system and multilateral economic and technical cooperation system; an economic globalization under which hegemony and power, the jungle law and zero-sum game are eliminated, and the guiding thought of achieving shared growth through discussion and collaboration that truly embodies democracy, equality, justice, and reasonableness is carried out; and an economic globalization that helps continuously promote world peace and stability and common development and prosperity. We should believe that, with the joint efforts of the governments and peoples of countries in the world, such new economic globalization, as an inevitable requirement for building a community with a shared future for mankind, will be sure to come and that it must be able to establish a broader world economic platform with greater vigor and vitality and lay more abundant material and technological foundation for building a community with a shared future for mankind.

Fifth, promoting new international cooperation development through the BRI is a strategic measure for building a community with a shared future for mankind.

It has been five years since President Xi proposed pursuing the BRI and began to implement it. Over the past five years, this new international cooperation development has become a broad consensus of the international community. More and more countries are participating in this cooperation development, and their cooperation projects are steadily increasing. This is a good beginning. As time goes on, the development of this cooperation will increasingly show its great vitality and bright prospects.

Why do we say the BRI is a new international cooperation development, and where is the "new"? First, countries along the Land and Maritime Silk Roads and those in other regions of the world can participate in this cooperation development. It has never been seen before in the world that they carry out international cooperation simultaneously on such a large scale and jointly participate in developing cooperation in various projects. Second, countries that participate in this cooperation development include developing and developed countries, as well as socialist and capitalist countries. With the BRI as an opportunity and principal axis, these countries, at different development levels and under different social systems, develop international cooperation simultaneously on such a large scale. This has never happened before in the world. Third, we are not sitting in a house designing the deployment and planning of the BRI; instead, we make determinations step by step and make continuous improvements. At the same time, such deployment and planning are closely connected with the existing construction and development in countries and regions along the Belt and Road and in countries and other regions of the world for the determination and implementation of cooperation projects. In other words, we are not starting everything from scratch but developing cooperation according to the actual development of each region and country. Developing large-scale international cooperation in a practical, realistic, planned, and step-by-step way is unprecedented. Fourth, the BRI is an international cooperation development that starts with and focuses on infrastructure development. For historical and realistic reasons, infrastructure along the Belt and Road in many developing countries and those in other regions is poor and weak, the biggest weakness hindering their development. So, top priority should be given to strengthening infrastructure construction. Also, some infrastructure in quite a few developed countries has aged and needs to be updated. Therefore, starting from infrastructure construction and taking it as a priority is not only a timely need for many countries to develop cooperation, but also is in great demand and has great potential. Meanwhile, cooperation in infrastructure construction is the basis for carrying out and expanding trade cooperation, technical cooperation, and other project cooperation. Only through cooperation in infrastructure construction in each region and country can we truly achieve interconnectivity in all respects and create the most essential and fundamental precondition for international cooperation in all respects. Therefore, this idea is neither proposed at the spur of the moment nor, as some people say, by China to output excess capacity. That is totally a distortion. In a word, it is unprecedented in the world to carry out infrastructure construction on such a large scale in the international community around the BRI. Fifth, the guiding thought and basic principles that the BRI follows are extensive consultation, joint contribution, and shared benefits. The cooperation development of all projects in all regions and countries is the result and benefit of all those involved in cooperation through joint negotiation, construction, and sharing. Such international cooperation development has never been seen before in the world.

Because of the above new features, international cooperation development will surely have new advantages and new vigor and vitality, and we can expect that it will be pushed ahead until final success is achieved.

With the development of practice, the BRI's pioneering and fundamental role and far-reaching significance in building a community with a shared future for mankind, and the bright future it demonstrates will increasingly emerge. Over time, like in 30, 50, and even around 100 years, as long as we follow the principle of extensive consultation, joint contribution, and shared benefits and pursue the BRI as a path, platform, and guidance, we will keep developing new international economic cooperation and new international political, cultural, and social cooperation in regions and countries along the Belt and Road and other regions and countries. Based on practice, people can see that economic, political, cultural, and social communities of shared interests can be formed and developed in regions and countries, and a community with a shared future can be built. If one after another community of shared interests and of shared future with respective features and a common value basis is being formed and developing from Asia to Oceania, Australia, Africa, Europe, and America, will it be far to achieve success in building a community of shared interests and shared future for mankind? It will be proved through practice that so far on our planet, countries have had different historical civilizations, development levels, and social systems. Some are advanced or backward, strong or weak, rich or poor, but as long as they treat each other equally, coexist peacefully, and adhere to the principle of achieving shared growth through discussion and collaboration to develop various cooperation, one day, this world will enter a realm of common development, prosperity and wealth. So, the BRI is a strategic measure and a major step for building a community with a shared future for mankind and a great testing ground, and its pioneering contributions in building a community with a shared future for mankind will be great and far-reaching.

Between Eastern and Western Civilizations: Mutual Learning and Joint Building of a Community with a Shared Future for Mankind*

Speech at the International Confucianism Forum · International Academic Conference in Copenhagen

August 26, 2019

Today, I feel honored and pleased to have the opportunity to come to Copenhagen, the capital of Denmark, a country renowned as a "fairy-tale land," to discuss with you the successful experience and modern inspiration of our civilizational exchanges between East and West. I would like to express my sincere gratitude to all our friends from 15 countries to present this symposium despite your busy

*   From August 26 to 28, 2019, the ICA, in collaboration with the Niels Brock Copenhagen Business College, jointly organized the International Confucian Forum in Copenhagen, Denmark, with the theme "Historical Experience and Realistic Insights of Exchange and Mutual Learning between Eastern and Western Civilizations." The conference was attended by more than 40 scholars from over 15 countries, including China, Denmark, the United Kingdom, Germany, the United States, France, Spain, Austria, India, Portugal, Finland, Slovenia, Czech Republic, Israel, and Singapore. This was the keynote speech at the opening ceremony on August 26, 2019. It elaborated on the foundations, characteristics, and advantages of the formation and development of ancient civilizations in the East and West. It summarized the main contents and indicators of the world's unprecedented changes today in ten aspects, highlighting the inevitability of building a community with a shared future for mankind during human historical development.

schedules. Since you are all experts and scholars who have attained remarkable achievements in various research fields, I believe that by putting our heads and strengths together, we will obtain fruitful results from this symposium.

Although far apart on the Earth, China and Denmark have witnessed a long history of exchanges. In 1674, the Danish merchant ship "Fortuna" departed from Copenhagen to Fuzhou, China, with a personal letter written by Christian V, King of Denmark, to Chinese Emperor Kangxi, marking the maiden voyage of friendship between China and Denmark. The time-honored history and culture of China and Denmark and our common aspiration for peace and a better life have closely linked our two peoples and forged a profound friendship that has stood the test of history. The splendid Danish culture has attracted great admiration from the Chinese people. For instance, the Danish writer H. C. Andersen's fairy tales, such as *The Ugly Duckling, The Little Match Girl, The Daughter of the Sea*, and *The Emperor's New Clothes*, have long since won hundreds of millions of readers in China. Looking back to 1919, a century ago, Chen Duxiu and Li Dazhao, two founders of the CPC, sponsored the *New Youth* and published a Chinese translation of *The Little Match Girl* in its first issue. Since then, many of Andersen's works have been translated into Chinese by Chinese writers and translators. Up till now, Andersen is still a household name in China, deeply loved by Chinese readers. Likewise, the Danish people have tapped into and appreciated the splendid culture of China, as shown in the album printed with verses and collages themed "China" designed by Andersen, Peacock Theatre in Tivoli Gardens that features a strong Chinese flavor, and the Chinese restaurants that can be found everywhere in Copenhagen. Throughout history, the cultural exchanges and mutual learning between China and Danmark have been graceful and highly appraised by men of letters. We will never forget that the Danish people have always expressed concerns and supported the Chinese people's great cause of revolution, construction, and reform. Denmark was one of the first Western countries to establish diplomatic ties with New China and the first Nordic country to establish a comprehensive strategic partnership with China. We believe that in the future, the friendship between our two peoples will continue to grow much closer, like brothers and sisters.

I. Foundations of the Making and Development of Eastern and Western Civilizations in History and Their Characteristics and Advantages

Ancient times witnessed the emergence of major civilizations, such as Mesopotamian, Egyptian, Chinese, Indian, Greek, Roman, and Mayan civilizations. These ancient civilizations, if divided according to the geographical locations, are mainly the Oriental civilizations represented by China, India, and West Asian countries, and the Western civilizations represented by Greece and other European countries. Despite different foundations, development, and characteristics, these civilizations communicate with and influence each other, jointly promoting the development and progress of human civilization for thousands of years.

1. Foundations of the making and development of Eastern civilizations in history and their characteristics and advantages

The Chinese civilization, for instance, emerged and developed on the basis of the longtime agricultural production and living. Since agricultural farming was a simple reproduction, the ancient economic and social development was low-paced but relatively stable, thus gaining gradual development and progress. Such civilization in the East lasted for thousands of years, greatly contributing to human civilization in the ancient world. From the perspective of social systems, the agricultural civilization of ancient China and other Oriental countries can be categorized as a pre-capitalist civilization.

The characteristics and advantages of ancient Chinese civilization can be summarized as follows.

First, it advocated and pursued harmony and diversity in unity. This is a fundamental principle in ancient Chinese philosophy in dealing with the relationship between different things. In other words, we should recognize and respect the diversity and contradiction, the unity of opposites, and the interaction and complementarity of different views on things, which constitute the emergence and development of new ideas and new things. As can be viewed from ancient Chinese books, "Harmony generates and sameness stifles vitality," "Be both opposite and complementary," "Everything under heaven as a whole," and so on.

Second, it advocated and pursued self-discipline and collective wisdom. This is an important thought established by ancient Chinese sages to understand the relationship between individuals and collectives in family, society, and country in a dialectical way. That is to say, we should attach importance to collectives in society and be aware that the interests of individuals and collectives are basically the same. When our individual interests conflict with the collective ones, we should remain self-disciplined to obey the collective interests prior to our own. Meanwhile, the collective should protect the legitimate interests of individuals and give full play to their subjective initiative and creativity to relate the collective cause to individual undertakings. Our predecessors' words of wisdom, such as "Draw on collective wisdom and absorb all useful ideas," "Work with collective wisdom and concerted efforts," "Collective purposes form a fortress," and "A common danger causes common action," and such famous saying as "I shall dedicate myself to the interests of the country in life and death irrespective of personal will and world," all reflect the Chinese people's advocacy and pursuit.

Third, it advocated and pursued people-oriented thought and peaceful governance. This is the core political ideology of governing the country and society in ancient China. That is to say, we must attach importance to the strength of the people and their common aspiration and hold that "Good governance pleases people's heart; bad governance thwarts people's will" and that "The people are the root of a country; the root firm, the country is tranquil. They demand that governors deliver amity, prosperity, security, and good neighborliness to the people and strive to alleviate and relieve people's poverty. This fundamental political concept, early established in the Shang, Zhou, Qin, and Han dynasties, has had a far-reaching influence on the development and progress of China over the past two thousand years.

Fourth, it advocated and pursued the "rule with virtue and moral" and "co-governance through virtue and law." This is an important political principle of state governance in ancient China. Emphasizing the indispensable role of moral education in the political life of a country, it demanded that the governors integrate the rule of virtue with the rule of law when managing national and social affairs. That is to say, we must combine moral education with legal punishment, internal self-discipline with external heteronomy, and take the rule of virtue, education, and self-discipline as the foundation of governance. Only in this way can the social contradictions be resolved and the harmony and stability of society be promoted. The principles, such as "illustrate one's virtue and be careful in the use of punishment," "morality guiding and punishment supplementing," and "virtue and rites remain the foundation of while punishment serves for politics and religion," are also embodied in ancient Chinese books.

Fifth, it advocated and pursued the doctrine of the mean and the truth sought from facts. This is the practical and wise governance explored by ancient Chinese sages. That is to say, we should understand and handle all national and social affairs by "listening to both sides and choosing the middle course" instead of "overdoing" and "underdoing" for extremes and deviating from actual circumstances. Also, people's cognition should change following the reality. That is to say, subjectivity, knowledge, and policy must be consistent with objectivity, practice, and reality. This is the truth of the ancient Chinese expositions such as "reaching its greatest height and brilliancy and following the path of the mean," "reality corresponds to the words," "seeking truth from facts," and "practice makes success and engenders truth."

Sixth, it advocated and pursued the unity of nature and man and ceaseless self-improvement. This is an in-depth understanding of the relationship between man and nature and the attitude of Chinese civilization toward life. That is to say, the sky belongs to nature, and so do those beneath the sky. All human activities should follow the objective laws of nature, so that man and nature will co-exist in harmony. Meanwhile, man is not helpless in the face of nature but can invent and create according to objective laws to constantly promote social progress. As written in ancient Chinese books, "Heaven rules as the people rule; heaven hears as the people hear," "The man of honor will strive constantly for self-improvement," and "Man can conquer nature" all carry the aspirational spirit of respecting the natural law and encouraging people to progress.

Seventh, it advocated and pursued a comprehensive approach and overall balance. This is a unique and sapiential way of thinking and studying pursued by Chinese civilization. That is to say, we should be adept at integrating all parts of things into a whole, analyzing, and inspecting from a comprehensive perspective so as to get the whole picture and guide people's actions. Meanwhile, it holds that people's thoughts and actions should be integrated and balanced, not being biased and running for extremes. This is what the ancient Chinese sages described and pursued as "Listen to both sides, you will be enlightened," "Be observant and alert in all directions," and "A single flower does not make spring, while one hundred flowers in full blossom bring spring to the garden."

Eighth, it advocated and pursued helping each other in times of trouble and the common interests of the whole world. This is an important political concept of Chinese civilization on our ideal society and how to realize it. That is to say, the ideal society of mankind should focus on the aspiration of all to achieve the ultimate harmony worldwide. Because "the world is shared by all mankind," those not serving the people will not achieve such things as "the whole world as one community" and "a world of great harmony." It advocated that people should stick to the spirit of unity and cooperation and make concerted efforts to help each other in the journey toward the great harmony of the world. Such a pursuit is reflected in the assertions of ancient Chinese scholars, such as "To know the people is to be wise, to serve the people is to be virtuous" and "Those who govern beneath the heaven must pursue commonwealth for all to achieve a great harmony."

Ninth, it advocated and pursued moral neighborliness, peace, and tranquility in all countries. This is the important wisdom of the Chinese civilization in handling relations between nations. That is to say, countries should live in good faith like virtuous neighbors, stand by and help each other, establish themselves, and reach out to others so as to engender peace for the whole world. In ancient China, thoughts such as "To win people by virtue will gain love and admiration; to win people by force will get disdain and resentment," "Not to deceive the few, not to bully the weak," "People brightly intelligent, the myriad states will be united and harmonized," etc., all expound this concept.

Tenth, it advocated and pursued innovation that was abreast with the times. This is an important ideological principle of Chinese civilization in our view of development and related theories. That is to say, everything in the world is developing and changing. People must emancipate their minds, bring forth the new instead of sticking to the stale, so as to comprehend correctly the development of things and historical stages, and always participate in practice in the forefront of the times. The expositions of ancient Chinese scholars, such as "Adjust measures to actual circumstances; formulating laws to the changing world; and keeping abreast with the times" and "If you can improve yourself in a day, do so each day, forever building on improvement," are the embodiment of this thought.

These characteristics and advantages of ancient Chinese civilization have become an important part of the wisdom of the Oriental civilization and wisdom. As long as they are integrated with the trends of the times and the economic and social development in today's world, along with creative transformation and innovative development, they will still contribute to the development and progress of human civilization nowadays.

2. Foundations of the making and development of Western civilizations in history and their characteristics and advantages

European civilization, for instance, especially in the period after the Renaissance, emerged and developed on the basis of longtime industrial and commercial production and living. Since industrial and commercial production expanded reproduction, the ancient economic and social development was fast-paced, even sometimes by leaps and bounds. Such civilization in the West also greatly contributed to human civilization in both ancient and modern times. From the perspective of social systems, the industrial and commercial civilizations of ancient Europe and other Western countries can be categorized as capitalist civilizations.

The characteristics and advantages of such a capitalist civilization in Europe in modern times can be summarized as follows.

First, it advocated and pursued natural human rights and personality liberation. This is the fundamental ideology of capitalist civilization in the West. That is to say, people have the innate right to live, seek freedom, and pursue happiness and property. Although the argument that human rights are "innate" is of no scientific sense, it still played a progressive and positive role in encouraging people to pursue personality liberation, overthrow the church hierarchy, and break away from the ignorance of the Middle Ages in guiding capitalists' democratic revolution against feudal autocracy in Europe.

Second, it advocated and pursued humanism, freedom, and equality. This is an important value of capitalist civilization in the West. Proposed during the Renaissance, it advocated that people are born free and equal, which affirmed the value of man and emphasized the dignity of mankind. It thus broke the medieval theology that ruled Europe for over 1,000 years. The transformation from "God-oriented" to "people-oriented" greatly liberated people's thoughts, stimulated people's subjective initiative and creative spirit, and laid the ideological and political foundation for the Bourgeois Revolution, the establishment of capitalist society, and the creation of industrial civilization.

Third, it advocated and pursued market competition and innovative development. This is the fundamental motive mechanism for the Western capitalist civilization to continuously realize the expansion of reproduction and material progress. That is to say, the market plays an important role in allocating resources and adjusting prices in economic development. Through the competition and regulation of the market, the resources and factors of production, such as land, minerals, capital, technology, and labor, can be effectively allocated among different sectors and fields during the production process, so as to improve their utilization efficiency. Meanwhile, the market mechanism of "survival of the fittest" through competition will also promote and encourage participants to give full play to their enthusiasm, initiative, and innovative spirit, thus improving production efficiency. History has proved that the market economy has made indispensable contributions. It can be viewed as an economic miracle, as Marx and Engels quoted, "The bourgeoisie, during its rule of scarce one hundred years, has created more massive and more colossal productive forces than have all preceding generations together"; the production model has evolved from natural economy to commercial and industrial economy, opening up a broad space for the development of productivity and material progress. Due to the spontaneity and hysteresis of market competition and the economic gap resulting from profit-driven capitalism, the government should take macro-control measures to intervene and adjust the market and improve social morality and public welfare undertakings to solve the problems brought by the market mechanism. Western countries have accumulated useful experience in this regard, which is worthy of learning from other countries' implementation of the market economy.

Fourth, it advocated the social contract and pursued democracy and the rule of law. This is an important political ideology of the Western capitalist civilization in dealing with the relationship between individuals, the state, society, and state governance. To realize effective governance, every natural person should give up and transfer some of his rights to society and the state and jointly draw up a common contract that is recognized and observed by all. The governance of democracy and the rule of law relies on the power of the state and society to safeguard every citizen's rights and property. This political ideology has laid a solid foundation for promoting the Bourgeois Revolution and constructing the capitalist system in the West.

Fifth, it advocated analytical methods and pursued empirical results. This is a unique and sapiential way of thinking and studying pursued by capitalist civilization in the West. That is to say, it is necessary to concretely analyze social and natural things and emphasize that they should be divided into separate parts and studied accordingly so as to achieve refinement and accuracy during research. It requires utilizing logical thinking in the study through numerous inductions and deductions so as to draw the ultimate conclusions. The conclusions shall also be taken into experiments to verify repeatedly to generate a scientific understanding of things. Such a method of thinking has played an important role in breaking the bondage of mysticism and empiricism and in establishing positivism with scientific study methods.

Sixth, it advocated pragmatism with a prior pursuit of utilitarianism. This is another ideological concept of Western capitalist civilization that deals with the relationship between knowledge and practice. That is to say, knowledge and experience should be utilized during practice and action. Practice must be measured by its function and effects. With utilitarianism as a priority, usefulness is thus deemed as truth. This ideology, under some specific historical conditions, can stimulate people's enthusiasm for practice and exploration, help to form a pragmatic environment, and promote social development. However, its essence is a sort of mechanical materialism, which separates the dialectical unity of cognition and practice. History proves that due to the limitation of both subjective and objective conditions, people may not always achieve success after applying their knowledge and experience. Failures, though occurring sometimes, always breed success. If we evaluate things simply with success and usefulness as standard, we will plunge into conservatism or narrow utilitarianism.

These characteristics and advantages of European civilization have become an important part of Western civilization and wisdom. Similarly, as long as they are integrated with the trends of the times and the economic and social development in today's world, along with creative transformation and innovative development, they will also contribute to the development and progress of human civilization.

Materialistic dialectics expounds that all things in the world have their strengths and weaknesses that co-exist at the same time. Both the Oriental and Western civilizations have their advantages and disadvantages, with essence and dross co-existing throughout history. Therefore, we should adopt a scientific attitude toward both civilizations, that is, selecting the essence and discarding the dross, carrying out the strengths and eliminating the weaknesses, and adhere to the principle of "adjusting measures to the changing times and actual circumstances," "seeking truth from facts," and "keeping pace with the times." By doing this, the two civilizations will jointly contribute more wisdom and strength to the common progress of mankind.

When we review and compare the formation and development of Eastern and Western civilizations, it is worth considering the following: If it were not for the emergence and brilliant development of ancient Chinese and Eastern civilizations, the progress of human civilization in the ancient world might have been much less, and the process could have been much slower. Similarly, if it were not for the emergence of the European Renaissance and the rapid development of the European capitalist civilization it engendered, the progress of human civilization in the modern world might also have been much less. In that case, it would not have been possible for the historical situation described by Marx and Engels to occur, "The bourgeoisie, during its rule of scarce one hundred years, has created more massive and more colossal productive forces than have all preceding generations together." Furthermore, one can imagine that if there had been no subsequent socialist revolutions in the Soviet Union, East Europe, China, and other Western and Eastern countries guided by Marxism, which created a new socialist civilization that competed, learned from, and influenced capitalist civilization, then the progress of human civilization in the contemporary world might also have been much less. It can be asserted that if China had not embraced socialism, it would not have been possible to rescue the old China in deep crisis nor to create a vibrant new China. The Chinese people would have had to endure an extended period in the darkness of the old society.

The above considerations are not intended as historical hypotheses, as history cannot be assumed. It's just an attempt to change the perspective for thinking, explaining, and emphasizing the following: From ancient times to the present, various forms of human civilization, regardless of the historical stage or the country and region in which they originated, always continue to forge ahead to secure their existence and development. This is something no difficulty or force can obstruct. It is a certainty of history and a kind of historical "eternity." From ancient times to the present, various forms of human civilization have always promoted common progress through mutual learning and influence. They have each made contributions to the development of human civilization. At the same time, different forms of human civilization are not produced and progressed simultaneously. They have a sequence of emergence and development, each with distinct values and contributions. They are not uniformly observable. In the world, no form of civilization can monopolize every historical stage of human society or dominate the social stage in all countries and regions. This, too, is a certainty of history and a kind of historical "eternity."

II. The Mainstream of Our Times and the Profound Changes Unseen in a Century

From the beginning to the middle of the 20th century, two world wars took place on the land we live on together, both of which originated in the West. The two world wars, launched by some Western imperialist countries to fight for markets, resources, spheres of influence, and colonies, brought great disaster to both the colonial and semi-colonial countries in Asia, Africa, and Latin America and the advanced capitalist countries in the West. The successive wars demonstrated the intensifying contradictions within the Western countries and their interrelations, as well as the deepening crisis of the capitalist economy, politics, and society. The deepening of these crises, though leading to the two world wars, still brought some favorable political results; that is, as the opposite of the capitalist system, socialism bloomed both in the West and East. For instance, the Soviet Union, the first socialist country, was born after the First World War, followed by a number of socialist countries in East Europe and East Asia after the Second World War. Also, under the influence and impetus of the worldwide socialist movement, the national liberation movement arose in Asian, African, and Latin American countries. These countries and nations successively realized their independence after the Second World War and gained the opportunity to develop their own economy and culture and realize social progress.

The three great forces, the people of socialist countries, nationally independent countries, and the West, who have experienced the bitterness of two world wars, have united a front against war and colonialism and formed the trend of our times featuring peace and development. After the Second World War, two political camps of socialism and capitalism took shape between the East and West. Though opposing and restricting each other, they also learned from and contended with each other. This new political pattern has made it impossible to wage a new world war and old-fashioned colonialism, thus basically creating peace and enabling all countries to speed up their development. Up to the end of the 20th century, despite the drastic changes in the Soviet Union and the socialist countries in East Europe, world peace and common development of all countries remained the aspiration of all people and the mainstream of our times.

As we enter the 21st century, the world pattern has undergone further profound and complex changes. Through an in-depth analysis of these changes, Chinese President Xi Jinping made the major judgment that "our world is undergoing profound changes unseen in a century" and has profoundly expounded on various occasions domestically and abroad. Policymakers and insightful people in many countries also pay close attention to and study the world pattern today.

As we may ask, what are the contents and gauges of these great changes in today's world? From my perspective, I would like to put forward the following ten aspects for discussion with you.

The first gauge is that the neoliberal policy in Western developed countries that imposed crippling crises on the economy, politics, and society was declared bankrupt.

Neoliberalism, also known as the "Washington Consensus," was put forward and implemented in the late 1970s after the economic crisis resulted from Keynesianism, which advocated strong government intervention in the market and expansionary fiscal policy. The basic idea of neoliberal policy is to allow more free competition in the market. The measures are as follows: to reduce government intervention to allow capitals, especially the monopoly capital, to pursue interests in the market and encourage the transfer from an entity economy to a more fictitious one featuring self-circulation; to cut tax for large monopolies and the wealthy and reduce investment in public welfare undertakings and social benefits enjoyed by the majority; to weaken the labor unions by restricting their activities in negotiating with employers on behalf of laborers and defending laborers' interests; to re-privatize the state-owned economic sectors, etc. These measures affected the economy and society in the following two aspects. First, it caused huge financial bubbles and debt crises. Since the fictitious economy was composed of financial derivatives, it had seriously nibbled at and hollowed out the real economy. This brought worries and crises to the economy and society, threatening and damaging the interests of the public. Second, it began an unprecedented disparity between the wealthy minority and the poor majority. In OECD countries, the richest 10% of the population earn 9.6 times the income of the poorest 10%. In the 1980s, this ratio stood at 7:1. In Italy, 20% of the richest people account for 61.6% of the social wealth; In Britain, the top 10% possess 54% of the country's wealth. In the US, the richest households, which make up just 0.1 percent of the population, possess almost as much wealth as the rest of ordinary families, which constitute 90% of the population. Stiglitz, a famous American economist, believes that the US is now "of the 1%, by the 1%, for the 1%," which is quite different from the society "of the people, by the people, for the people" proposed by President Lincoln. Such a huge financial bubble and the income disparity triggered the 2008 economic recession in the West. The crisis then extended from the economy to society, which was marked by longtime protests such as "Occupy Wall Street" in many Western countries since 2008.

Here, I would like to quote Wendy Brown, professor of Political Science at the University of California, Berkeley, who commented on neoliberalism in his new book, *In the Ruins of Neoliberalism*. She pointed out that neoliberalism intended to destroy the ideal of social justice in concept, system, and practice. Some neoliberal politicians regarded state regulation and redistribution as improper interference in the market and invasion of freedom, so they adopted the methods of social privatization, large-scale reduction of social welfare, and deconstruction of the administrative state to govern the country. Neoliberal policies aimed to loosen political control over economic entities and markets and replace regulation and redistribution with market freedom and tough proprietorship. Both former US President Reagan and former British Prime Minister Margaret Thatcher, holding that "Government is not the solution to our problems, Government is the problem," dealing with economic and social issues by cutting taxes, reducing social welfare, and deregulating capital in the market. Neoliberalism demonized nationalism, aggravated the principle of "abandoning the government" into hostility toward politics, opposed the "government-regulated" society, policies, and public goods, and sought to place political power under economic metrics to meet the market's demands. In a word, neoliberalism cannot lead to long-lasting prosperity and social justice.

Facing the serious economic and social crisis caused by the neoliberal policy, some people of insight in the West began to question the political system of Western countries. Some even proposed another political force that can represent the interests of the majority and enable them to participate in the country's governance. For instance, David Rothkopf, an American political scientist, proposed the political concept of a "new American majority." Thomas Friedman, an American political commentator at *The New York Times*, wrote in the German magazine *International Politics and Society (IPS)* that "There is a potential new American majority out there to be assembled to meet these challenges." No long-term and well-thought-out policy can be devised if the two parties govern in rotation, with the ruling party in office and the other placing obstacles. He also quoted Mark Mykleby, a retired Marine colonel, saying, "At no time in our history have our national challenges been as complex and long-term as those we face today. But the most salient feature of our politics of late has been our inability to respond coherently and effectively to obvious problems before they become crises. How will we fulfill the promise of and our obligation to secure the Blessings of Liberty to ourselves and our Posterity?" The emergence of these political views and phenomena in the US and other Western countries is attracting people's attention. We may conclude that the failure of neoliberal policy in Western countries and the serious economic, social, and political crisis it brought about was an unprecedented change in the progress of Western countries and their capitalist civilizations.

The second gauge is that many Western countries are seeking new development patterns. The principle and practice features strengthening the constructive role of the government in economic and social progress and further integrating government regulation with market competition, economic growth, and social stability and equity.

At present, some Western governments hold that they should "rely on a stronger government for warmth" to advance the economy and maintain political and social stability. For example, Ralf Stegner, Vice-President of the Social Democratic Party of Germany (SPD), said: "The state needs to become much more involved in key areas such as work, pensions and health care." Marcel Fratzscher, head of International Policy Analysis at the European Central Bank, said: "European countries need fundamental reforms that focus on empowering people and on stopping the market abuse of firms and lobby groups." French President Macron recently said, "We are facing a market economy crisis like never before" when discussing issues related to the Western market economy. He added, "The 'distorted' market economy that has reached a crossroads has led to severe wealth inequality and polarization, disrupting our political order."

The French government, in order to ease social tensions, such as massive street protests, has taken steps to lower the personal income tax on low-income groups and replace it with higher taxes on enterprises. Also, the individual pension rates below 2,000 euros are linked to inflation to ensure the livelihood of low-income retirees; Germany is also increasing social spending to improve social welfare that covers the majority. Some SPDs also proposed an "unconditional pension policy" to provide security for those who do not contribute enough to the social security system. Pedro Sánchez, Secretary-General of the Spanish Socialist Workers' Party (PSOE) and Acting Spanish Prime Minister, won elections in Spain and the EU for substantially raising the minimum wage, the level of social benefits, and taxes on corporations. In Denmark, the ruling Social Democratic Party is also adjusting its economic and social policies to raise taxes on the wealthy and businesses, increasing public spending, and amending pension policies to allow early retirement. In the UK, the listed Corporate Governance Code has been revised to require the consideration of the voices of employees as stakeholders in business operations. Leader of the Labour Party Jeremy Corbyn said the state would take control of water, electricity, gas, and railway operators, as well as the Royal Mail and the Royal Bank of Scotland, and raise funds for nationalization by issuing treasury bonds. In the United States, on August 19 of this year, the chief executives of 181 top American companies convened at the Business Roundtable meeting in Washington, D.C., where they collectively signed the Statement on the Purpose of a Corporation. This statement redefines the purpose of corporate operations, asserting that shareholder interests are no longer the sole objective of the company. The primary mission of the company is declared to be the creation of a better society. The statement emphasizes that as socially responsible entities, corporate leadership teams should be committed to achieving several goals: delivering value to customers, investing in employees by hiring diverse groups and providing fair treatment, adhering to business ethics when dealing with suppliers, actively engaging in societal causes, prioritizing sustainability, and creating long-term value for shareholders. The Business Roundtable was established in 1972 and brings together influential business leaders from major US companies such as Amazon, Apple, Boeing, General Electric, PepsiCo, Walmart, JPMorgan Chase, and others. Since 1997, each statement issued by the organization has supported the principle of "shareholder primacy," highlighting that the company's primary task is to benefit shareholders and maximize profit. Jamie Dimon, CEO of JPMorgan Chase and Chairman of the Business Roundtable, stated in the declaration that an increasing number of major companies were now turning to invest in their employees and communities because, in the long run, it was the only way for companies to succeed. Alex Gorsky, CEO of Johnson & Johnson and Chairman of the Business Roundtable's Governance Committee, commented at a press conference that the new statement better reflects the operational approach modern businesses should adopt, and the company will play an important role in improving society by meeting the needs of all stakeholders. *The New York Times* commented on this, saying, "This statement signifies that the American business community is reflecting on its rightful role in the 21st century." American economist Joseph E. Stiglitz remarked, "The statement signed by the Business Roundtable has caused quite a stir." He further stated, "Certainly, the new stance of the most influential CEOs in the United States is welcome," and asked, "Is this a huge change, or is it a huge change?" He concluded with the observation, "We must wait and see." Stiglitz believed market forces might lead to short-sightedness and insufficient investment in employees and communities. Therefore, it is heartening that these corporate leaders, who should have profound insights into the economic functions, have finally grasped the essence of the modern economy, even though it took them 40 years to do so. French scholar Alain Peyrefitte believed that if wealth is excessively concentrated, such as the total compensation of top executives of American companies exceeding 200 times the median employee income, this mode of growth and distribution is unsustainable. He predicted that, if not changed, an era would come when "99% of the world's population will feel extremely angry."

The practices and principles of the above-mentioned countries demonstrate that they are increasing the government's regulation and control of the market, strengthening the country's leading role in economic and social progress, especially the construction of public welfare undertakings, and adjusting social distribution to relieve income disparity. This saliently differs from neoliberalism, which has prevailed in the West for decades in the policy for development model. *The Wall Street Journal (WSJ)* wrote that the Washington Consensus, featuring laissez-faire, advocated by American and British leaders 40 years ago, opened an era. Yet, the current policy marks the end of this era. As early as 1998, former French Prime Minister Lionel Jospin said that France is "yes to the market economy, no to a market society." That is to say, the role of market mechanisms is limited only to the socio-economy and cannot be transferred to other social spheres. As to public welfare undertakings, the government should not perform under the rule of the market mechanism but allocate resources and guide its development. This development model, which is now promoted in Western countries to further integrate government regulation with market competition and economic growth with social stability and equity, differs from both Keynesianism and neoliberalism. It is likely to facilitate a significant reform in the progress of capitalism, marking a great change in the Western world. The new economic and social pattern it will bring to the Western capitalist society and even the capitalist civilization is worthy of attention. It should also be learned from and studied by all developing countries and socialist countries.

The third gauge is that some Western developed countries have taken the lead in inciting unilateralism and protectionism to solve their own economic and social crises. Against the historical trend of economic globalization, these behaviors are doomed to failure, harming others and themselves.

Economic globalization is a historical trend that the world economy can not resist. It has accelerated the circulation of production factors among countries and regions, facilitated people-to-people exchanges, and promoted mutual learning among civilizations. This is determined by the social productive forces under today's economic and cultural development, which is beyond man's will. However, some Western developed countries, mainly the US, have failed to implement neoliberalism. In order to extricate itself from economic and social crises and preserve its own interests, it performed against the historical trend by inciting unilateralism and protectionism. It waged so-called "sanctions," additional tariffs, technical blockades, and various economic and trade frictions against other countries in an attempt to channel the waters in the economic ocean back into isolated lakes and creeks. This is turning back the wheel of history.

Unilateralism and protectionism are nothing new. They have existed for a long time, but neither have survived. Therefore, these resurgent thoughts and practices in the international community were immediately resisted and criticized by many dignitaries and insightful people in both the East and West. Manfred Grund, German politician of the Christian Democratic Union (CDU), said, "Free trade paves the way for global prosperity," "We firmly oppose unilateralism and protectionism. The additional tariffs will not help solve the problem, and tariff barriers against other countries will also be detrimental to our own development." Danilo Türk, Former President of Slovenia, stated, "Unilateralism and protectionism bring no benefit. We need interconnectivity and cooperation based on mutual respect, equality, and common benefits." Mario Rendulić, President of the Chinese Southeast European Business Association (CSEBA), said: "The international trade norms under the WTO mechanism have been endorsed by over 160 members, contributing to the international trade and global economic growth and serving the interests of people around the world. Protectionism and discriminatory policies not only undermine the normal global supply chain system but, more seriously, blow the confidence of all in free trade and international cooperation." Abbas Mousavi, Spokesman of Iran's Ministry of Foreign Affairs, said: "The imposition of illegal and unilateral sanctions against nations is doomed to failure and do not correspond with the international pyramid of power given the current fast developments." Rascal Kupman, the South African economist, said: "Isolationism and unilateralism pose a serious challenge to free trade. Imposing additional tariffs will inevitably lead to long-lasting trade frictions, which may bring a series of chain reactions and harm global interests." Hor Namhong, Deputy Prime Minister of Cambodia, said: "At present, the world is experiencing profound and complex changes, and the global economy has also been affected by trade protectionism and unilateralism. Facing such challenges and difficulties, we must strengthen cooperation, which is the fundamental way to solve the problem."

Nowadays, the economic, cultural, and social ties between countries and regions are becoming closer, and an interdependent and indivisible situation of "sharing a stake in each other's future" has long been formed. The outdated national egoism featuring unilateralism and protectionism will obstruct the world's economic and social progress, leading those suffering from economic and social crises to nowhere. Although this is another form of "change," it will not bring long-lasting benefits. It will neither stop the wheel of history nor change the unprecedented progressive trend conducive to the world economy and human civilization.

The fourth gauge is that the trend of economic globalization is irreversible. Due to its accumulated and increasingly apparent drawbacks, the international community has achieved consensus to call for new patterns, paths, rules, and

ideas so as to make economic globalization more open, inclusive, balanced, and beneficial to all and ensure justice and equity.

Economic globalization has greatly contributed to the world economy and international society and profoundly changed the historical process of mankind. However, due to various factors, some drawbacks have accumulated that need to be dealt with. To sum up, these drawbacks are mainly reflected in the following three aspects. First, the leading pattern is outdated. So far, economic globalization has been dominated by one or more Western powers, namely, the capitalist developed countries. Their contributions and constructive role in promoting economic globalization should be affirmed. Yet, this pattern does not advance with the times. Without the extensive participation of developing countries and joint regulations on economic globalization, the principle of democracy in international relations will not be truly attained. Second, the concrete measures are off the track. When promoting trade exchanges and economic and technological cooperation, some countries ignore the general rules of economic globalization, such as trade liberalization and the multilateral trade system, and incite unilateralism, protectionism, and egoism, which seriously hinder the running and development of economic globalization. Third, the rules and concepts are founded on drawbacks. In the hundreds of years since the beginning of economic globalization, the jungle law and the zero-sum game featuring "winner takes all" prevailed for a long time, resulting in a huge disparity concerning wealth and sustainability between developed and developing countries and even within these countries themselves.

Over time, these drawbacks have become increasingly prominent, shackling and obstructing the healthy development of economic globalization. Facing these drawbacks, the international community increasingly realizes that it is time to improve the previous patterns, paths, rules, and ideas of economic globalization to sum up and draw lessons from the past, conform to the trend of the times featuring peace, development and win-win cooperation, so as to make economic globalization more open, inclusive, balanced, and beneficial to all and ensure justice and equity. What should be the new features of today's economic globalization? Many insightful people around the world believe that today's economic globalization should allow all countries to play their constructive roles and jointly make regulations. It should continue to uphold and protect trade liberalization and the system of multilateral trade that have been proven to be correct and effective and welcome creative transformation and innovative development. It should develop without hegemony, jungle law, and zero-sum game, and follow the principles of extensive consultation, joint contribution, and shared benefits, thus realizing democracy, equity, justice, and fairness around the world. It should constantly promote world peace, stability, tranquility, and common development and prosperity for all.

The international community's profound understanding of the drawbacks of economic globalization, together with its expectations and requirement for improved patterns, paths, rules, and ideas in the new era, has constituted a major change that has decisive significance in promoting the healthy development of economic globalization, maintaining lasting peace in the world and advancing the progress of human civilization.

The fifth gauge is that the emerging economies among the developing countries in the East and South are changing the world's economic and social progress.

Since the 14th century, by the capitalist mode of production and economy generated by the Renaissance, Industrial Revolution, and Bourgeois Revolution in Western Europe, the West has gradually led world development, especially after the 17th century, and became the center of the world that long dominated the world economic, political, cultural, and social development. This pattern was described by the American historian Immanuel Wallerstein as follows: based on the international division of labor, the capitalist world system has established a global pattern featuring the "core," "semi-periphery," and "periphery." That is to say, in this global pattern, the core refers to Western developed capitalist countries, the periphery to the dependent developing countries of Asia, Africa, and Latin America countries that were colonized by the Western countries, and the semi-periphery defines states that are located countries between core and periphery.

This pattern has existed for centuries in the world. Since the mid-20th century, thanks to the founding of a number of socialist countries and the national liberation movements blooming worldwide, the colonial and semi-colonial countries in Asia, Africa, and Latin America have achieved independence, and the previous colonial system finally collapsed. These newly independent Asian, African, and Latin American countries have become an important political and economic force in the international arena through their arduous efforts to revitalize and develop their economies and improve people's livelihoods. Especially since the second half of the 20th century, through years of development, a large number of developing countries and emerging economies are rapidly rising, profoundly changing the pattern of the world economy. Here, we can focus on two sets of data: in the first decade of the 21st century, emerging economies grew by an average of more than 6%. Among them, China, India, and Russia have achieved an average growth rate of over 10%, 7%, and 6%, respectively, and the BRICS countries over 8%, which is much higher than that of 2.6% in the Western developed countries and 4.1% of the world economy. Emerging economies and developing countries have already contributed 80% of the growth of the global economy. Another is that calculated by the exchange rate, these emerging economies and developing countries account for nearly 40% of the global economic output. Maintaining the current development pace, they will expand even to half of the world's total in a decade.

These data demonstrate that the eastern and southern parts of the world, specifically the emerging economies and developing countries in Asia, Africa, and Latin America, have played a critically constructive role in driving the global economy. More importantly, the data manifests a new trend in the world economy; that is, the Western industrial center and development center have been shifting and spreading to other regions in recent centuries. The "Atlantic Era" or "West-Centered Era," which had lasted for centuries, is evolving into a new era in which the Atlantic Ocean and Pacific Ocean countries, the West and the East, and the North and the South, are developing side by side. We can conclude that the era when global development relied mainly on a single region is now coming to an end. The world economy and society are entering a new landscape in which the East and the West, the South and the North, the developing countries and the developed countries, and the socialist countries and the capitalist countries jointly promote exchanges and cooperation and facilitate mutual learning, so as to attain common progress. Isn't this change yet another sign of the great changes that have not occurred in a century?

The sixth gauge, after the drastic changes in the Soviet Union and East Europe, the so-called "end of history," that is, the world would be unified in capitalism as some Western scholars predicted, did not come into being. Also, the cause of world socialism represented by socialism with Chinese characteristics was opening up a new development path and a new situation full of vigor and vitality.

The so-called "end of history" was put forward by Japanese-American Francis Fukuyama in the late 1980s and early 1990s in response to the drastic changes in the Soviet Union and the socialist countries in East Europe and the serious set-backs in the cause of world socialism. The main viewpoints are as follows: the collapse of the Soviet Union and East European socialism and the end of the bipolar structure resulting from the Cold War marked the end of communism and the victory of capitalism. The changes demonstrated that the only way for human development was through the market economy and democratic politics of Western capitalism. The history of human development is a "universal history of mankind oriented toward a liberal democratic system." The Western-style liberal democracy is "the end point of mankind's ideological evolution, and the universalization of Western liberal democracy as the final form of human government," and human society will end up in capitalism. His argument prevailed for a time, as if history had ended like that.

However, nearly 30 years have passed. What is the world like today? The world's development did not rely merely on Western capitalism. Socialism, as we know, stays vigorous in the world. Moreover, after such setbacks occurred in the Soviet Union and East Europe, the cause of world socialism went through a rough patch, drew lessons from the past, and gained new development. Socialism with Chinese characteristics remains a prominent representative. Thanks to the CPC's leadership and the Chinese people's efforts in reform and opening-up, our great achievements in the economy and society have attracted worldwide attention. Socialism with Chinese characteristics has entered a new era, demonstrating a bright future of the great rejuvenation of the Chinese nation, an enriched and developed Marxism, and the great vitality of scientific socialism. Also, it broadens the path for developing countries to achieve modernization and for those countries and nations who want to speed up their development while maintaining their independence. By contributing Chinese wisdom and solutions to the common problems facing mankind, the achievements and contributions of socialism with Chinese characteristics are widely recognized and praised by the international community. American economist Shamik Dhar said, "When the West is experiencing a crisis of collective confidence, China offers an alternative to the traditional Western model of freedom." German scholar Frank Sieren said, "In just a few decades, China has risen from one of the poorest countries to the world's largest trading power and largest economy in terms of purchasing power parity (PPP), which has never taken place in history." Peter Nolan, Director of the University's Centre of Development Studies, University of Cambridge, said, "China has been a world leader in innovation and creativity for thousands of years. The government takes over responsibilities that the market cannot undertake, while the market is supervised by the government and guided by the Chinese philosophical tradition. China's major giants are now rather competitive in the world market. China's economic growth has been the basis for improving the material and mental well-being of its people. China still has a long way to go, facing various internal and external challenges. Still, the Chinese people and its leadership have found a way to overcome difficulties and contribute to global sustainability." Venezuelan scholar Sergio Rodríguez Gelfenstein said: "In 1991, British Prime Minister Margaret Thatcher told the Chinese President that it was impossible to establish a system combining socialism with the market economy. The market economy must be based on capitalism and privatization." However, the Chinese Communists have proved by facts that within the framework of Marxism, they can also run a market economy. "Since Marxism was introduced in China, the Chinese Communists used the scientific theory to find solutions to the country's problems and overcome various difficulties, concretely contributing to the development of Marxism-Leninism." Dominique Meeus, an expert at the National Secretariat of the Workers' Party of Belgium, said, "China has made great achievements in recent years. China's success furthers the development of Marxism and provides a different path for the world."

The understanding of history is always deepened through comparison between things. While China and other socialist countries, together with all developing countries, have made progressive achievements, the developed capitalist countries in the West are also developing on their own track. But the world did not end up as smoothly and inevitably as predicted by the theory of the "end of history." They have not yet recovered from the previous economic and social crises. In recent years, "Marxism Mania" and "*Das Kapital* Mania" emerged in Western countries, which is unprecedented in Western history. German historian Joachim Bauer commented on this phenomenon, "The world has indeed changed a lot, but the analysis on *Das Kapital* is still of practical significance." Although he didn't give up his "end of history" theory, Fukuyama admitted that "The end of history has been postponed, and at present, this is not true for many people." The *Foreign Affairs* of the US wrote, "A better era is slowly unfolding." Such a "better era," undoubtedly, will not be what Fukuyama predicted as the "end of history." It is foreseeable as follows: the two major civilizations, socialism and capitalism, through competition and mutual learning, jointly promote human civilization to achieve new progress, in which socialist civilization will make much greater contributions.

The seventh gauge is that by waging the "color revolution" and local wars, some Western developed countries promote their so-called "universal values," interfere in the internal affairs of other countries, incite ethnic divisions to quell the "clash of civilizations," insincerely and strive to create a "successful model" of Western-style liberal democracy in developing countries. But all their intentions have failed or are failing as never before. It demonstrates that the era encouraging hegemony and power politics is gone for good.

Since the end of the 1980s, especially after the collapse of the Soviet Union and the end of the Cold War, the United States has become the only superpower in the world, with its hegemony and power politics remaining salient in the world. In order to dominate the world, the US incited several Western countries to intervene in developing countries through political and military measures. The insidious trick is to launch so-called "color revolutions" in regions of developing countries, such as South Europe, Central Asia, West Asia, and North Africa. It sponsored rebellion in these regions by overthrowing the current regime via so-called peaceful and nonviolent means and by establishing new regimes that conform to their "universal values" and the Western-style liberal democracy. The direct actions include waging military strikes and local wars against regions in South Europe and the Arab world of West Asia and North Africa, thus overthrowing their current regimes and fostering pro-American and pro-Western forces as new regimes. How did these evildoing come out? Have they brought the promised "flowers and spring" to these countries and regions? Have they realized "democracy and liberty"? Have they achieved economic and social progress? Have they provided regional security and national unity? None. On the contrary, these regions only witnessed chaos, depression, cultural rupture, ethnic division, religious conflicts, social unrest, and a disastrous mess of poor people. By waging military attacks and local wars, the US and some other Western countries have also suffered from loss of human, material, and financial resources, destroying the lives and interests of their people. Facing the above results, some Western media and intellectuals cannot but admit the hypocrisy of the US and other Western countries in pursuing hegemonism and power politics and the evil consequences they have brought about. "It is the external forces that have played the most important role in the so-called 'Arab revolutions,'" Eric Denécé at the French Intelligence Research Center said in an interview on Arab issues. "People in these regions now realize that they were being manipulated and exploited unconsciously. In fact, all countries that experienced the 'Arab Spring' are now facing worsening political, economic, social, and security situations than they had in 2010."

As hegemonism and power politics have been completely exposed in the above-mentioned developing regions, people with conscience and a sense of justice and insight from both developing countries and developed countries are more aware that hegemonism and power politics have brought nothing but destruction and calamity to the world. As a result, their evildoing did not achieve what they wanted. Hegemonism and power politics have never been so troubled and isolated as they are now. Isn't this change yet another significant sign of the great changes that have not taken place in a century?

The eighth gauge is the long-existing excessive industrialization and urbanization and other over-exploitation of human activities, constituting a predatory pattern of economic growth. Global destruction, pollution, and

waste of natural resources and ecological environment have reached unprecedented levels, posing ever-increasing threats to the survival and sustainable development of people around the world. Maintaining and rationally using natural resources and improving and protecting the ecological environment have become the most urgent calls and the strongest demands of all countries.

All people live on the same Earth. Our survival and development rely on the abundant natural resources and suitable ecological environment provided by the Earth. Without these basic elements, human beings will not be able to survive, not to mention achieving economic and social development. Since the Industrial Revolution, humans have created a splendid industrial civilization in modern times by exploiting and utilizing natural resources, facilitating industrialization and urbanization, and promoting economic and social progress. But on the other side, human activities have now far exceeded the Earth's carrying capacity due to long-term excessive exploitation, predatory destruction, and a population explosion. Many natural resources have been overused to depletion, and the ecological environment continues to deteriorate, causing serious problems for resources and the environment.

For instance, due to excessive carbon dioxide emissions, global warming is now causing more extreme weather. According to statistics, the concentration of carbon dioxide has increased by 25% over the past few centuries, and global carbon dioxide emissions reached a record 33 billion tons in 2018. The growing concentration of carbon dioxide causes the greenhouse effect, eventually resulting in a rise in global temperature. It further affects global atmospheric circulation and weather systems, leading to frequent weather extremes such as typhoons, rainstorms, high temperatures and severe cold, melting glaciers and permafrost, sea-level rise, etc., greatly endangering the balance of the natural ecosystem and the food supply and living environment of human beings.

Likewise, freshwater resources are in a serious crisis due to plenty of abuse, waste, pollution, and uneven regional distribution. According to the *2018 UN World Water Development Report (WWDR 2018)*, the global demand for water resources is increasing at an annual rate of 1% due to population growth, economic development, and changes in consumption patterns. And that rate will surge significantly over the next 20 years. Nowadays, nearly half of the 3.6 billion world's population lives in water-scarce areas, which is expected to grow from 4.8 billion to 5.7 billion by 2050.

Moreover, impacted and destructed by human activities, forests and wetlands continue to decline, along with the expanding deserts. According to statistics, forests account for at least 7.6 billion hectares of the Earth. Yet, it reduced to only 4.128 billion hectares in 1990 and 3.99 billion hectares in 2015. Since 1900, about 64%–71% of the global wetland areas have disappeared due to human activities. By the end of the 20th century, the desertification area had reached 36 million square kilometers, accounting for 1/4 of the Earth's land, equal to the total land area of Russia, Canada, China, and the US. Over 100 countries are now affected by desertification, which is increasing at an annual rate of 50,000 to 70,000 square kilometers. Moreover, the frequent acid rain, energy shortages, cultivated land pollution and degradation, festering garbage, biodiversity reduction, and other disasters remain serious up to now.

These resources and ecological disasters damage people's lives and health and threaten the living environment and the sustainability of the world economy and society. Frederick Engels pointed out, "Let us not, however, flatter ourselves overmuch on account of our human victories over nature. For each such victory, nature takes its revenge on us." The traditional pattern featuring reckless predatory and high pollution on the economy and society at the cost of over-exploitation of natural resources and damage to the ecology can no longer be sustained. Otherwise, our only home, the Earth, will no longer be habitable, and mankind will have to swallow the bitter fruits of its own brewing. The solution to the common crises of resources and ecology lies not merely in one country or region. Solutions can only be achieved through the governments' and all peoples' joint efforts, coordination and cooperation, collected wisdom, and long-term struggle. Facing the crises and changes in resources and environment that have not occurred in the past century, no country will allow hands-off and beggar-thy-neighbor approaches for their nations' own good.

The ninth gauge is the rapidly developing technological and industrial revolutions. They bring about a bright future for global development and people's livelihood, yet also pose unprecedented challenges to national and social governance. It is a new and huge task that governments and all peoples

must face and solve together, that is, fully utilizing the revolution brought by new technologies and industries to serve people's well-being and the world's progress while effectively preventing potential worries and abuses.

Nowadays, science and technology are developing in keeping with the times, which constitutes a progressive landscape as never before. The technological integration of information, biology, new energy, and new material is triggering a new technological and industrial revolution, giving birth to various new industries, formats, and production and management modes. Among them, the information technology revolution represented by the Internet, the IoT, AI, big data, cloud computing, and quantum communications is the core of the new technological and industrial revolution. They are profoundly changing people's way of thinking, learning, and producing, as well as employment, lifestyle, and social communication. The rapidly developing technological and industrial revolution will undoubtedly promote the world's progress and human civilization with unprecedented energy and impetus. Therefore, reform and innovation are required in the concepts, rules, paths, and patterns of economic, political, cultural, and social activities. New challenges will come along concerning the state and social governance in many facets and aspects.

For instance, the transparency, flattening, and speediness features of the Internet, big data, and AI, among other infotech, may challenge the hierarchy system of today's institutions setting and state governance. When issuing policies, the government is required to consider these new situations so as to make corresponding reforms and innovations. John Naisbitt, an American scholar, mentioned in his *Megatrends: Ten New Directions Transforming Our Lives* that "Information itself is a powerful force that generates equal treatment among people" and "The computer will shatter the hierarchical pyramid: it will keep track of the movement of people and business information, and organizations will no longer need hierarchies." Likewise, the emergence and application of new industries, such as AI and IoT, will equip the real economy with up-to-date information, impetus, and vitality so as to improve production efficiency. Yet, it will inevitably reduce jobs, especially those of manual workers. How to arrange these redundant workers and secure their future employment and livelihood has become a new subject that needs to be studied in advance. What's more, the previous economic development mode centered on real enterprises for production. However, in the future, the new economic formats featuring virtual, intensive, interactive, and platform-based production and management will increase as time goes on. How to strengthen effective supervision and make them serve our economy remains another subject that must be studied in advance. Moreover, infotech, especially the Internet, provides new means and favorable conditions for the government to keep abreast with social progress, better understand people's needs, improve social governance, and facilitate the public's expressions of their views. But on the other side, worries and challenges are hidden behind. With a smartphone, everyone becomes a "journalist," even a "spokesperson" of the press who can broadcast social events to the world anytime and anywhere, make comments at their own will, and even fabricate social events and information. Some may even fabricate events and information out of thin air, which is bound to negatively influence public opinion and people's sentiments. How will the government deal with these new problems? Also, the developing biotech, such as "clone technology," may bring unexpected worries and challenges to human reproduction, social ethics, and so on. What measures will the government adopt to deal with and effectively prevent them? Still another, the current technological and industrial revolution equips military actions with new infotech, biotech, energy technology, and material technology, greatly improving today's weaponry and combat patterns. To all countries and regions, conducting modern combats via new military technology while reducing the concomitant threats to others is another major issue that needs to be solved. Another, besides technological blockades on emerging economies and developing countries, some developed countries have imposed sanctions and crackdowns on others' scientific and technological innovations in an attempt to monopolize science and technology and even take advantage of their high-tech to penetrate, undermine, and subvert other countries. How are the developing countries and the international community supposed to deal with and prevent these issues?

All these technological and industrial revolutions have brought both opportunities and challenges to the economy and society, along with many urgent issues that need to be solved through global efforts in both developing and developed countries. The current revolution, different from those in history, is happening worldwide in many fields of technology and industry. Therefore, it calls for joint efforts and collected wisdom between governments, scientific and technological personnel, and ordinary people of all countries so as to promote cooperation, joint study, and mutual learning to solve the common problems the world is facing. All things, including social revolutions, are mixed blessings during their making and development. Taking advantage of the gains while removing the losses is the general principle to scientifically deal with the interrelationship of all things, including social revolutions, in order to facilitate healthy development. The same is true of the current technological and industrial revolutions. How can the government take advantage of the current revolution to provide high-efficiency and quality services for all countries while promptly and effectively guarding against the concomitant worries and abuses that they may bring about? This will be a worldwide test calling for better performance and wisdom of all governments, scientific and technological personnel, and ordinary people when coping with the great changes in science, technology, and industry that have not taken place in a century.

The tenth gauge is the global governance system and rules, which have been dominated by Western countries for centuries, have accumulated drawbacks and can not effectively deal with the increasing problems facing the world's development today. Therefore, reforming and improving the governance system, rules, and patterns and establishing a new international order featuring justice and fairness in politics and economy have increasingly become a common aspiration and requirement of people around the world.

After the Bourgeois Revolution and Industrial Revolution entered into the climax in Europe and the US in the 18th century, the world's development was centered on the West till the mid-20th century. The global governance system, rules, and patterns, along with the economic and political order, were established and led by the Western capitalist countries. By the mid-20th century, after the Second World War, the rise of socialist countries and nationally independent countries had impacted and partially improved the Western-led global governance order and the economic and political order. However, the overall pattern remained unchanged, with drawbacks accumulating even more serious. One of the main drawbacks is economic inequalities, with the law of the jungle prevailing in the world. Economically, the disparity in development between and within countries has been widening. The vast number of developing countries, in particular, are still suffering from bully and exploitation in various forms and degrees. Politically, the world does not see true democracy. Major international economic, political, and cultural affairs have long been decided by the Western powers. Hegemonism and power politics have run rampant, restraining the developing countries from expressing their own voices, not to mention conducting a leading role. Culturally, the Western countries impose the so-called "universal values" on others. They regard the people of developing countries featuring uneven development and different social systems as dissidents and wantonly interfere with and contain these developing countries. This unequal, unjust, and irrational world order seriously runs counter to the themes of our times of peace and development, the general trend of world development, the common aspiration of all the peoples, and the law of civilizational progress. The world shall no longer run on this order. Calls for a change in this abnormal world order have spread to people from both developing and developed countries. This is another significant feature of the great changes that have not occurred in a century.

Here is a quote from a recent speech by French President Emmanuel Macron discussing the issue of Western dominance in the world order and the promotion of hegemony: "We are witnessing the end of Western hegemony. Western hegemony was the French hegemony that went through the Enlightenment in the 18th century, the British hegemony that went through the Industrial Revolution in the 19th century, and the American hegemony that emerged with economic and political dominance after the two world wars in the 20th century. But now, everything has changed." Frank Sieren wrote in an article published by the German weekly *Congress* on August 12 this year that the West should no longer decide the governance rules alone, which has been taken for granted for centuries. The Europeans ruled the world from the 17th to the 19th century, and in the 20th century, the Americans. If we comprehensively think about the right to decision-making at the global level, we may conclude that we should no longer exclude ourselves at the global level and impose our concept of world order on the majority of the world's population. The global center is now clearly shifting toward Asia, especially China. What China demands is just an era featuring global equality. Today, many more emerging countries from Asia, Latin America, and Africa are willing to participate in the BRI. The sooner we adapt to the current situation, the more ideas we can present for the new world order. Macron's realization and this commentary by Sieren are far-sighted perspectives that conform to the requirements of the times, which is worth deeper thought.

What should we think of these contents and signs of the current great changes? When observing things or history, we should view beyond their present situation and, more importantly, predict their future trends and development momentum so as to get a more comprehensive and scientific understanding. The same remains true when observing the current changes.

The changes are rather diverse and intertwined for their particular circumstances in different fields, regions, and countries and in the social and political forces that drive behind them. The "different fields" refer to the natural and social ones covering ideology, politics, economy, culture, science and technology, military and society, etc. The "differences regions and countries" refer to both developed and developing countries, or capitalist and socialist countries, including Europe, America, Asia, Africa, Oceania, etc.; The different "social and political forces that drive behind" refer to the progressive strengths, as well as conservative forces. Yet, viewed as a whole, regardless of the above differences and specific approaches, it is the people around the world that promote concrete changes and determine the future trend, momentum, and ultimate results. People of every country and region, living in whatever ethnic group and social system, all hope for economic and social progress, peace and tranquility everywhere in the world, and a better-off life. This is the common will and demand of the peoples of the world, which also shows that the fundamental will and interests of the peoples of the world are the same. History has always proved that it is the people who fundamentally promote social development and ultimately determine the source, paths, and results of all events. Through the awakening and unity of the people, as well as their initiative and creativity, all changes that conform to the common aspiration and the trend of the times will be promoted and protected by the people, eventually leading to victory. In contrast, those changes that run counter to the common aspiration and the trend of the times will be opposed and struggled against by the people, resulting in nothing but failure.

We should analyze and observe, under the viewpoint and method of historical materialism, the current "profound changes unseen in a century," together with those specific and concrete changes. Their present situation and future orientation conform to the trends of the times, peace and development, and the requirements of world progress and human civilization, and are therefore beneficial and favorable to mankind. That is to say, the favorable and beneficial changes constitute the mainstream, and those unfavorable and harmful changes are the tributaries. Generally speaking, most of the concrete changes in the world conform to the will and aspirations of all people around the world. Those running counter to people's common wish are impeding the wheel of history, which cannot hamper the mainstream from advancing toward progress and victory.

As long as all insightful people in political circles and all sectors of society, together with all international and regional organizations pursuing world peace and development, jointly serve for the common aspiration of all peoples, draw on their wisdom and strength, adhere to the global principle on governance and democracy featuring "extensive consultation, joint contribution, and shared benefits," thus properly handle the following relationships on a global scale, the current worldwide social changes will definitely open up a new phase for human civilization. We should properly handle the following relationships. First, the relationship between the unification and specialization of the global market. All countries and regions constitute an integral part of a unified global market. The construction of national and regional markets should be conducive to and serve the stability and development of the global market and should not engage in protectionism and egoism that separate the unified one. Second, the relationship between the countries' different roles, that is, the unified and divided roles, in global governance. The separate governance of each country and region should be conducive to and serve global governance. It should not engage in separatism and isolationism that run counter to the current rules and requirements. Third, the relationship between various countries on a global scale. The principles of common progress and prosperity based on equality, cooperation, and mutual benefit should be upheld and implemented in both developed and developing countries or capitalist and socialist countries. Both should oppose any form of hegemonism or power politics that bully the weak, harm the neighbors, discriminate, destroy, endanger, or even subvert other countries, the approaches of which should all be waved out from history. Fourth, the relationship between removing stereotyped thoughts and bringing forth new ones. All stereotyped ideas, rules, mechanisms, and orders that have proved to be obsolete in practice should be dismantled and abandoned. Moreover, those that meet the requirements of the times and the common interests of all people should be put forward. No forces of conservatism and historical retrogression that will block global progress and social changes will be allowed in today's world.

In a word, by properly handling these relationships on a global scale, we will be able to advance the "profound changes unseen in a century" so as to help promote healthy economic globalization, improve global governance, establish a new international order featuring justice and fairness, and build a community with a shared future for mankind. Although many risks, obstacles, and even upheavals exist along the thorny way, the truth will always prevail over fallacy, progress over backwardness, and brightness over darkness, which have been embodied in the dialectic of historical development. We will certainly realize the magnificent goals of achieving common prosperity for all peoples and new progress in human civilization.

III. Building a Community with a Shared Future for Mankind Remaining the Historical Necessity of Human Civilization

After the 18th National Congress of the CPC, President Xi Jinping proposed an initiative to build a community with a shared future for mankind, which has been widely recognized and endorsed by the international community and has been written into the UN documents many times. The initiative is generating an increasingly far-reaching influence in the world. I would like to talk about the following opinions regarding this initiative.

First, the initiative of building a community with a shared future for mankind has profound historical and cultural deposits. It conforms to the

demands of the times, directing the correct path for the future development of the world and the progress of human civilization. "The whole world as one community" and "a world of great harmony," advocated by the traditional Chinese culture, "Man should live in harmony with each other" by the ancient Greek philosopher Aristotle, and the "cosmopolitanism" by European scholars during the Enlightenment in the 18th century, "one world, one family" by former Indian Prime Minister Nehru, etc., all constitute the historical and cultural basis and thought foundation for this initiative. With the development of economic globalization and social informatization, all countries and regions today enjoy more frequent and closer inter-linkages and interdependence than in any periods of history. The world is increasingly becoming a community with close dependence and shared interests. Peace, development, cooperation, and mutual benefit have become irreversible trends of the times, which are the realistic basis and common political foundation for building a community with a shared future for mankind. The development of the world and the progress of human civilization should no longer re-experience the period featuring discrimination, disruption, incitement of bullying, and huge income disparity that have been proved to bring only pain and catastrophe to the world. Instead, we should create a new era featuring mutual respect, cooperation, equality, mutual benefit, and common prosperity. Only in this way can we conform to the historical laws of world development and the progress of human civilization, which is precisely the direction forwarded by the initiative of building a community with a shared future for mankind.

Second, the most suitable platform for building a community with a shared future for mankind is to carry out a new type of international cooperation on constructing the "Belt and Road." The "Belt and Road" was named after the ancient Land and Maritime Silk Roads. The "Belt and Road" construction has been widely responded to and supported. It has become an important practical platform for building a community with a shared future for mankind due to its deep roots in history and answering to realistic needs. The ancient Silk Road stretched tens of thousands of miles. It lasted for thousands of years, connecting ancient Chinese, Indian, Persian, Mesopotamian, Egyptian, Greek, Roman, and Mayan civilizations, and integrating the East and the West, the South and the North. In promoting the economic, political, and cultural exchanges and the communication and mutual understanding of different civilizations in various parts of the ancient world, the spirit of the Silk Road emerged with peace and cooperation, openness and inclusiveness, mutual learning, and mutual benefit and win-win results at its core. From ancient to modern times, the historical merits and spirits of the ancient Silk Road have been familiar to people of all countries and regions along the road. Therefore, when President Xi Jinping proposed building the "Belt and Road" and advocated constructing a new type of international cooperation, it aroused strong repercussions and heartfelt excitement in all countries and regions along the "Belt and Road" and beyond. The core connotation of this new type of international cooperation is to carry out infrastructure construction and inter-connectivity construction that are urgently needed by all parties along the "Belt and Road" and beyond, strengthen mutual economic policy coordination and development strategy docking, and promote mutual synergy and linkage development, in order to achieve economic progress and prosperity of all parties. It is expected that through the infrastructure construction and the economic win-win cooperation, a community of interests shared by different countries and regions will certainly be created, thereby facilitating the constant significant material foundation for the construction of a community with a shared future for mankind from various fields. Today, the construction of the "Belt and Road" is progressing in a solid and orderly manner in various countries and regions, which powerfully demonstrates that it is and will continue to build an important practice platform for building a community with a shared future for mankind.

Third, to build a community with a shared future for mankind, it needs to determine the correct principles it should adhere to so as to ensure its future practice. Building a community with a shared future for mankind is a brand new and great cause in the history of social development. To realize such a great cause, we must determine the correct principles of its construction by profoundly understanding and grasping the laws governing the development of human society. Looking at the entire history of social development, especially the historical experience since economic globalization, we may propose the following basic principles that guide the construction of a community with a shared future for mankind. The first is the principle of common development and common prosperity, for building a community with a shared future for mankind should correctly grasp its fundamental purpose and development direction; the second is the principle of equal communication and mutual learning, for building a community with a shared future for mankind should correctly absorb the historical wisdom of different civilizations of the world; the third is the principle of the balance between rights and interests, and reciprocal benefits, for building a community with a shared future for mankind should properly handle the relationship between righteousness and interest and the mutual interests of the nations of the world; the fourth is the principle of "extensive consultation, joint contribution, and shared benefits," for building a community of shared future for humankind should correctly apply the methodology of uniting the global forces to join efforts and the concept of improving global governance; the fifth is the principle of coexistence featuring common peace, for building a community with a shared future for mankind should correctly handle the security relations of all countries and regions to achieve global peace and tranquility. These principles certainly call for the study, complement, and improvement of all parties in the world. They will be tested in the concrete practice of building a community with a shared future for mankind.

Fourth, building a community with a shared future for mankind cannot be accomplished in one stroke. The ultimate victory requires a long struggle for all mankind. We should be aware of the uneven development of countries around the world, especially between developed and developing countries. Hegemonism and power politics still exist, unilateralism, protectionism, and narrow nationalism resurge from time to time, and traditional security and non-traditional security issues are intertwined. The above problems show that the construction of a community with a shared future for mankind cannot be achieved overnight; it needs joint efforts, long-term struggle, and perseverance of all peoples to finally achieve the ambitious goal that we have pursued for a long time. It requires countries of different parts of the world, with different levels of development and social systems, to gradually accumulate experience through tests based on their actual conditions and specific needs so as to build a community with a shared future for mankind in different scopes, levels, and scales, to continuously lay down and strengthen the foundation for the ultimate victory of building a community with a shared future for mankind.

Fifth, China initiated the building of a community with a shared future for mankind and the BRI and will unswervingly pioneer its great cause with a consistent and conscious spirit. This is determined by the fine traditions of the Chinese civilization that the Chinese people inherited, as well as the essence and mission of the Chinese socialist system created by the CPC leadership. The Chinese nation and Chinese people have developed since ancient times, over 5,000 years ago, and have always been pursuing and inheriting concepts of concordance, peace, and harmony, such as "harmony in diversity," "seeking goodwill with neighbors," "harmony is precious," and "harmony with all nations." In the blood of the Chinese nation, there has never been a cultural gene of invading and bullying others or seeking hegemony and exclusively dominating the world, which is evidenced by the history of China's development and the progress of Chinese civilization. Today, China is a socialist country, and the CPC adheres to Marxism. The highest ideal of Marxism is to liberate mankind and lead them to a communist ideal society without exploitation, oppression, and bullying, but featuring equality, harmonious coexistence, and shared happiness. Socialist China, under the leadership of the CPC, has always been pursuing an independent foreign policy of peace, holding high the banner of internationalism of peace, development, cooperation, and win-win, and striving to promote the great cause of common development, common progress, and common prosperity for mankind. This is also evidenced by the 100-year history of the arduous work of the CPC and the 70-year history of the development of socialist China. As President Xi Jinping has pointed out, the development of China "brings the world with opportunities but not threats, peace but not turbulence, and progress but not retrogression. Napoleon said that China is a sleeping lion, and when the sleeping lion wakes up, the world will tremble. This lion has woken up, but it is a peaceful, amiable, and civilized lion."

The construction of a community with a shared future for mankind is an unprecedented great cause for the future development of human society. As long as the people of all countries join their efforts and persist and persevere, this great cause will surely achieve an ultimate victory.

Becoming a Research Mentor and a Practice Exemplar[*]

Foreword to *On Confucianism and Modern Society*

Confucianism remains the backbone of traditional Chinese culture and the guiding ideology of state governance in ancient China. Originating and developing in China, it has now influenced Asia and the rest of the world. In addition to the splendid civilization it created in ancient China, Confucianism, at present, still enlightens people with wise and time-tested solutions to the issues and problems facing both China and the international community. Therefore, the study of Confucianism should set its sights on the past and the present. Based on our own national and regional conditions, we should also view beyond the whole world.

Since its founding, the ICA has adhered to the principle of "studying the ideas, inheriting the essence, and carrying forward the spirit of Confucianism for the good of freedom, equality, peaceful development, and lasting prosperity of mankind." It actively carries out research, education, publicity, application, and communication of Confucian culture in various countries and regions and also endeavors to promote mutual learning between these civilizations. So far, we have attained remarkable achievements. To further promote the study of Confucianism in the international community and fully express its universality despite time and space, we published this *Collection on Academic Researches of the International Confucian Association*. We hope this collection will serve as an

---

[*] This is the foreword to *On Confucianism and Modern Society* by Prof. Tan Eng Chaw, a famous Singapore scholar and honorary adviser to the ICA.

ideal platform for scholars from various countries and regions to present their research on Confucianism and provide a critical perspective on the development of Confucian culture.

I recently read the *On Confucianism and Modern Society* by Prof. Tan Eng Chaw, a famous Singapore scholar and honorary adviser to the ICA, whose works greatly impressed me and aroused my admiration. This book collects Mr. Tan's academic papers after 2000 and speeches at some major academic conferences. It elucidates the profound implication of Confucianism and its great value of practical use in modern society. Mr. Tan has taught and conducted academic research at the National University of Singapore for over 50 years. He has endeavored to promote the revival of Confucianism and the exchange of different cultures in Singapore. Thanks to frequent exchanges with scholars from the Chinese mainland, Hong Kong, Taiwan, and countries such as Korea, Japan, Britain, and America, Prof. Tan has published numerous papers and articles, greatly contributing to the cause of Confucian culture.

This book manifests two remarkable features in Mr. Tan's study on Confucianism: First, he based the research on the current society and the times. Through studying the inheritance and development of Confucianism in East Asia history and integrating the historical materials with modern theories, he extends research over the whole of history, untiringly exploring and expounding the ideological wisdom and humanistic spirit of Confucian culture so as to meet the development demands of society and the times. These articles summarize and embody Confucianism's ideological wisdom and humanistic spirit, precisely as he has always advocated. Second, when carrying forward Confucianism, he keeps integrating research with relevant education and application, which conforms to the fine tradition of "unity of knowledge and practice" advocated by Confucian scholars in history. Some other articles summarize and sublimate his practice and experience in imparting and applying Confucianism. Wang Anshi, a renowned Confucian scholar in the Song Dynasty, once proposed that "the study of Confucian classics precisely facilitates state governance," and Zhu Xi, another Confucian master born decades later, also said that "scholars shall shoulder the responsibility of current affairs." They both advocated that scholars should use what they learn and study to improve the governance of "statecraft and social affairs" so as to play the dual role of research mentor and practice exemplar. I believe Prof. Tan Eng Chaw and other famous Chinese scholars in East Asia who carry these two traits deserve to be called great mentors and exemplars for studying and practicing Confucianism.

Index